AF412002

Johannes Hüppi

JEAN-CHRISTOPHE AMMANN (Hrsg.)

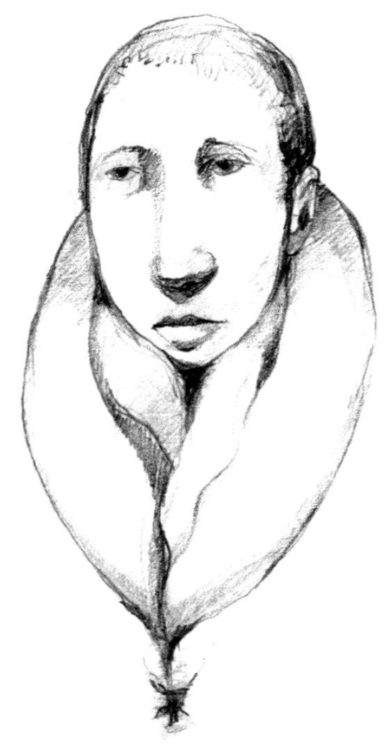

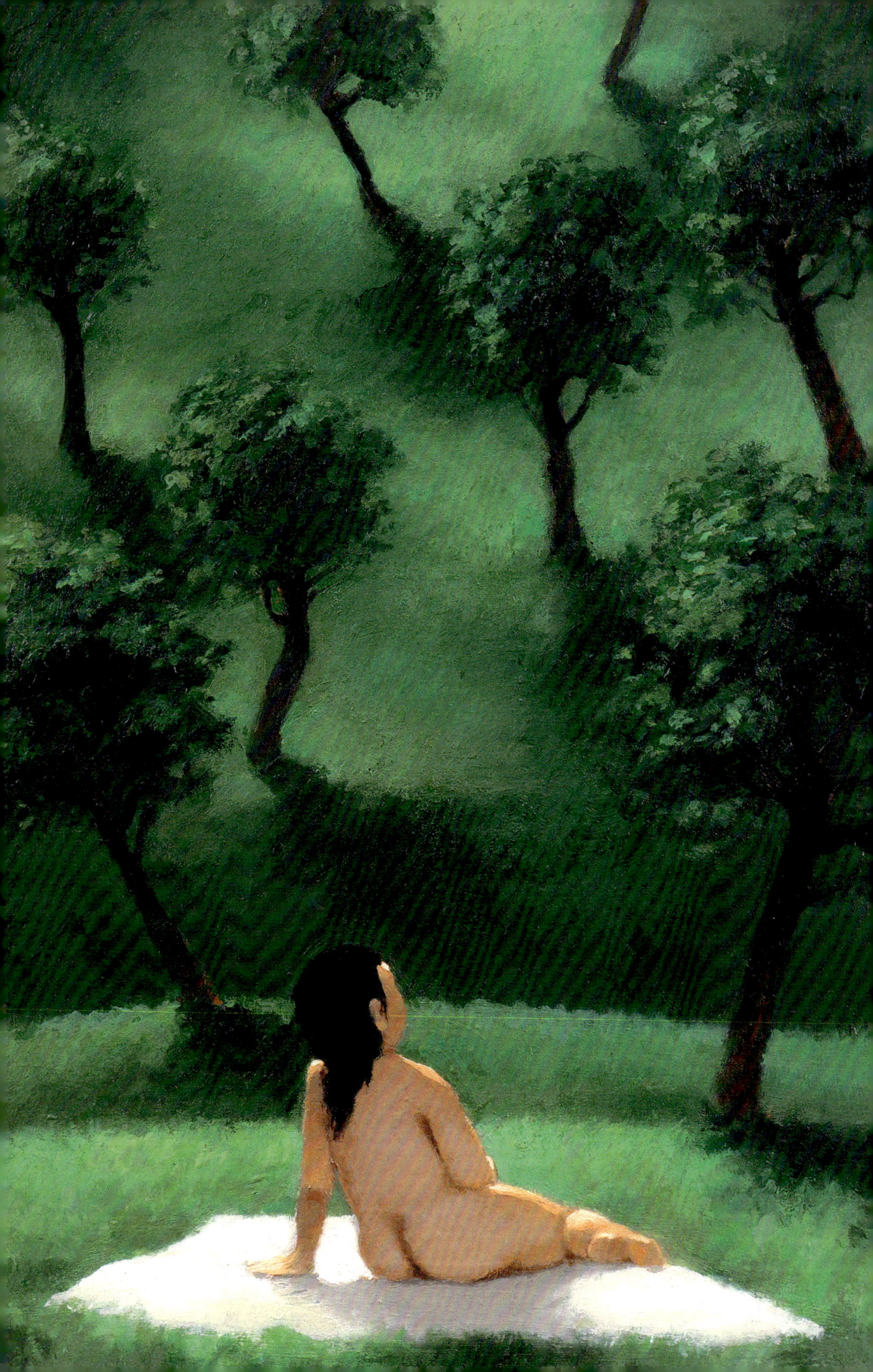

ZWISCHEN LICHT UND SCHATTEN

JOHANNES HÜPPIs
HELL-DUNKLE GESCHICHTEN
AUS DER LIEBESWELT

In dem Maße, wie die Kunst ins Leben drängt,
wird das Leben zur Kunst.[1]

In den Nachbildern, die die Betrachtung von Johannes Hüppis Malerei
vor dem geistigen Auge entstehen lässt, taucht immer wieder das Ge-
sicht einer Frau auf. Man hat sie im Werk des Schweizer Malers viele
Male gesehen, auf frühsommerlich lichter, von dunklem Tannenwald
gesäumter Wiese. Schlafend im Bett. Als streng blickende Kellnerin.
In Gesellschaft von Tieren. Aus der Ferne, aus der Nähe. Allein und
in der Menge, in der alle um sie herum wie Doppelgängerinnen sind.
Mal begegnet man ihr in Liebesumarmungen, dann wieder als autar-
kes Einzelwesen, die Aufmerksamkeit durch den Künstler auf Augen
und Mund gelenkt, jene Attribute eines Gesichts, aus denen Liebe und
deren Ende am eindringlichsten zu sprechen vermögen. »Sie schrei-
tet, sie liegt. Sie ist nackt, sie ist wunderbar angezogen«[2]: Wie die von
Elias Canetti schillernd portraitierte »Erfundene« alias Venus, Göttin
der Schönheit und der Liebe, vereint Hüppis immer gleiche und sich

doch immerfort wandelnde Frauengestalt unterschiedlichste Eigenschaften und bleibt sich dabei stets treu. Sie ist, wie der Maler gesagt hat, »Mutter, Geliebte, Muse«[3] in einem. Ein Ideal, das in der Wirklichkeit fußt und insofern Tatsache und Erfindung zusammenführt. »Die einen suchen in allen Frauen ihren eigenen, subjektiven und stets gleichen Traum von der Frau«[4], hat Milan Kundera den »lyrischen« Liebhaber in seinem Bestseller *Die unerträgliche Leichtigkeit des Seins* charakterisiert und ihm den »epischen« Frauenheld, der ständig das Neue sucht, gegenübergestellt.[5]

Hüppis Heldinnen entsprechen in dieser Hinsicht eher dem »lyrischen« Modell. Sie sind Repräsentationen des Weiblichen, die einem durchgängigen Grundtraum entspringen, auch wenn ihre Züge und Eigenschaften variabel sind wie die Liebesgeschichten, denen der Künstler in seiner Malerei Ausdruck verleiht. Seine filmästhetisch durchdrungene, zwischen höchst subjektiv und kühl-distanziert oszillierende Bildsprache nimmt die Betrachter mit auf eine intime Reise durch Landschaften und Interieurs, Alltags- und Traumregionen, in denen seine Protagonistinnen warten und flanieren, sich ausruhen und der Liebe hingeben. Der romantische Realist Hüppi, der über viele Jahre unermüdlich unterwegs gewesen ist zwischen Ländern und Kontinenten, bevor er sich mit Frau und Kind im Schweizer Idyll niedergelassen hat, erzählt seine Geschichten von Liebeslob und Liebesverlust nicht in Gänze und schon gar nicht zu Ende. Sondern überlässt das Weiterspinnen der Phantasie seines Publikums und dessen Erfahrungshorizonten, die so ebenfalls Teil seiner Kunst werden. Dass nicht fortwährend alles eitel Sonnenschein ist in der von Hüppi ausgebreiteten Liebeswelt, liegt in der Natur des Menschen und der Liebe. Der Maler hat auch den dunkleren Kehrseiten des Liebesglücks, das ebenso wie das Leben selbst potenziell auch die eigene Vergänglichkeit in sich birgt, wiederholt Form gegeben. Das lassen auch die Schatten erahnen, die sich gelegentlich wie schwere Wolken über waldige Landschaften legen oder sich düster in die Gesichter von schlafenden Liebenden einzeichnen wie schwarze Masken, vom scharfkantigen Schein einer unsichtbaren Lampe kreiert. Viel Licht, viel Schatten. Hüppis Bilder künden davon, dass das eine ohne das andere nicht denkbar ist. »Die Welt ist helldunkel«, hat der Philosoph und Kunsttheoretiker Hannes Böhringer treffend bemerkt. »Manches ist klar, vieles unklar. Was klar ist, wird auf Dauer ein wenig deutlicher. [...] Das Dunkle hellt sich auf, das Helle wird fleckig. Die Wirklichkeit ist gemischt, helldunkel.«[6] Genau in diesem aus der Wirklichkeit in die Kunst übertragenem Chiaroscuro aus Licht- und Schattenspielen gewinnen Johannes Hüppis Liebesgeschichten inklusive ihrer Akteure ihre vielgesichtige und dabei unverwechselbare Gestalt.

BELINDA GRACE GARDNER

1. Aus: Hannes Böhringer, Attention im Clair-obscur: Die Avantgarde, in: *Aisthesis. Wahrnehmung heute oder Perspektiven einer anderen Ästhetik*, hrsg. v. Karlheinz Barck, Peter Gente, Heidi Paris, Stefan Richter, Leipzig 1990, S. 31.
2. Elias Canetti: *Der Ohrenzeuge. Fünfzig Charaktere*, Frankfurt/M./Berlin/Wien 1979, S. 104.
3. Vgl. Gespräch mit Johannes Hüppi in der vorliegenden Publikation, S. 19.
4. Vgl. Milan Kundera: *Die unerträgliche Leichtigkeit des Seins*, aus. d. Tschechischen v. Susanna Roth, München/Wien 1985, S. 192.
5. Vgl. ibid., S. 191f.
6. Vgl. Hannes Böhringer, Leipzig 1990, S. 14.

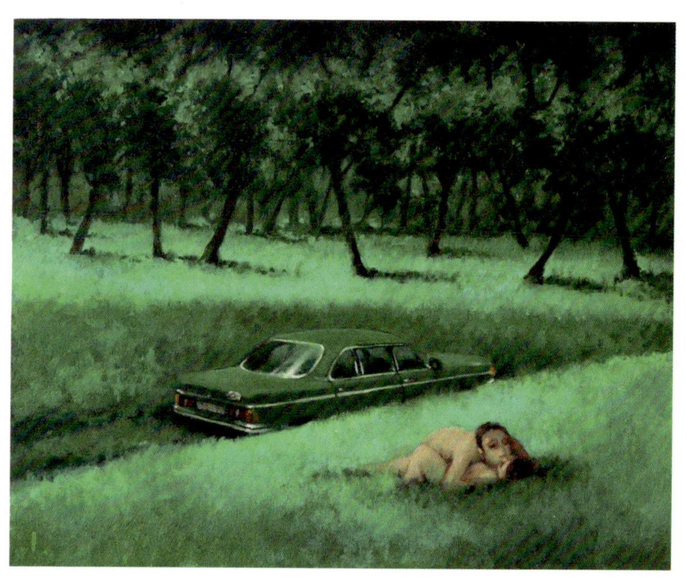

o.T. / *Untitled*,
Öl auf Holz/oil on wood
30 × 37,5 cm, 2010

BETWEEN LIGHT AND SHADOW

JOHANNES HÜPPI's
CHIAROSCURO STORIES FROM
THE WORLD OF LOVE

To the extent that art invades life,
life becomes art[1]

In the afterimages, which Johannes Hüppi's paintings evoke before one's mind's eye, the face of a woman keeps reappearing. One has seen her many times in the work of the Swiss painter, lying supine on a field of luminous, early-summer grass framed by dark fir trees; on a bed, sleeping, as a stern-faced waitress, or in the company of animals; from the distance and at close quarters; alone and in a crowd, in which everybody else resembles her like mirror reflections. We encounter her in a lovers' embrace, then again as an autonomous individual, our attention having been drawn to her eyes and mouth by the artist, those very attributes of the face with the strongest capacity for speaking of love and its demise. "She is striding, she is reclining. She is naked, she is dressed in beautiful garments"[2]: in the same manner as in the case of Elias Canetti's ambiguously portrayed "Invented Woman," alias Venus, goddess of love and beauty, Hüppi's unchanging and yet constantly metamorphosing female figure possesses a wide range of characteristics and yet continues to remain true to herself. As the painter has remarked, she incorporates the roles of "mother, lover, and muse,"[3] all in one: an ideal, which is rooted in reality, thus conflating fact and invention. In his bestseller *The Unbearable Lightness of Being*, Milan Kundera characterized the "lyrical" lover as the kind of man who is always seeking in every female his subjective, invariable dream woman[4], and posited as the counterpart of the former the "epic" type who relentlessly seeks the new in every woman he meets.[5]

In this respect, Hüppi's heroines are more in accordance with the "lyrical" model. They are representations of femininity, which spring from a consistent, fundamental dream, even if their features and traits are variable like the love stories the artist gives expression to in his paintings. His pictorial language, oscillating between highly subjective and coolly detached, and permeated by a cinematic aesthetic, takes the viewer on an intimate journey through landscapes and interiors, the realms of everyday life and the regions of dreams, where his female protagonists are waiting and walking, resting and abandoning themselves to the power of love. The romantic realist Hüppi, who traveled tirelessly between the countries and continents for many years before settling down with wife and child in idyllic Switzerland, never discloses the climax or conclusion of his tales about the glory and loss of love. But rather leaves their further elaboration to the imagination and personal horizons of experience of his audience, which in this manner also becomes included in his art. The fact that not everything is sunshine and roses in the world of love, which Hüppi unfolds in his works, lies in the nature of both humanity and love. The painter has also repeatedly given shape to the darker aspects of love's bliss, which just like life itself potentially encompasses its own transience. These implications are also conveyed by the shadows, which occasionally move across the landscape like heavy clouds or are inscribed in the faces of sleeping lovers like black masks, created by the sharply contoured glow of an invisible lamp. Much light, much shadow. Hüppi's paintings bear witness to the fact that the one is inconceivable without the other. "The world is both light and dark," as the philosopher and art theoretician Hannes Böhringer has stated. "Some things are clear, many are unclear. In the long run, that, which is clear, becomes more pronounced. [...] What is dark becomes lighter, what is light becomes mottled. Reality is a blend of light and dark."[6] It is exactly in this chiaroscuro with its interplay of light and shadow, transposed from reality into the realm of art, that Johannes Hüppi's love stories and their protagonists assume their simultaneously multi-faced and distinctive shapes.

BELINDA GRACE GARDNER

1. From: Hannes Böhringer, Attention im Clair-obscur: Die Avantgarde, in: *Aisthesis. Wahrnehmung heute oder Perspektiven einer anderen Ästhetik*, Karlheinz Barck, Peter Gente, Heidi Paris, Stefan Richter (eds.), Leipzig, 1990, p. 31.
2. Elias Canetti: *Der Ohrenzeuge. Fünfzig Charaktere*, Frankfurt/M./Berlin/Vienna, 1979, p. 104.
3. Cf. conversation with Johannes Hüppi in this publication, p. 29.
4. Cf. Milan Kundera: *Die unerträgliche Leichtigkeit des Seins* (The Unbearable Lightness of Being), from Czech into German by Susanna Roth, Munich/Vienna, 1985, p. 192.
5. Cf. ibid, p. 191f.
6. Cf. Hannes Böhringer, Leipzig, 1990, p. 14.

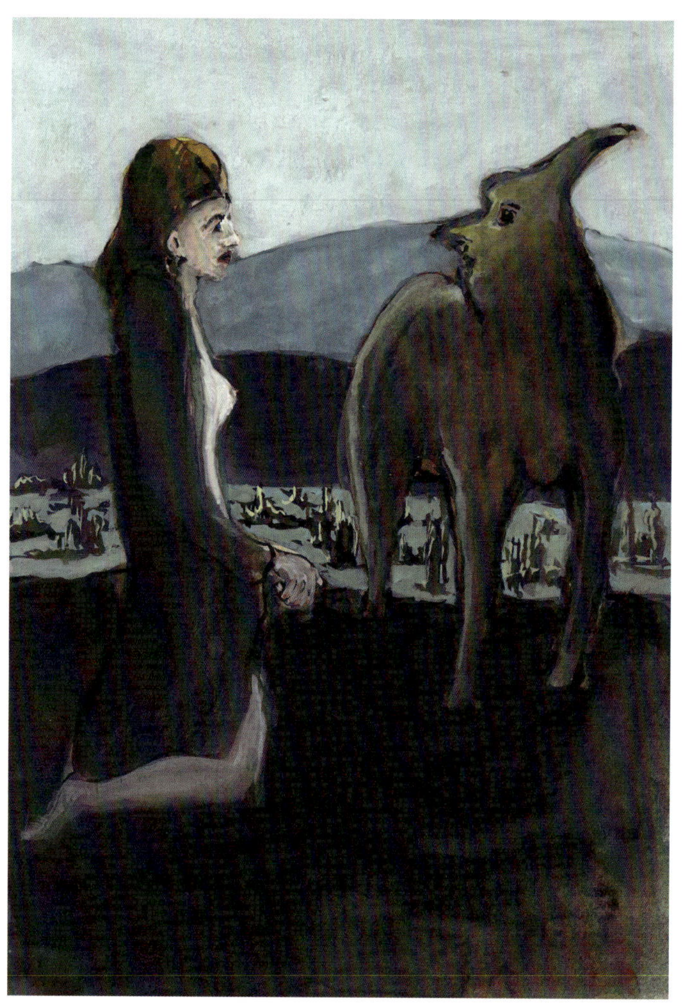

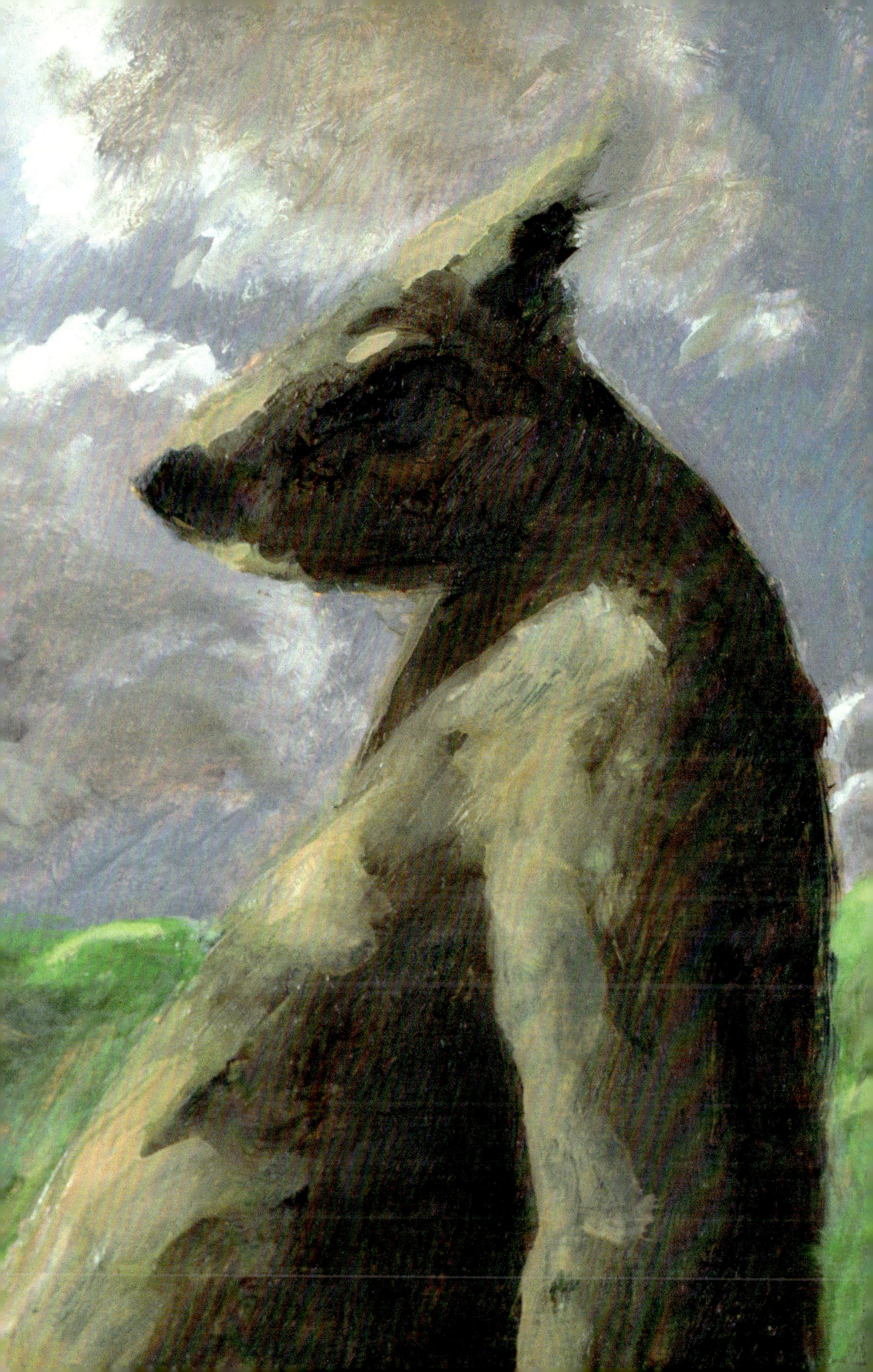

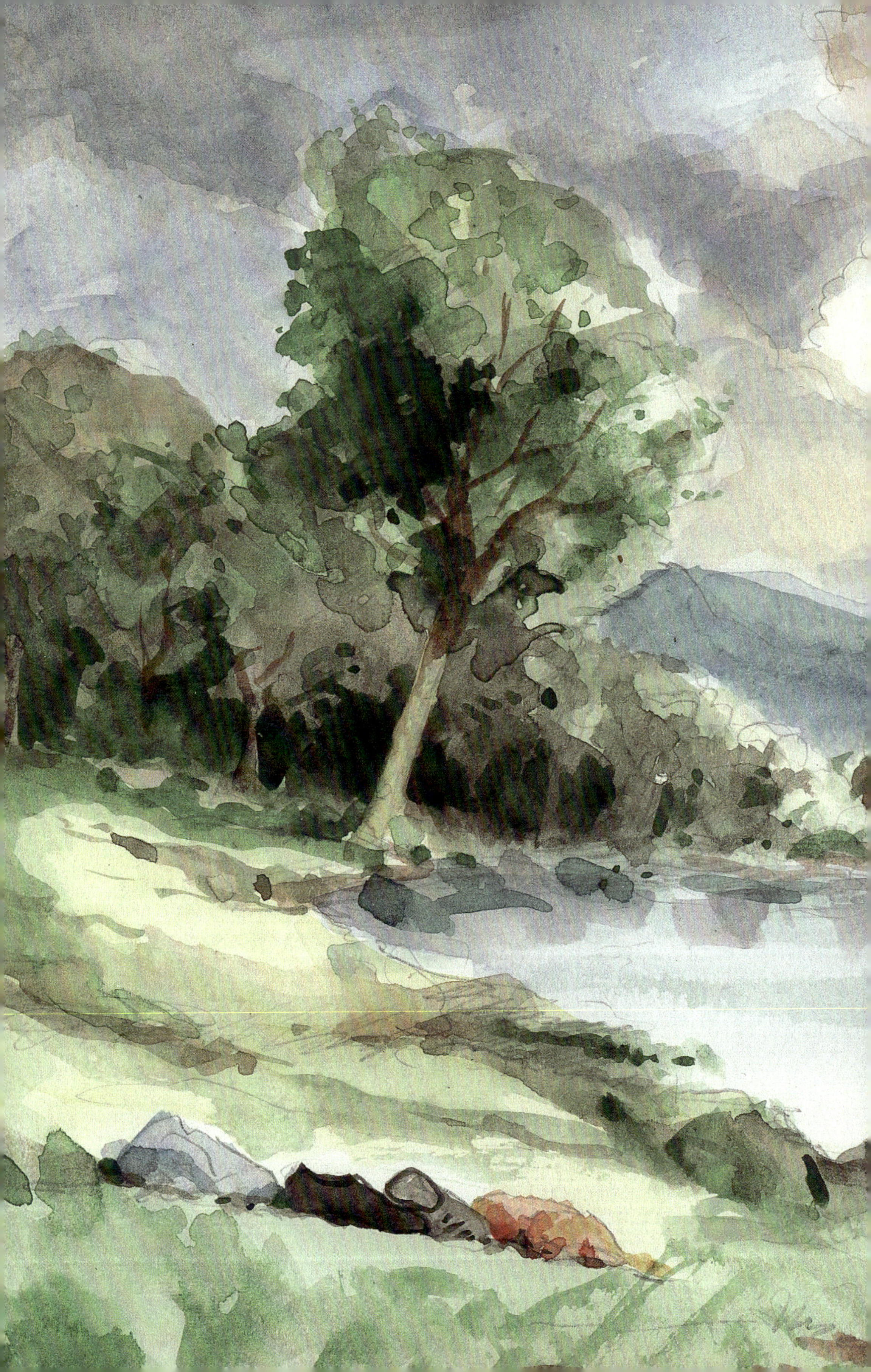

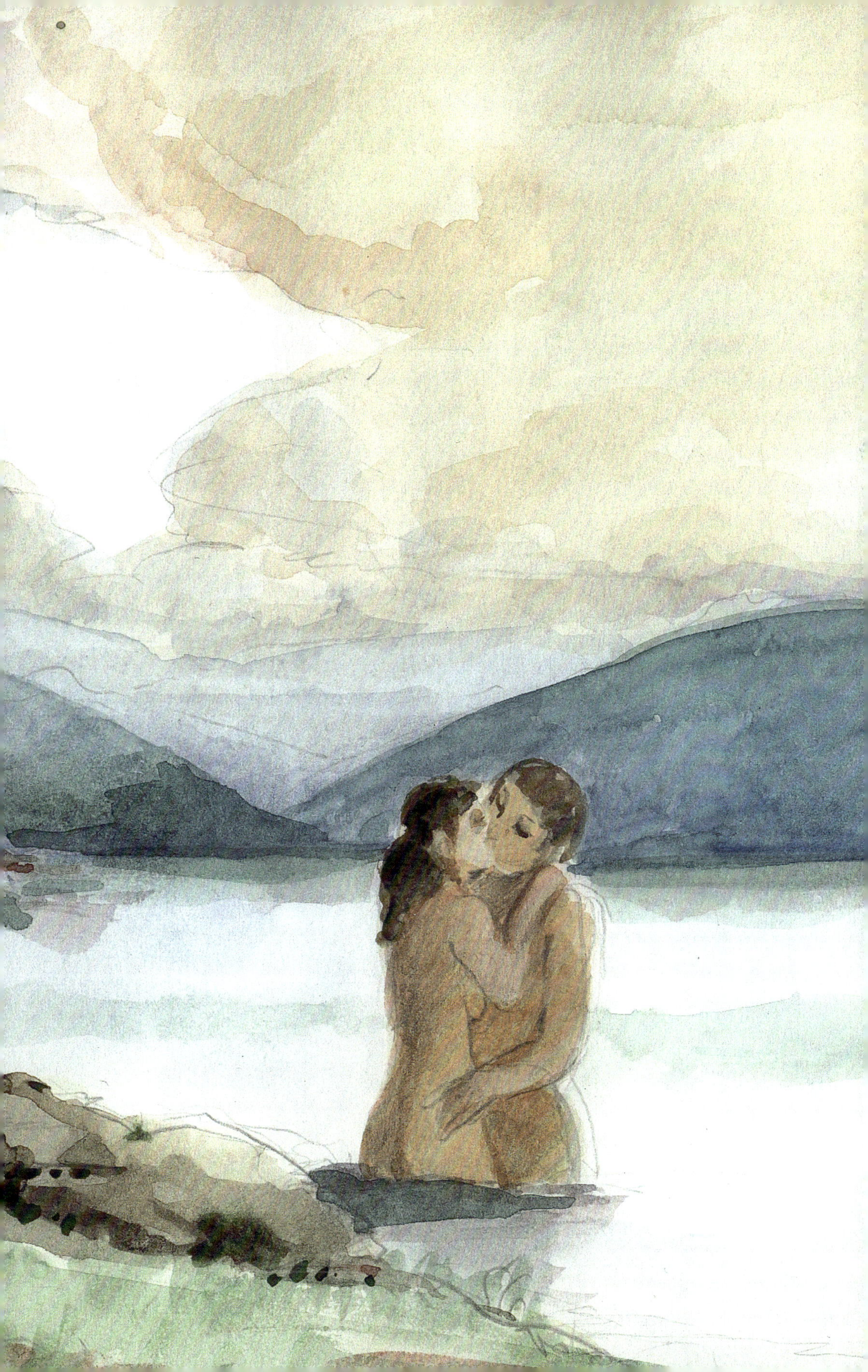

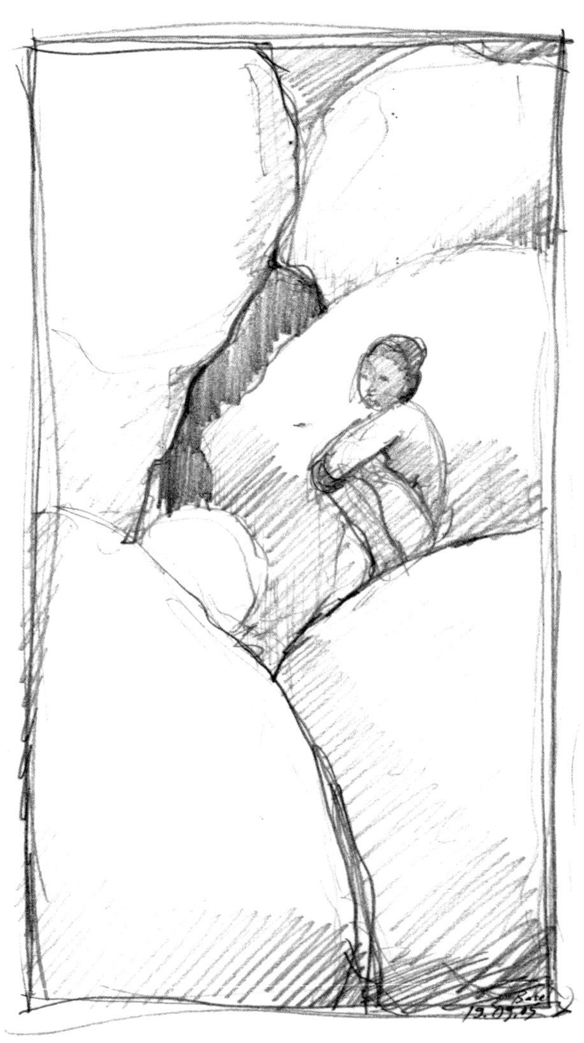

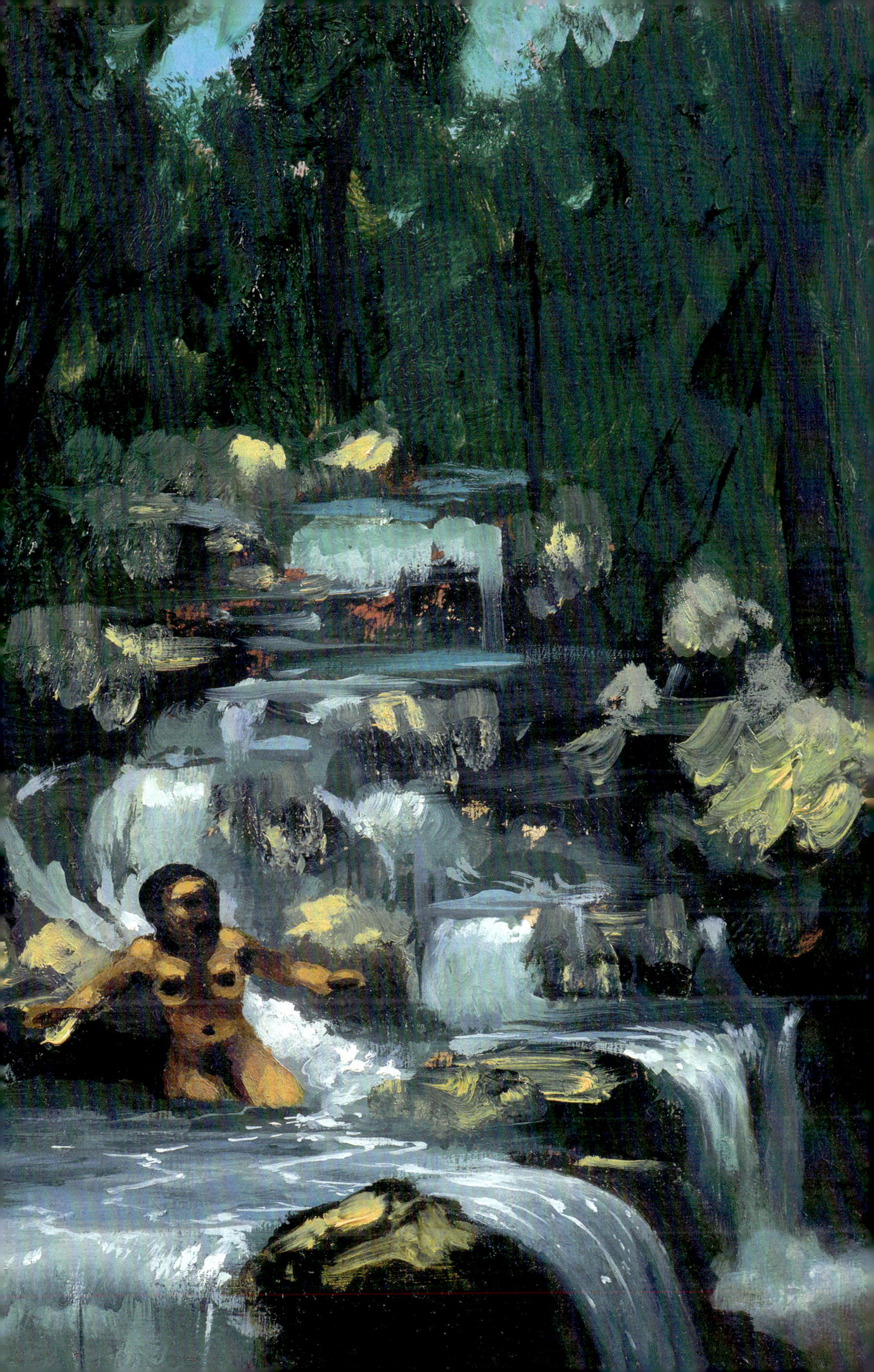

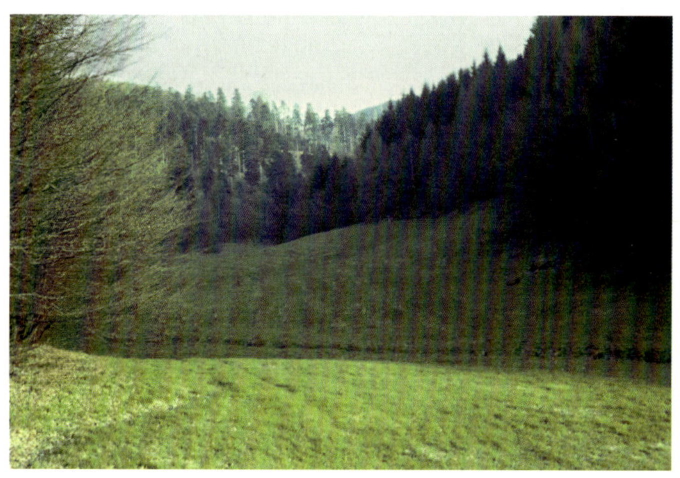

Baden-Baden, im Übelbachtal, 1984

BÜHNEN FÜR GROSSE GEFÜHLE

JOHANNES HÜPPI IM
GESPRÄCH MIT
BELINDA GRACE GARDNER
ÜBER DIE KUNST STIFTENDE
KRAFT DER LIEBE[*]

BELINDA GRACE GARDNER: *Betrachtet man die Arbeiten in der Zusammenschau, scheinen sich darin magische Geschichten zu entfalten, die immer wieder um die Liebe kreisen. Handelt es sich dabei um Idealbilder, die kraft der Kunst zur Anschauung kommen?*

JOHANNES HÜPPI: In meiner Malerei geht es im weitesten Sinne um Begegnung, Neugierde, Anziehung und Abweisung. Die direkte Anschauung der Realität und das Kennenlernen einer Situation in ihren unterschiedlichen Facetten sind dabei entscheidend. In den Bildern sind oft Beobachtungen aus vielen Jahren eingefangen.

BGG: *Die teils phantastisch anmutenden Szenarien wurzeln also in der Wirklichkeit?*

JH: Ja, in jedem Fall sind die Bilder autobiografisch, aus der eigenen Erfahrung, dem eigenen Leben gegriffen. Insofern enthalten sie auch eine soziale Komponente. Die Auseinandersetzung mit der

Wirklichkeit und die menschliche Begegnung scheinen mir gerade in einer globalisierten Welt besonders wichtig. Meine Bilder enthalten Emotionen, haben einen entsprechenden Schwung, eine Vibration. Insofern ähneln sie vielleicht auch Kinofilmen über das große Gefühl.

BGG: *Weibliche Figuren, mal allein, mal als Teil eines Liebespaars, spielen im gesamten Werk eine dominante Rolle. Sind diese Frauengestalten, die alle mehr oder weniger einem Schönheitsmuster gehorchen, Prototypen?*

JH: Der Grundtypus bleibt gleich. Ohne psychologisieren zu wollen, sind die Frauengestalten mit ihren dunklen Haaren und den Mandelaugen meiner Mutter oder auch mir selbst ähnlich.

BGG: *Ist dieser Typus also eine Art Urbild?*

JH: Tatsächlich repräsentiert er die Frau schlechthin als Mutter, Geliebte, Muse. Es ist alles darin enthalten, darum geht es in meiner Geschichte. Und diese Frau ist mal blond, mal brünett, mal dunkelhäutig, mal asiatisch...

BGG: *Sie bekommt immer wieder eine eigene persönliche Note?*

JH: Ganz genau.

BGG: *Wie hat sich das Werk inhaltlich entwickelt, was hat sich an der Erzählweise der Bilder verändert?*

JH: Früher war es möglich, meine Bilder eins zu eins zu lesen, es gab eine einfache Geschichte, etwa so: Ein Auto fährt in die Landschaft, ein Paar legt sich auf die Wiese, es gibt eine Liebesszene, das Auto fährt wieder raus aus der Landschaft. Es ging oft um meine eigene Verliebtheit, da war die Liebesgeschichte eng mit meiner Person verknüpft. Heute muss man tiefer in die Bilder hinein gehen, man muss die Ikonografie, auf die sie sich beziehen, die Geschichte der Malerei und ihrer Akteure – von Salomé bis zum Heiligen Georg – kennen. Aber ich habe auch schon früher mit kunsthistorischen und literarischen Motiven gearbeitet, etwa in einer Arbeit von 1987, die auf eine groteske Erzählung aus dem Band *Nachtschatten* des italienischen Autoren Tommaso Landolfi zurückgeht.

BGG: *Welche Einflüsse schlagen sich heute in den Bildern nieder?*

JH: Ganz unterschiedliche: Allegorien und biblische Geschichten, Stoffe aus Büchern, Filmen, und der 2000-jährigen Geschichte der Malerei, allerdings immer von meiner persönlichen Perspektive aus betrachtet.

BGG: *Das eigene Leben wird mit der Kunst- und Literaturgeschichte kurzgeschlossen?*

JH: Ja, das Eigene wird für mich so neu erlebbar und zugleich entsteht eine Spannung zwischen Nähe und Distanzierung.

BGG: *Gibt es auch konkrete künstlerische Vorbilder?*

JH: Mit 15 Jahren habe ich die berühmte Straßenszene von Balthus aus dem Jahr 1933 im New Yorker MoMA im Original gesehen. Der ehemalige Leiter der Kunsthalle Baden-Baden Dietrich Mahlow, mit dessen Sohn Pol ich befreundet war – übrigens ist auch er Künstler geworden –, hat uns durch die New Yorker Museen und etliche Künstlerateliers geführt. Ich war tief beeindruckt von diesem Werk und halte Balthus für einen ganz großen Maler. Um die darin enthaltene atmosphärische Dichte zu erzeugen benötigt man im Film gleich mehrere Sequenzen. Balthus hat dafür ein einziges Bild gereicht – es ist eine sensationelle Malerei.

BGG: *Balthus' Werk* Die Straße *hat etwas Unheimliches, Alptraumartiges.*

JH: Nun, man würde sich beim Nacherzählen dieses Traums verhaspeln. Balthus hat darin seine Figuren flach durchgemalt und damit Neuland betreten. In ihrer Zweidimensionalität, die unterschiedliche Stimmungen und Dichten in sich vereint und in der die Figuren unproportional zueinander auftreten, wirkt die Szene tatsächlich alptraumartig, wie eine somnambule Filmsequenz. Kitaj hat ja auch eine bekannte Straßenszene gemalt, die aber lange nicht an das Irre von Balthus' Werk heranreicht. Kitaj hat versucht, die Szene vielschichtig anzulegen, kompliziert zu machen, bleibt aber in der Psychologie viel einfacher.

BGG: *Wie wichtig sind solche Stimmungsmomente im eigenen Werk?*

JH: Der Wechsel zwischen Schärfe und Unschärfe, beispielswei-
se, ist in meiner Malerei ein wichtiger Faktor. Es gibt auch bei mir gru-
selige, unheimliche Aspekte und das Anliegen, die Psychologie einer
Situation zu vermitteln, wie bei der Serie der Kellnerinnen, die durch
das unsichtbare Gegenüber hindurchgucken. Genau diesen Blick habe
ich versucht einzufangen. Mir geht es vor allem darum, dass man sich
als Betrachter mit dem Bild auf einer Ebene befindet und der Wirklichkeit des Bildes glaubt, obwohl man es besser weiß, wie im Kino.

BGG: *Die Bilder wirken teils sogar wie gemalte Film-Stills, in denen
sich eine Situation emotional verdichtet. Ist das Kino ein besonders
wichtiger Bezugspunkt für die Kompositionen?*

JH: Ich habe mal eine Zeitlang an meinem eigenen Filmlexikon
geschrieben und mich sehr intensiv mit Filmgeschichte beschäftigt.
Da kommt sehr viel Information her. So habe ich den bekannten Film-
kuss von Grace Kelly und James Stuart in Alfred Hitchcocks *Fenster
zum Hof* in andere Situationen übertragen. Die Spannung, bevor sich
die Lippen der beiden überhaupt berühren, ist enorm. Ein weiterer
wunderbarer Film-Kuss ist der aus *Vom Winde verweht*, aber ersterer
ist unübertroffen.

BGG: *Gibt es weitere Lieblingsfilme?*

JH: Mich interessiert eigentlich die gesamte Bandbreite, von
Fritz Lang über den Film noir bis hin zu John Schlesinger. Aber auch
frühe Filme von Luis Buñuel faszinieren mich. Die Szene mit dem
durchschnittenen Auge aus dem *Andalusischen Hund* lässt einen
selbst bei der hundertsten Betrachtung noch frösteln. Das ist eine
geniale Bilderwelt. Überhaupt haben gerade die Film-noir-Klassiker
noch eine ungeheure Kraft. Ich habe kürzlich *Reporter des Satans* mit
Kirk Douglas gesehen, ein Schwarzweiß-Film von 1951, ohne großar-
tige Action. Doch sind mir dabei die Tränen gekommen. Wann weint
man schon mal? Das kriegen kaum Realsituationen hin, geschweige
denn gemalte Bilder. Wann freut man sich, wann lacht man so richtig
von innen heraus? Das ist schon selten. Wenn man das durch Bilder
hinkriegt, ist es großartig, und darauf hebe ich selbst auch ab.

BGG: *Auf die Darstellung und Hervorrufung von Gefühlen?*

JH: Ja, genau. Es ist ein Bedürfnis in mir, dem nachzugehen, aber ich erkenne das Bedürfnis auch bei anderen. Allerdings ist es heute kaum gestattet, über die eigenen Emotionen – ob Wut, Trauer, oder Freude – zu sprechen, sich diese einzugestehen.

BGG: *Sind die Bilder Bühnen für Gefühle?*

JH: Ja, richtig.

BGG: *Der Schweizer Kunsthistoriker und Kurator Jean-Christophe Ammann hat bemerkt, dass die Bilder von einem Liebenden gemalt seien. Stimmt das?*

JH: Es ist das Menschsein, das dabei im Vordergrund steht. Aber die Malerei ist, wie gesagt, auch eine Reaktion, die persönlicher Erfahrung entspringt, und nicht irgendwelchen prototypischen Vorstellungen von Malerei nacheifert. Die Bilder entstehen oft in Serien, weil ich so ein Thema von verschiedenen Seiten aus beleuchten kann, wie in einem Gespräch, bei dem viele Meinungen einen Gedanken hervorbringen.

BGG: *Ist die Auseinandersetzung mit der Liebe, beziehungsweise die Haltung des Liebenden auch eine Form der Selbsterforschung?*

JH: Die Liebe hat immer etwas Eindimensionales.

BGG: *Wie bei unzähligen Dichter-Liebenden der Vergangenheit, allen voran Francesco Petrarca, die im Namen der Liebe Abgründe durchlitten und Höhen durchflogen haben.*

JH: Die größten Abenteuer spielen sich im Kopf ab. Bei der Liebe ist man selbst in der innigsten Liebesbeschwörung unsicher, ob es tatsächlich so ist, ob man selbst wirklich daran glaubt. Aber so oder so ist die Liebe hauptsächlich eine Projektion.

BGG: *Sind die Tiere, die gelegentlich in den Arbeiten weiblichen Figuren beigesellt sind, auch Projektionsflächen? Sie haben ja meist etwas sehr Menschliches.*

JH: Die Tiere sind Identifikationsfiguren. Wie bei Courbets *Selbstbildnis in Gestalt einer Pfeife* von 1858 handelt es sich bei mir um Selbstportraits, allerdings in der Gestalt eines Hundes oder Bärs. Im übertragenen Sinne könnte das bedeuten, dass die Liebe zwischen mir in Gestalt eines Hundes und meinem weiblichen Gegenüber quasi von der Gattung her unmöglich ist, ein auswegloses Unterfangen, da es einfach nicht zusammenpasst.

BGG: *Mann und Frau sind zwei Welten?*

JH: Das weiß ich nicht, *ich* bin eine andere Welt als mein Gegenüber. Biografisch geht die Figur des Hundes übrigens ganz konkret auf einen Schweizer Sennenhund aus meiner Kindheit zurück.

BGG: *Die Tiere haben aber auch etwas Märchenhaftes.*

JH: Ich habe mal in meiner Jugend Märchen geschrieben. Dieter Roth, der öfter bei uns zuhause zu Besuch war, hat mich dazu ermuntert. Ich bin im Schwarzwald aufgewachsen – das ist ja ein reiner Fichtenwald mit vielen düsteren Ecken, den Hölderlin und viele andere Dichter vor und nach ihm durchwandert haben. Es herrscht dort eine süße landschaftliche Schwermut und es ist völlig windstill. Deswegen bin ich kein großer Freund des Meeres, es ist zu laut, zu windig.

BGG: *Auch in den Bildern spürt man bisweilen eine Schwermut, auch wenn die dargestellten Waldstücke oft sattgrün und frühlingshaft statt düster sind. Doch gibt es ja auch Serien, in denen eine dunklere Unterströmung mitschwingt und der Schatten der Vergänglichkeit wie eine Vanitas-Warnung ins Liebesidyll einbricht. Steht in den Bildern Thanatos neben Eros?*

JH: Auch die Vanitas-Symbolik entspringt realen Situationen. Vielleicht enthalten die Bilder heute mehr Irritationsmomente, obwohl die persönlichen Dramen früher größer waren. Doch die Auseinandersetzung mit dem Tod ist eine spätere Entwicklung. Das Licht der Nachttischlampe, das in einer meiner neueren Serien auf das dargestellte Paar im Bett fällt, hat auch etwas Düsteres...

BGG: *...das Licht ist hell und dunkel zugleich und kippt atmosphärisch latent ins Bedrohliche.*

JH: Ja, es ist eine eigene Ikonografie. Ich muss hier an Giovanni Segatinis *Alpentriptychon* denken: *Werden–Sein–Vergehen,* das anhand

von landschaftlichen Details den Kreislauf des Daseins thematisiert.
Ich kann mich erinnern, dass mir seit frühester Jugend ein Leben nie
gereicht hat. Ich denke, dass auch deshalb der Vanitas-Gedanke immer wieder bei mir auftaucht. Ein Leben verhindert das andere. Man
kann nicht gleichzeitig viele Leben führen, aber man kann so tun als
ob. So wie dies angesichts eines spannenden Films geschieht. Dann
ist man ja auch mittendrin in einem anderen Leben. Es gibt ganz we-
nige Menschen, die sich von Anfang an damit beschäftigen, dass man
sterben muss. Man denkt stattdessen an Pension, Absicherung und
an die vage Möglichkeit, dass es einen vielleicht irgendwann in ferner
Zukunft einmal erwischen wird, aber nicht, dass es jederzeit soweit
sein kann. Doch genau diese Idee finde ich sehr wichtig. Das führt zu
ganz anderen Ausschöpfungen von Realität.

BGG: *Wie hat sich das im eigenen Leben ausgewirkt?*

JH: Ich habe viele Reisen gemacht, um irgendwo anzukommen
und dort zu leben. Ich war acht, neun Jahre in den USA, habe in Italien,
Frankreich, Mexiko, Spanien, der Schweiz, in Deutschland und auch
in Kanada gelebt und dachte immer, dass ich dort für immer bleibe.
In Oregon habe ich großes Liebes- und Lebensglück gefunden, einen
Freundeskreis, eine Galerie und so weiter. Und bin dann doch wieder
fort gegangen, um woanders wieder ganz neu anzufangen. Sich selbst
komplett umzukrempeln geht nur, wenn keiner weiß, wie und wer
man ist. In einer neuen Umgebung kann man sich wieder ganz neu
definieren. Es geht um Lebensexperimente. Vor sieben Jahren bin in
dann in der Schweiz gelandet, wo es so gesund und heimelig ist, eine
richtig heile Welt. Im Innersten bin ich meinem Prinzip der Erneu-
erung treu geblieben, aber das äußert sich jetzt nach meiner Heirat
und mit Kind nicht mehr so massiv in Form ständiger Aufbrüche. Es
hat sich in die Bilder hinein verlagert.

BGG: *Und wie manifestiert sich das?*

JH: Wie schon erwähnt, ist die erzählte Geschichte nicht mehr so
wichtig wie die Geschichten, die dahinter stecken. Heute muss man
tiefer gehen, es tun sich mehr Möglichkeiten auf, man kann die Bilder

nicht einfach nacherzählen. Vorher waren sie vielleicht bequemer, direkter. Heute versuchen sie einen zu packen, am Hosenbein.

BGG: *Auch bei den Liebespaaren ist kein Stillstand eingekehrt, es gibt sogar eher einen Zuwachs an Spannung, scheint mir. Bis hin zum abgetrennten Männerkopf, der von der weiblichen Heldin auf dem Tablett serviert wird wie einst das Haupt des Heiligen Johannes. Ist die Liebe zum Scheitern verurteilt?*

JH: Man kann keinen logischen Grund dafür finden, warum man jemanden liebt. Und man gerät auch in Erklärungsnot, wenn man eine Person nicht mehr liebt. Das Ende ist in der Liebe immer schon mit eingebaut. Aber das ist nicht mein Thema – Verlustangst habe ich nicht. Es geht einfach um das Erzählen einer Geschichte. Am Ende steht dann der abgetrennte Kopf, als Sinnbild dafür, dass die Liebe nicht funktioniert. Johannes der Täufer, das bin vielleicht ich selbst.

BGG: *Vielleicht steht der männliche Kopf auf dem Servierteller ja auch dafür, dass die Liebe per se ein kopfloser Zustand ist...*

JH: ...oder es ist, wie eine Sammlerin gesagt hat, die einzige Art, in der man Männer heute noch genießen kann.

*DAS GESPRÄCH FAND AM 31. JANUAR, 2011, IN HAMBURG STATT.

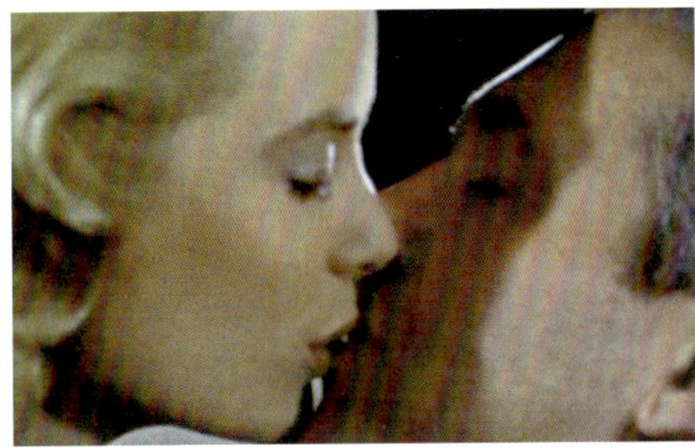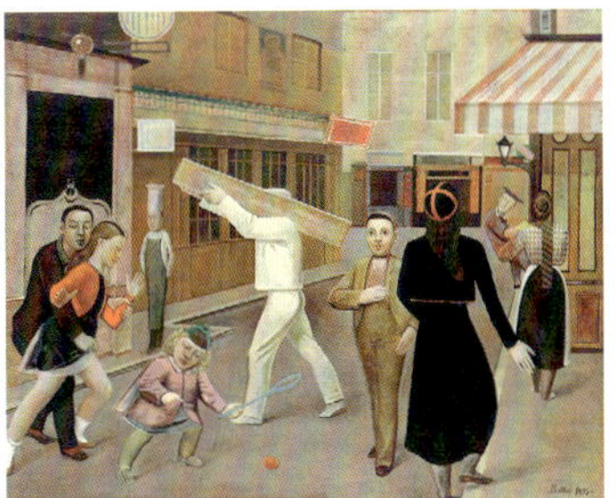

Film-Still aus / from: Alfred Hitchcock: *Das Fenster zum Hof / Rear Window*, USA, 1954
Film © 1954 Patron Inc. Renewed 1982 Samuel Taylor and Patricia Hitchcock O'Connell
as Co-trustees. Alle Rechte vorbehalten / All rights reserved.

Balthus, *La Rue / Die Straße / The Street*, 1933, Öl auf Leinwand / oil on canvas,
195 × 240 cm, The Museum of Modern Art, New York.

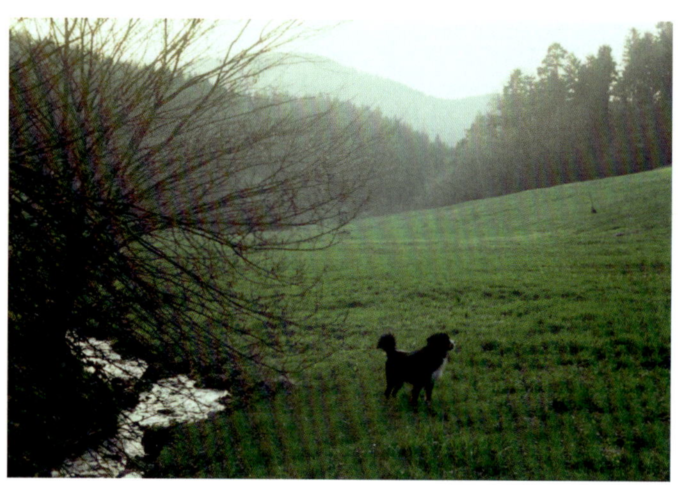

Baden-Baden, im Übelbachtal, 1984

STAGES FOR INTENSE EMOTIONS

JOHANNES HÜPPI
IN A CONVERSATION WITH
BELINDA GRACE GARDNER
ABOUT LOVE's POWER
AS A CATALYST FOR ART*

BELINDA GRACE GARDNER: *Regarding your works as a whole, magical stories seem to be unfolding in them, which usually revolve around love. Are you evoking ideal images through the power of art?*

JOHANNES HÜPPI: In the broadest sense, my paintings deal with encounters, curiosity, attraction, and rejection. The decisive factors here are a direct confrontation with reality and getting to know a situation in its various facets. The paintings often capture the observations of many years.

BGG: *Accordingly, the scenarios, some of which appear quite fantastic, are in fact rooted in reality?*

JH:　Yes. The paintings are always autobiographical, extracted from my own life experiences. In this respect they also contain a societal component. In my view, in a globalized world the investigation of reality and human encounters are of particular importance. My paintings contain emotions and are correspondingly infused with a specific verve and aura. In this respect, they have a certain kinship to emotionally charged movies.

BGG: *In your entire work, female figures, sometimes depicted alone, sometimes as part of an amorous couple, play a dominant role. Do these females, which more or less all follow a consistent pattern of beauty, represent a prototype?*

JH: The basic type remains consistent. Without wanting to overly stress psychological aspects, with their dark hair and almond eyes the female figures resemble my mother and also myself.

BGG: *Is this then a kind of personal archetype?*

JH: Indeed, it represents the woman per se as mother, lover, and muse. It encompasses everything. This is what my story is about. And this woman is sometimes blond, sometimes brunette, sometimes dark-skinned, and sometimes Asian…

BGG: *She always has her own personal attributes?*

JH: Exactly.

BGG: *In which manner has your work developed with regard to subject matter? What has changed in terms of the paintings' narrative style?*

JH: In the past, it was possible to take my paintings at face value. There was a simple story, for example: a car drives into the landscape, a couple lies down on the grass and makes love, the car drives out of the landscape. Often, I was addressing my own feelings of being in love, and the love story was closely related to my own personal life. Today, one has to get involved with the paintings on a deeper level. One has to be familiar with the iconography to which these refer, with the history of painting and its protagonists, ranging from Salomé up to Saint George. But I already worked with art-historical and literary themes earlier on, for instance in a work from 1987, which goes back to a grotesque story from a prose collection by the Italian author Tommaso Landolfi.

BGG: *Which influences find expression in the works today?*

JH:	A large variety of influences: allegories and biblical stories, themes from books, films, and the 2000-year-old history of painting, yet always viewed from my personal perspective.

BGG: *You short-circuit your own life with art and literary history?*

JH:	Yes. Thus, my own life becomes conceivable to me in new ways, while simultaneously tension develops between closeness and the creation of distance.

BGG: *Are there also concrete artists who have influenced you?*

JH:	As a 15-year-old, I saw Balthus's famous street scene from 1933 in the original for the first time at the MoMA in New York. The former director of the Kunsthalle Baden-Baden, Dietrich Mahlow, whose son Pol was a friend of mine—incidentally, he also became an artist—took us on a tour of the museums and a number of artist studios in New York. I was deeply impressed by this work and consider Balthus a great painter. In films, in order to create the atmospheric density that his work contains, you need a whole number of sequences. For Balthus, a single picture was sufficient—it's a sensational painting.

BGG: *Balthus' work* The Street *has an uncanny, nightmarish quality.*

JH:	Well, one would probably have problems recounting this particular dream. Here, Balthus has painted his figures in an entirely flat manner, thus entering previously uncharted territory. In their two-dimensionality, which unites a wide range of atmospheres and densities and in which the constellation of the represented figures defies the rules of proportion, the scenario indeed appears nightmarish, like a somnambulistic film sequence. Kitaj, in fact, also painted a well-known street scene, which, however, is a far cry from the bizarreness of Balthus's work. Kitaj attempted to conceive a multilayered scene, to make it complex, yet its psychology is much simpler in comparison.

BGG: *How important are atmospheric aspects in your work?*

JH:	The shift, for instance, between sharply focused and diffuse representation is an important factor in my painting. There are also eerie and uncanny aspects in my work, and the desire to convey the psychology of a situation, as in the series with the waitresses, which look right through their invisible counterpart. I tried to capture precisely this gaze. My concern is first and foremost that the viewer is on one level with the painting and believes in the reality of the picture, even though he or she knows better, just like when watching a movie.

BGG: *Some of the works even appear like painted film stills, in which a situation is emotionally condensed. Is the cinema a particularly important point of reference for your compositions?*

JH: I worked on my own film encyclopedia for a while and intensively studied film history. I have gathered a lot of information from these pursuits. Thus, I transposed the famous movie kiss between Grace Kelly and James Stuart in Alfred Hitchcock's *Rear Window* into other situations. The tension before their lips even touch is enormous. The kiss from *Gone With the Wind* is another wonderful movie kiss, but the former is unsurpassed.

BGG: *Do you have any other favorite movies?*

JH: I'm actually interested in the entire spectrum, ranging from Fritz Lang to Film Noir movies and up to John Schlesinger. But I am also fascinated with Luis Buñuel's early films. The scene with the severed eye in *Un Chien Andalou* makes you shudder even if you have seen it a hundred times. That's absolutely brilliant imagery. In general, the Film Noir classics still have enormous power. Just recently, I saw *Ace in the Hole* with Kirk Douglas, a black-and-white movie from 1951, which doesn't really have lots of action. And yet it brought tears to my eyes. When does anyone ever weep? Not even real-life situations manage to have this effect very often, not to mention painted pictures. When does one actually rejoice or laugh about something from the depth of one's heart? That's pretty seldom. If one can arouse this reaction with pictures, it's wonderful. It's something I also attempt to do.

BGG: *That is, to represent and evoke emotions in your work?*

JH: Exactly. It's an inner need to pursue the force of feelings, and I also recognize this need in others. Yet today it is hardly accepted to talk about one's emotions—regardless whether dealing with anger, sadness, or happiness—or to even admit these to oneself.

BGG: *Are your paintings stages for emotions?*

JH: Yes, indeed.

BGG: *The Swiss art historian and curator Jean-Christophe Ammann has remarked that your paintings could only have been produced by "a man who loves." Is this true?*

JH: It is the human existence as such that has priority in my work. However, as already mentioned, it is also a reaction arising from personal experience, and does not emulate some kind of prototypical notion of painting. I often produce my works in series because in this manner I can illuminate a theme from various angles, similar to a discussion where many opinions bring forth an idea.

BGG: *Is the exploration of love or the stance of the lover also a form of self-analysis?*

JH: Love is always in a way one-dimensional.

BGG: *As in the case of countless poet-lovers from the past, with Francesco Petrarca leading the way, who in the name of love plunged into the deepest abysses and were elevated to the highest peaks.*

JH: The greatest adventures take place in one's mind. But in the case of love even in its most ardent incantation one questions whether it is really true, whether one really believes in it. In any case, love is primarily a projection.

BGG: *Are the animals, which occasionally accompany the female figures in your works, devices of projection as well? They often have almost human features.*

JH: The animals are representations of my own identity. As in Courbet's *Self-Portrait in the Form of a Pipe* from 1858, these are self-portraits, yet in my case these take the shape of a dog or a bear. In a figurative sense, this could signify that due to the difference in species a love relationship between myself in the shape of a dog and my female counterpart is quasi impossible; it is a hopeless endeavor since the two simply don't fit together.

BGG: *Do men and women represent two different worlds?*

JH: I don't know, but *I* am a different world than my counterpart. Biographically, by the way, the figure of the dog very concretely refers to a Swiss mountain dog from my childhood.

BGG: *The animals also have a fairytale-like character.*

JH: In my youth I wrote fairytales for a while. Dieter Roth, who visited our home from time to time, encouraged me to do so. I grew up in the Black Forest, which consists entirely of spruce trees and has many dark areas, which Hölderlin and many other poets before and after him wandered through. The landscape is determined by a sweet melancholy and is absolutely calm. This is why I am not a great friend of the ocean. It's simply too loud and windy.

BGG: *The paintings as well occasionally convey a certain melancholy, even if the depicted forest areas are often lushly green and vernal instead of somber. Yet there are also series in which a darker undercurrent is resonant and the shadow of mortality enters the idyll of love like a* vanitas *warning. Are Thanatos and Eros intertwined in your work?*

JH: The *vanitas* symbolism also has its source in situations from real life. Perhaps today, the paintings contain more disruptive elements, although the personal dramas used to be more vehement. In any case, the interest in the phenomenon of death is a later development. The light of the bedside lamp, which in one of my more recent series illumines the depicted couple, also has a somber note…

BGG: *…the light appears simultaneously luminous and dark, and atmospherically evokes the sense of something latently threatening.*

JH: That's right, it represents a distinct iconography. I have to think here of Giovanni Segatini's *Alpine Triptych*, entitled *Life—Nature—Death*, which addresses the cycle of existence through details in the depicted landscape. I can remember that since my earliest youth one life never seemed enough to me. I think this is also the reason why the *vanitas* notion keeps reappearing in my work. One life prevents another life. One cannot lead many lives simultaneously, but one can pretend to do so. Just like one does when watching an exciting movie.

In that case one also becomes immersed in another life. There are very few people who deal with the fact that all of us must die from the very beginning. Instead, many think of their retirement pension, financial security, and the vague possibility that at some distant point in the future something might happen to them, but not that this could be the case at any time. But I find precisely this notion extremely important. It leads to an entirely different engagement with reality.

BGG: *How has this affected your own life?*

JH: I took many journeys with the objective of arriving and settling down somewhere. I spent eight, nine years in the United States, lived in Italy, France, Mexico, Spain, Switzerland, Germany, and also in Canada, always assuming that I would stay there forever. In Oregon I found much happiness in matters of life and love, including a wonderful circle of friends, a gallery, and so on. And still I eventually left again to start anew somewhere else. Turning your life inside out is only possible if nobody knows who or what you are. In a new environment, one can entirely redefine oneself. My objective has always been to experiment with life. Seven years ago, I finally landed in Switzerland, where life is wholesome and cozy. It's a truly idyllic world. At heart, I have remained true to my principle of renewal. But now, after getting married and having a child to take care of, this no longer expresses itself so massively in the shape of constant departures. It has shifted into the realm of my paintings.

BGG: *And how does this manifest itself?*

JH: As already mentioned, the story that is being told is no longer as important as the stories behind it. Today, one must delve more deeply, more possibilities open up, and one can't simply recount the paintings. Beforehand, they were perhaps more easygoing and direct. Today, they attempt to grab hold of you.

BGG: *The couples have obviously also not stagnated. There even appears to be an increase in tension, extending to the severed male head, which the heroine serves on a platter like the head of Saint John. Is love doomed to fail?*

JH: One cannot find a logical reason for loving someone. And one also comes under quite some pressure if one is to explain why one no longer loves a person. Always, in love, the end is already incorporated. But this is not my issue—I do not have separation anxiety. I just want to tell a story. At the end, the man with the severed head might be a metaphor for the notion that love does not work. I myself may be John the Baptist.

BGG: *Perhaps the male head resting on the serving platter also stands for the fact that love per se is a rather headless or mindless state...*

JH: ...or perhaps, as a female collector once observed, nowadays, it is the only manner in which men can still be enjoyed.

*THE CONVERSATION TOOK PLACE ON JANUARY 31, 2011, IN HAMBURG.

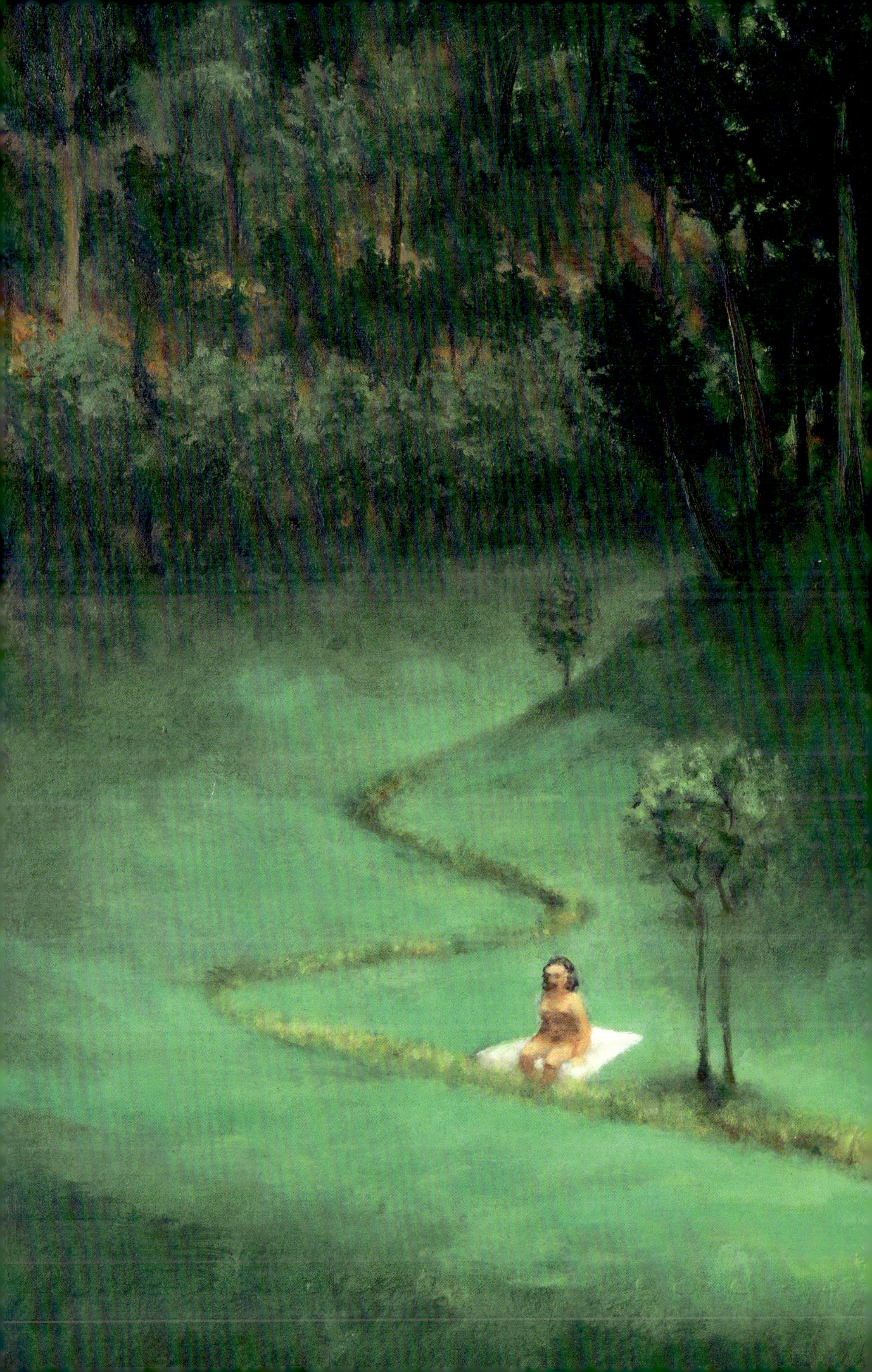

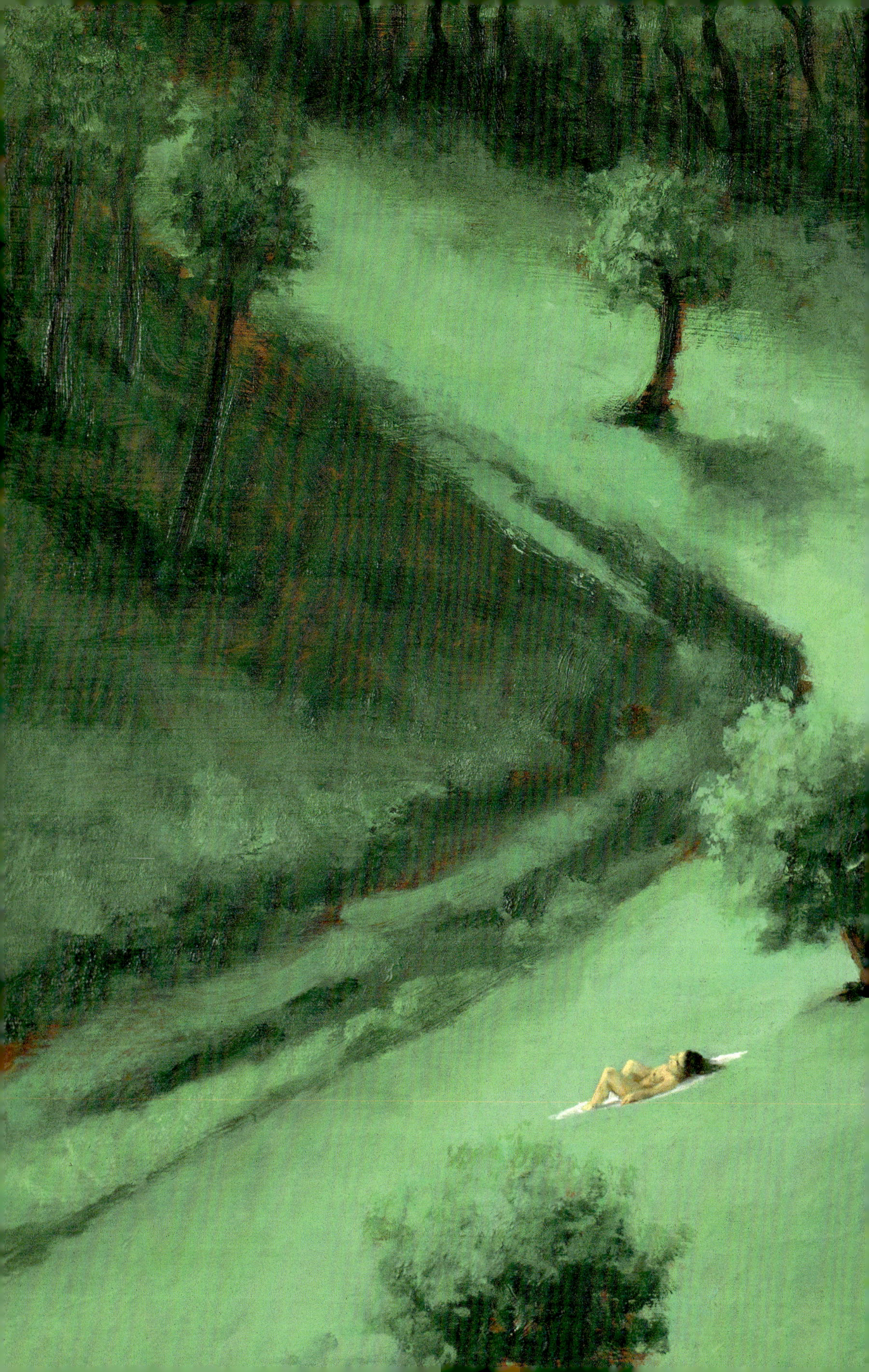

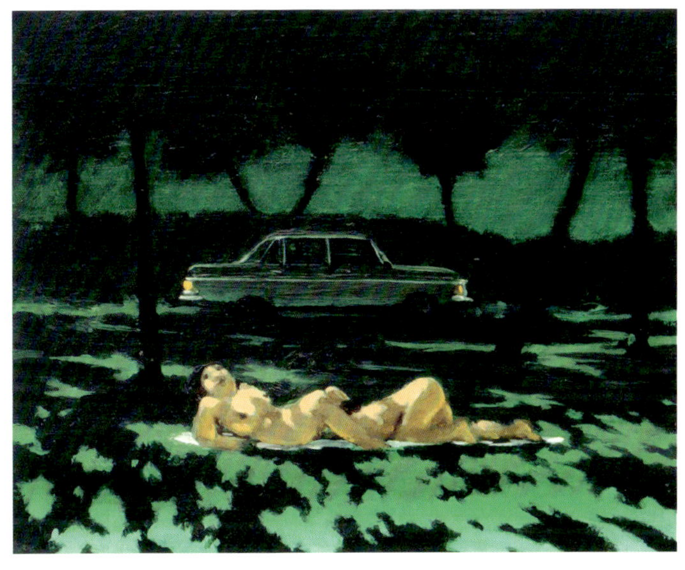

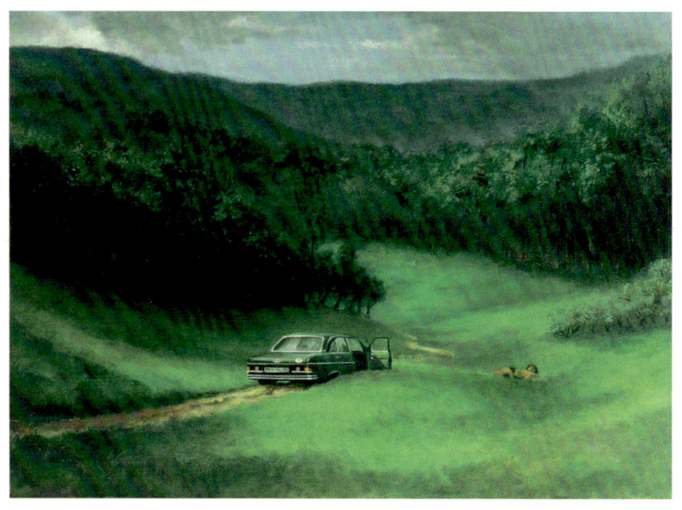

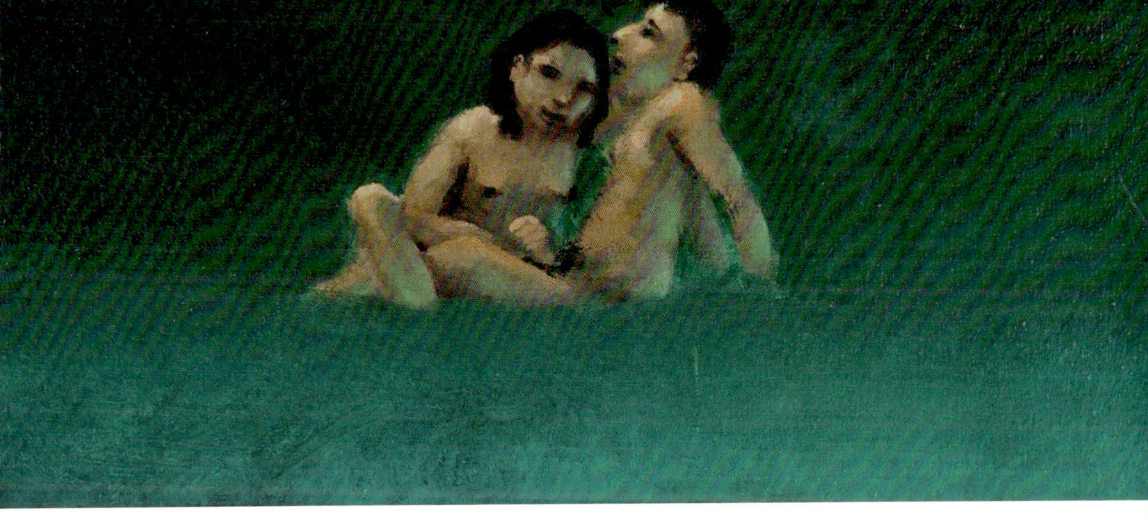

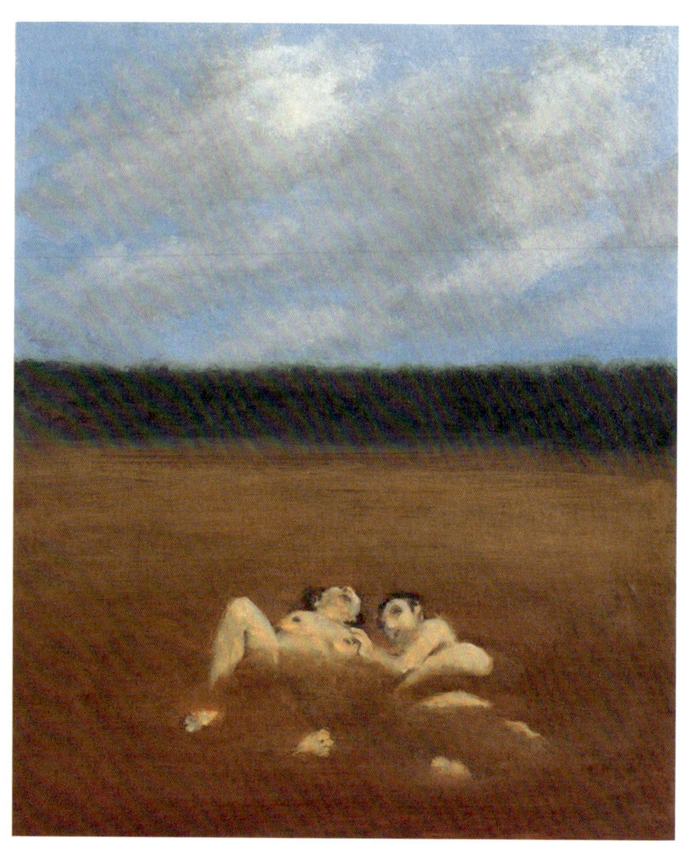

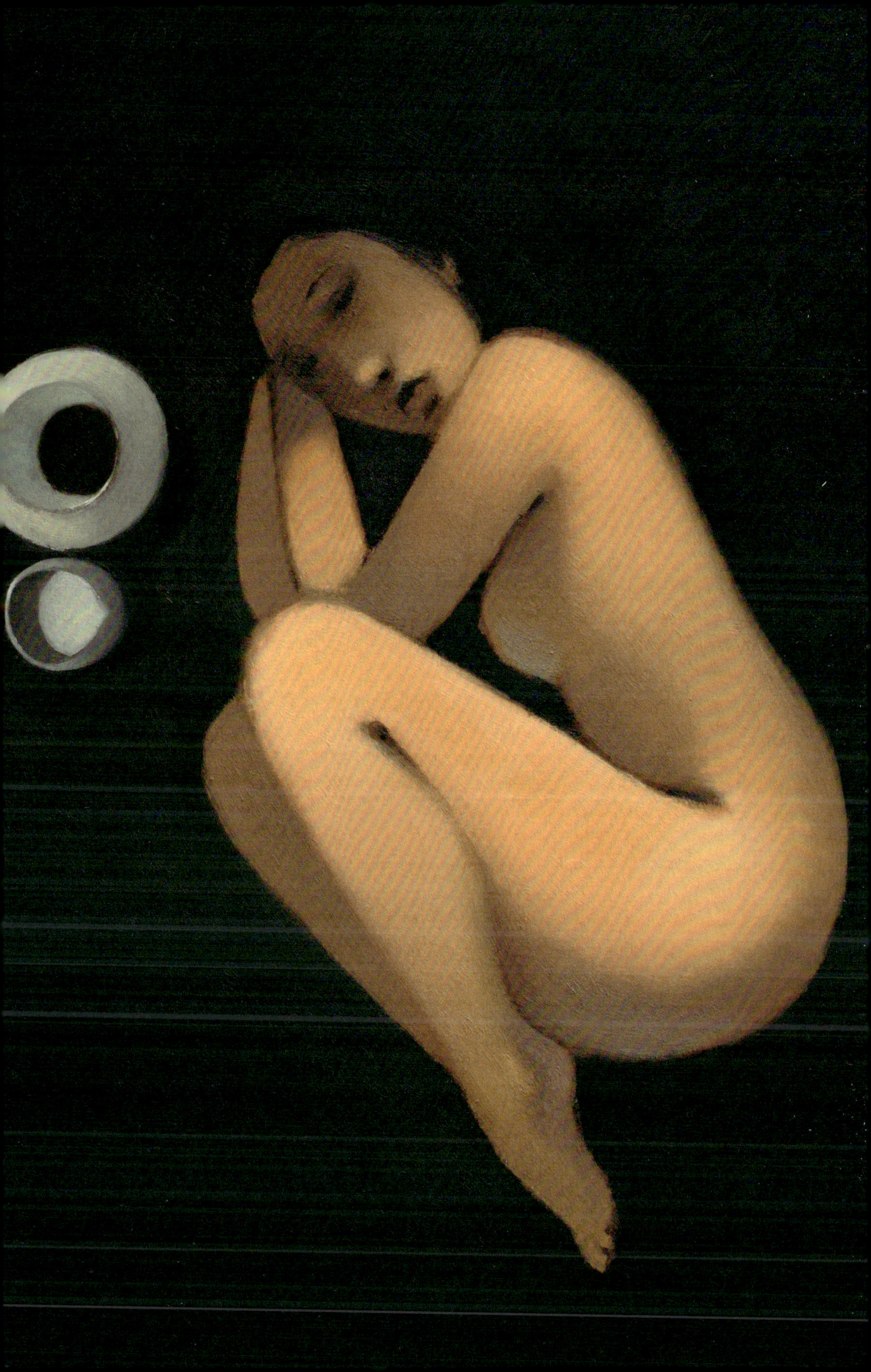

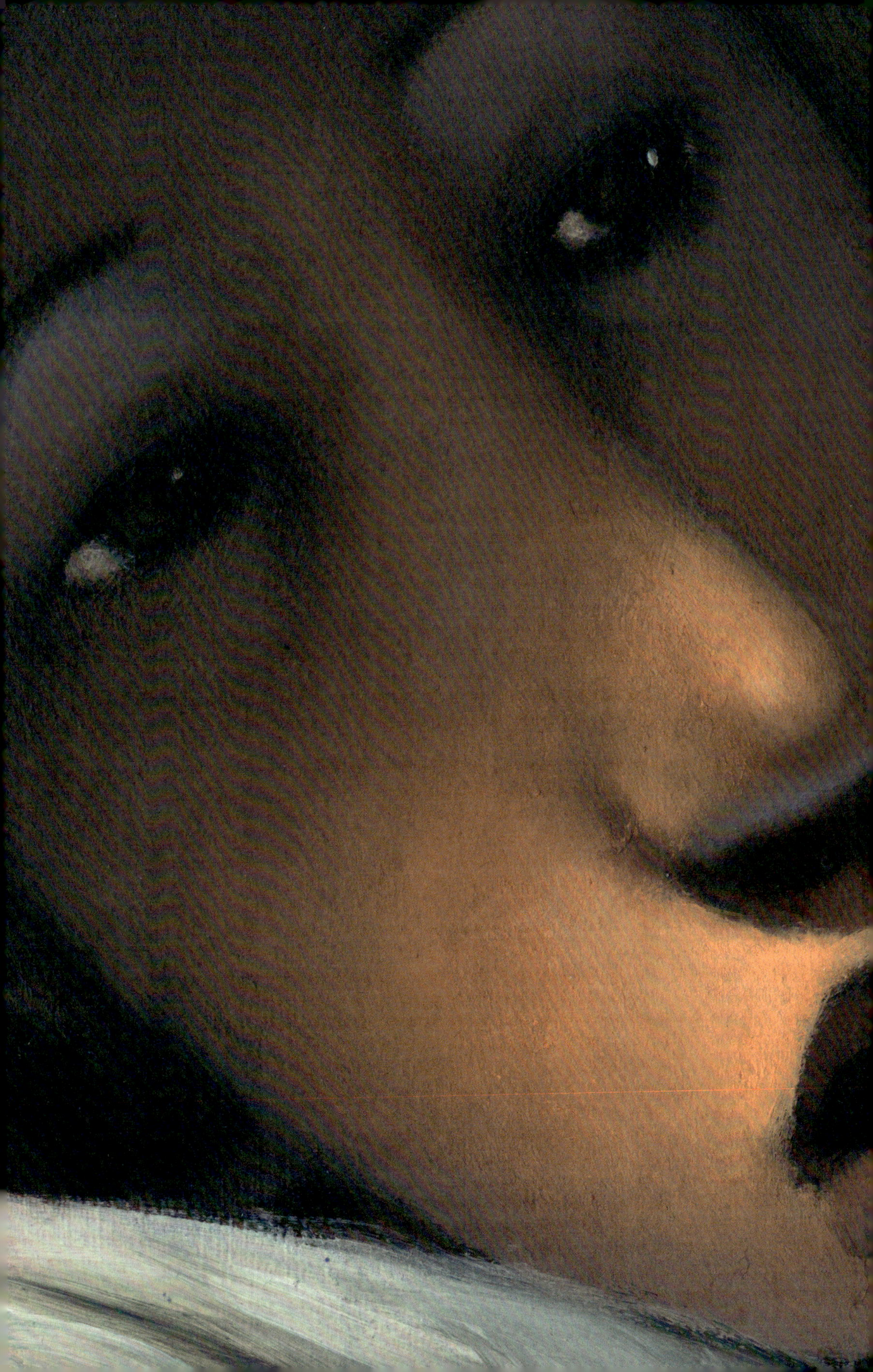

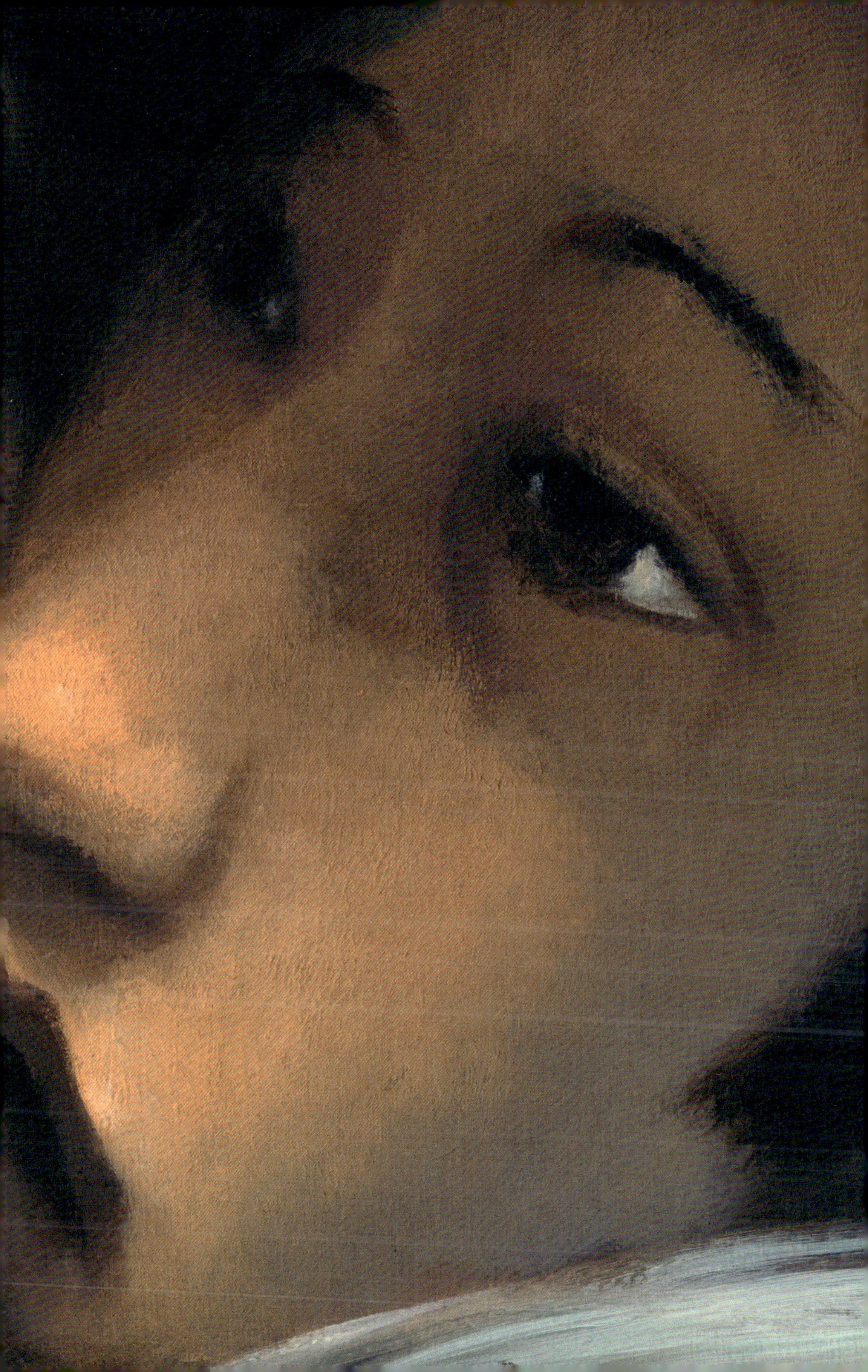

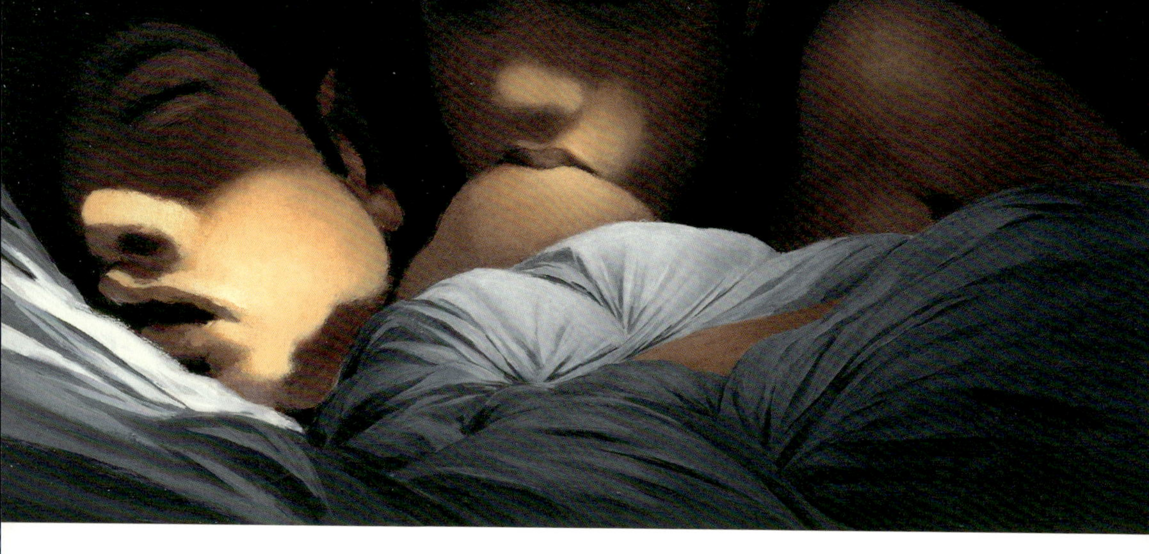

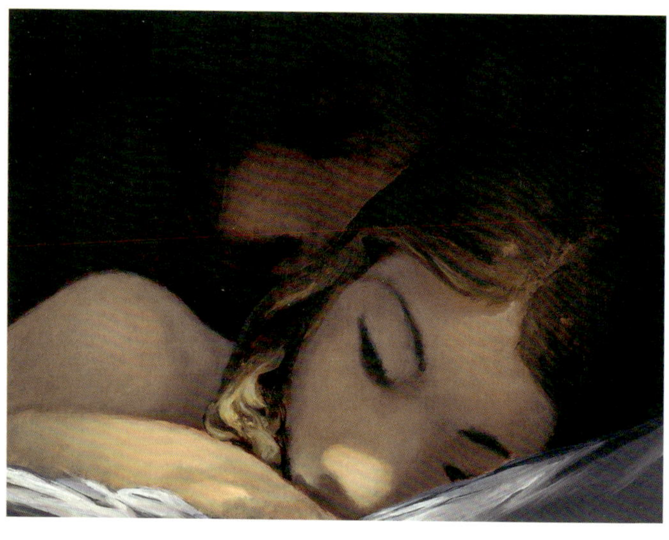

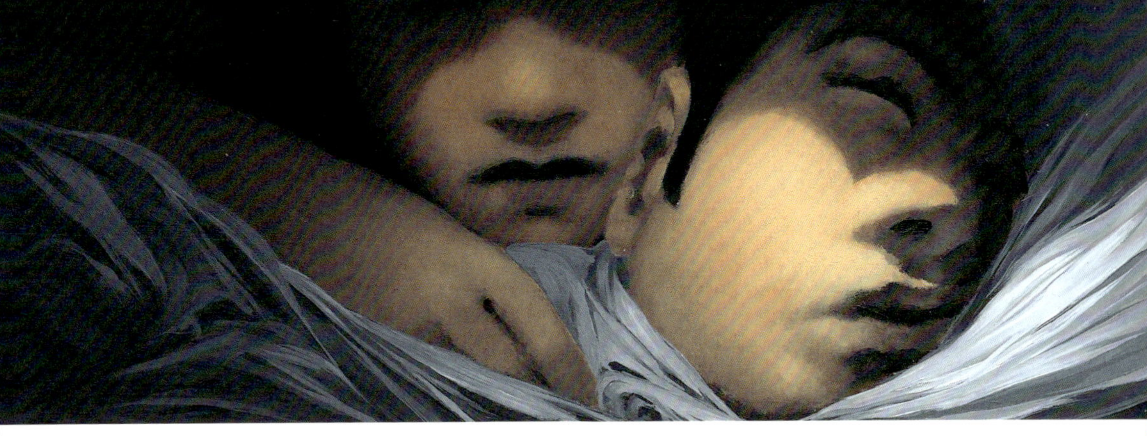

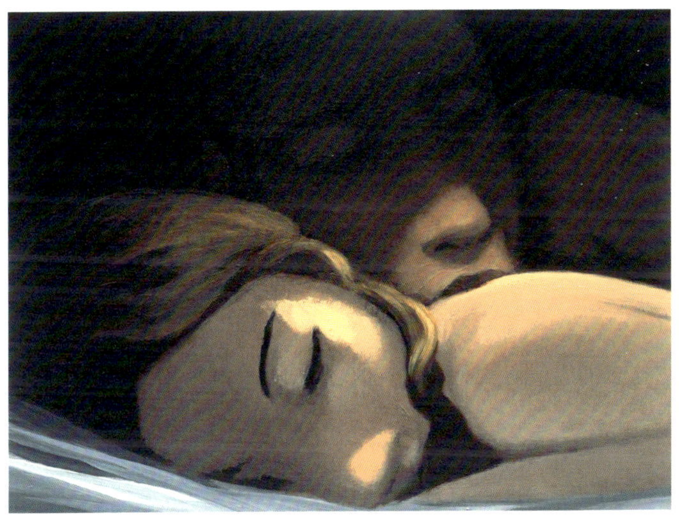

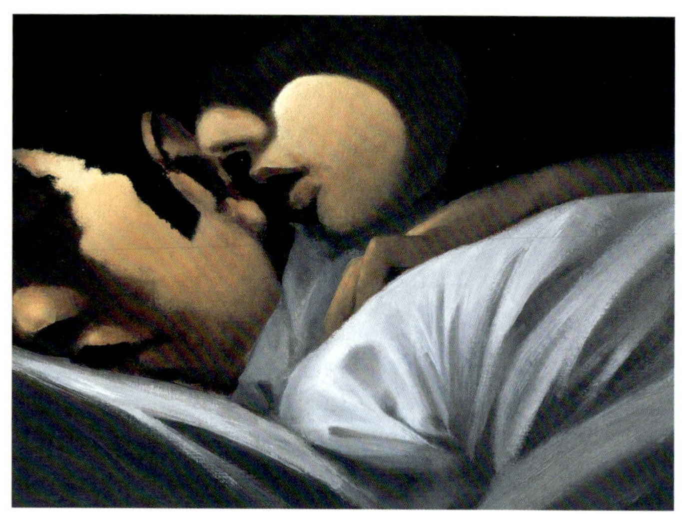

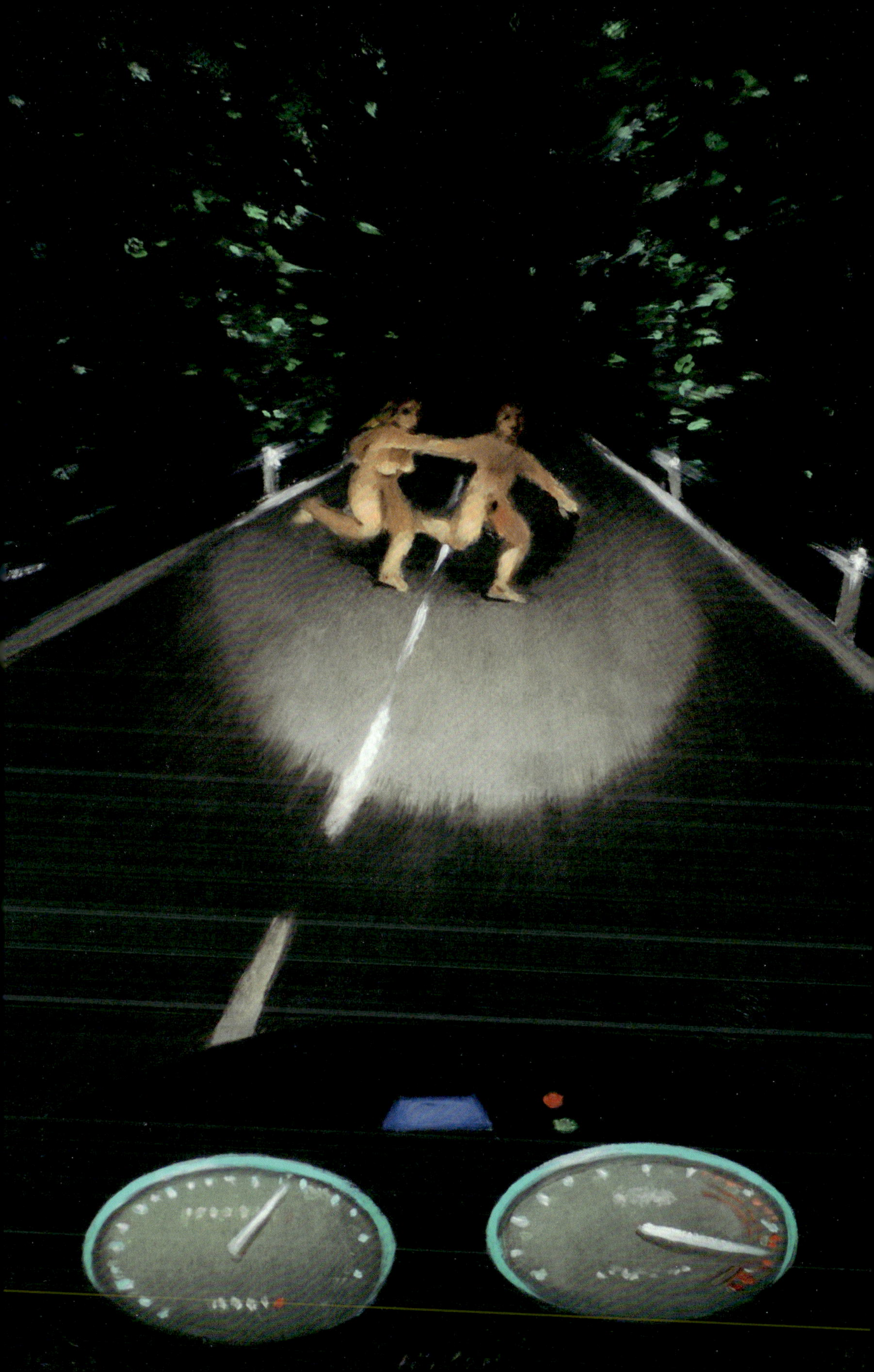

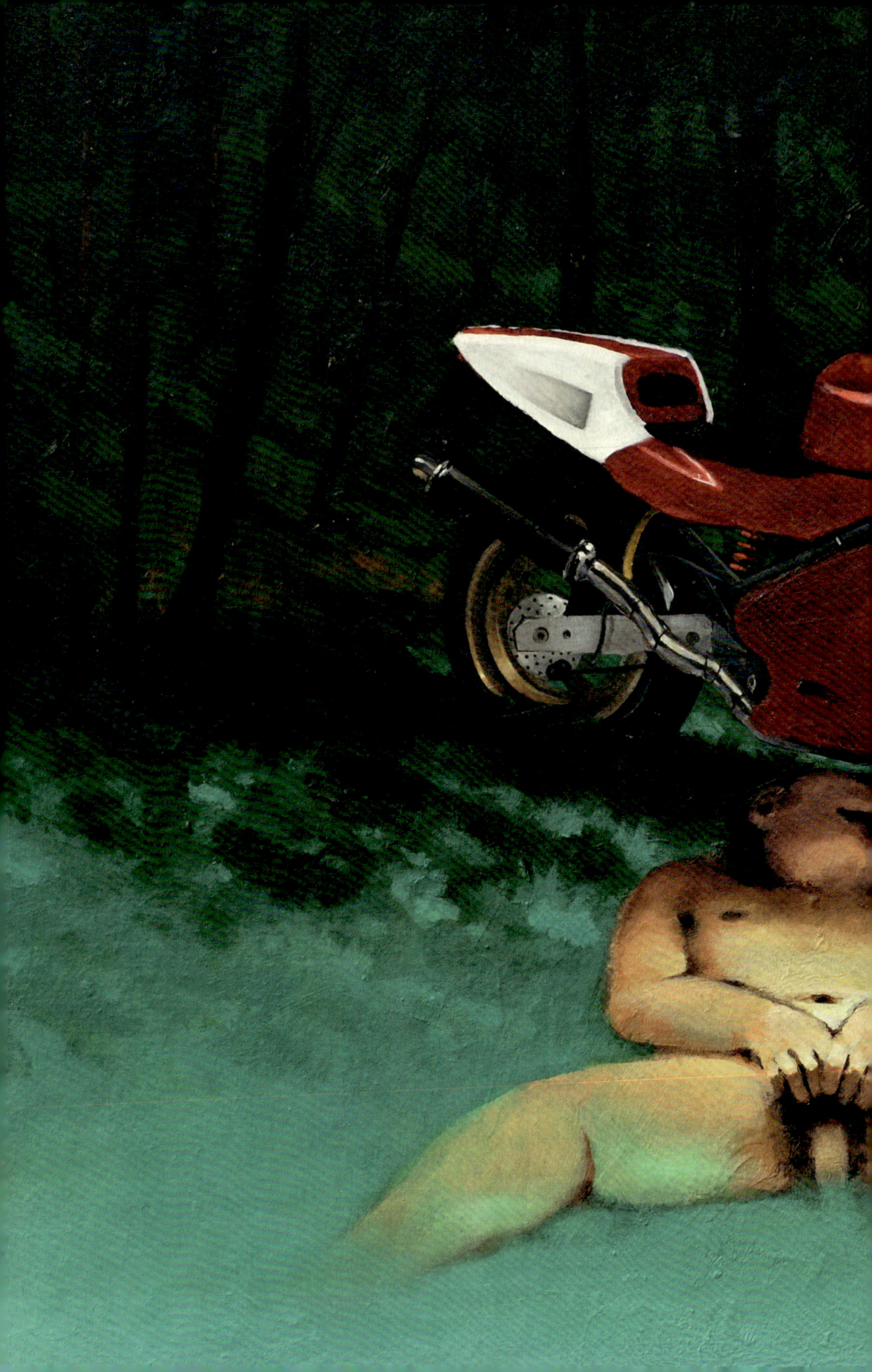

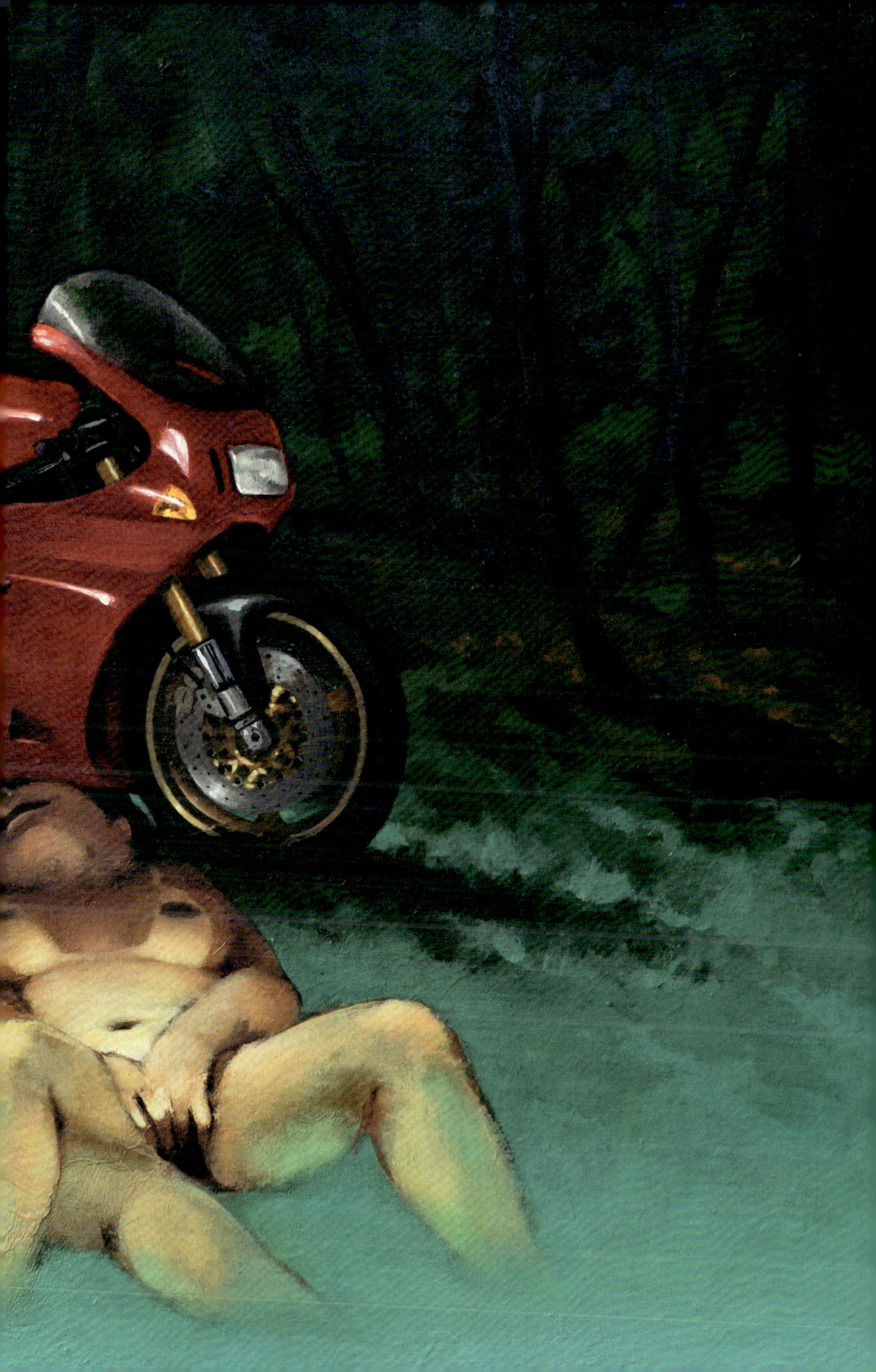

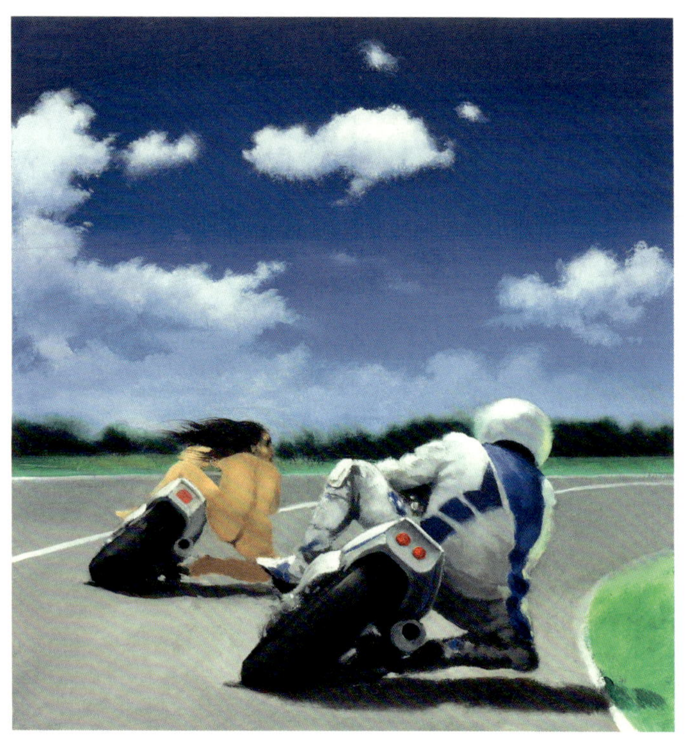

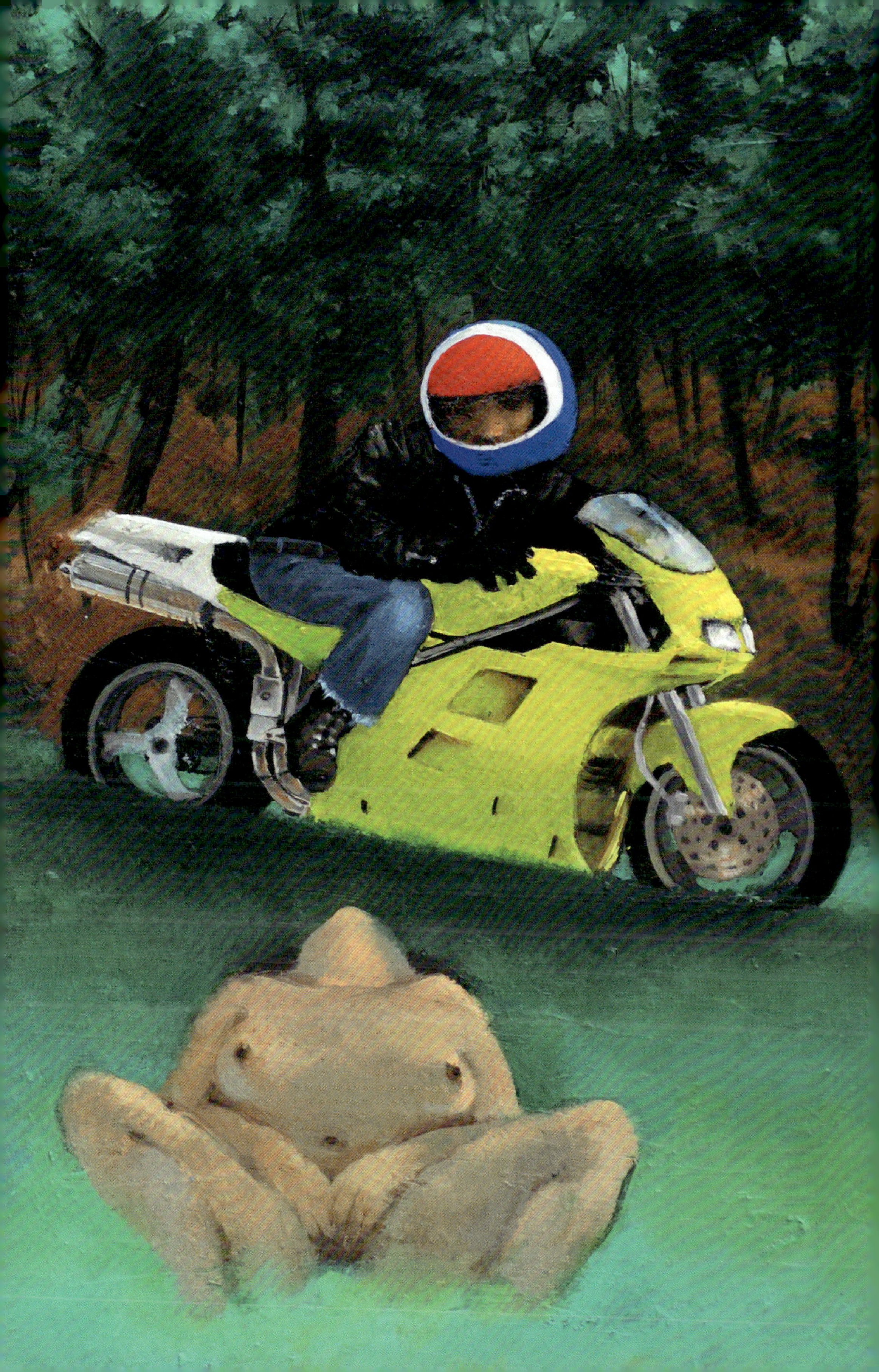

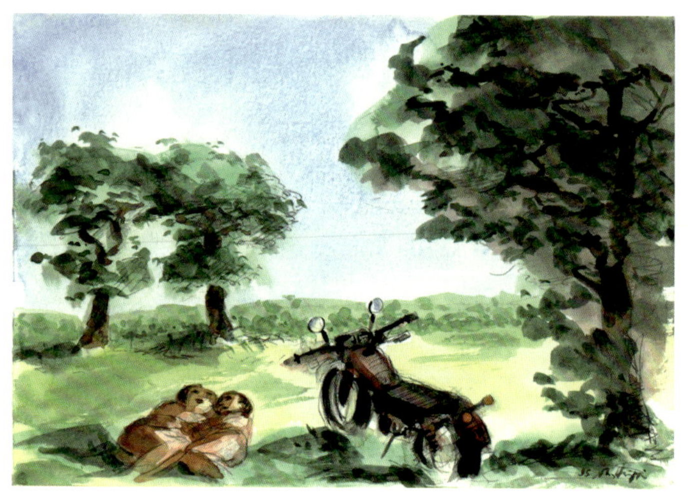

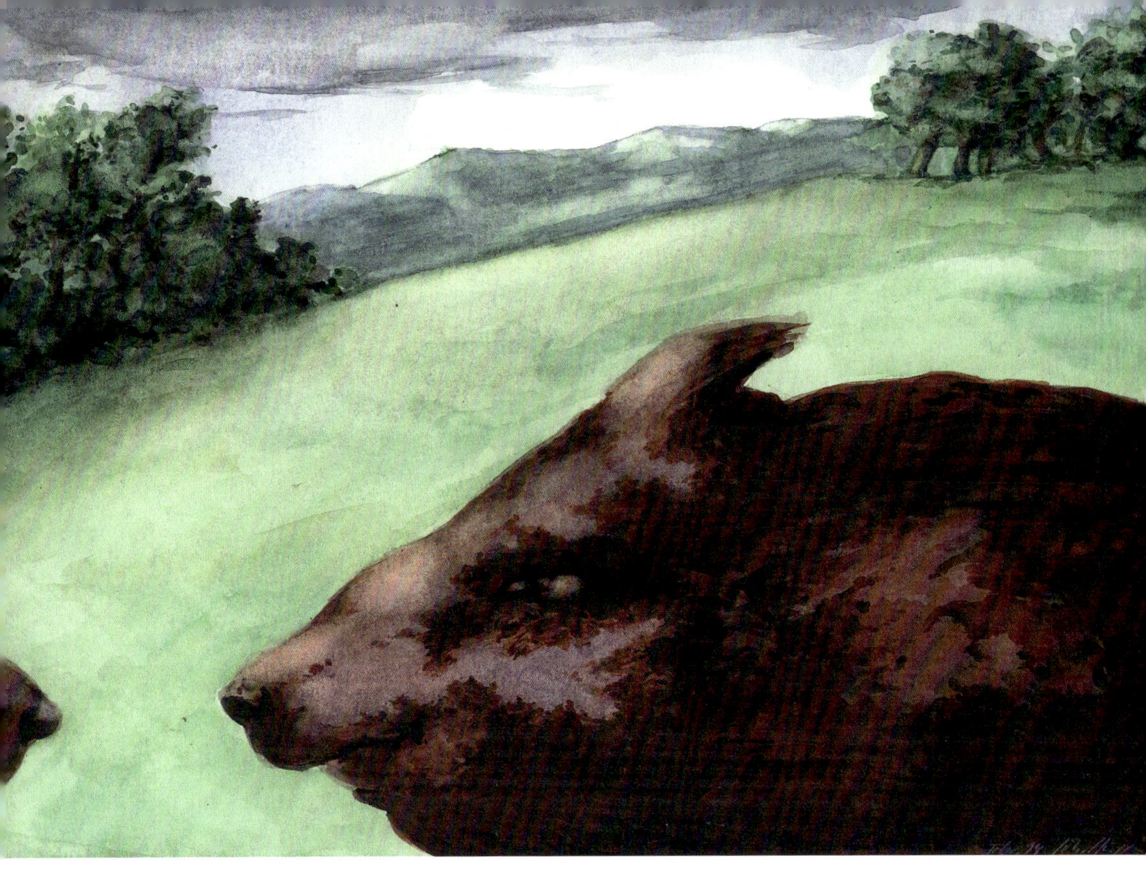

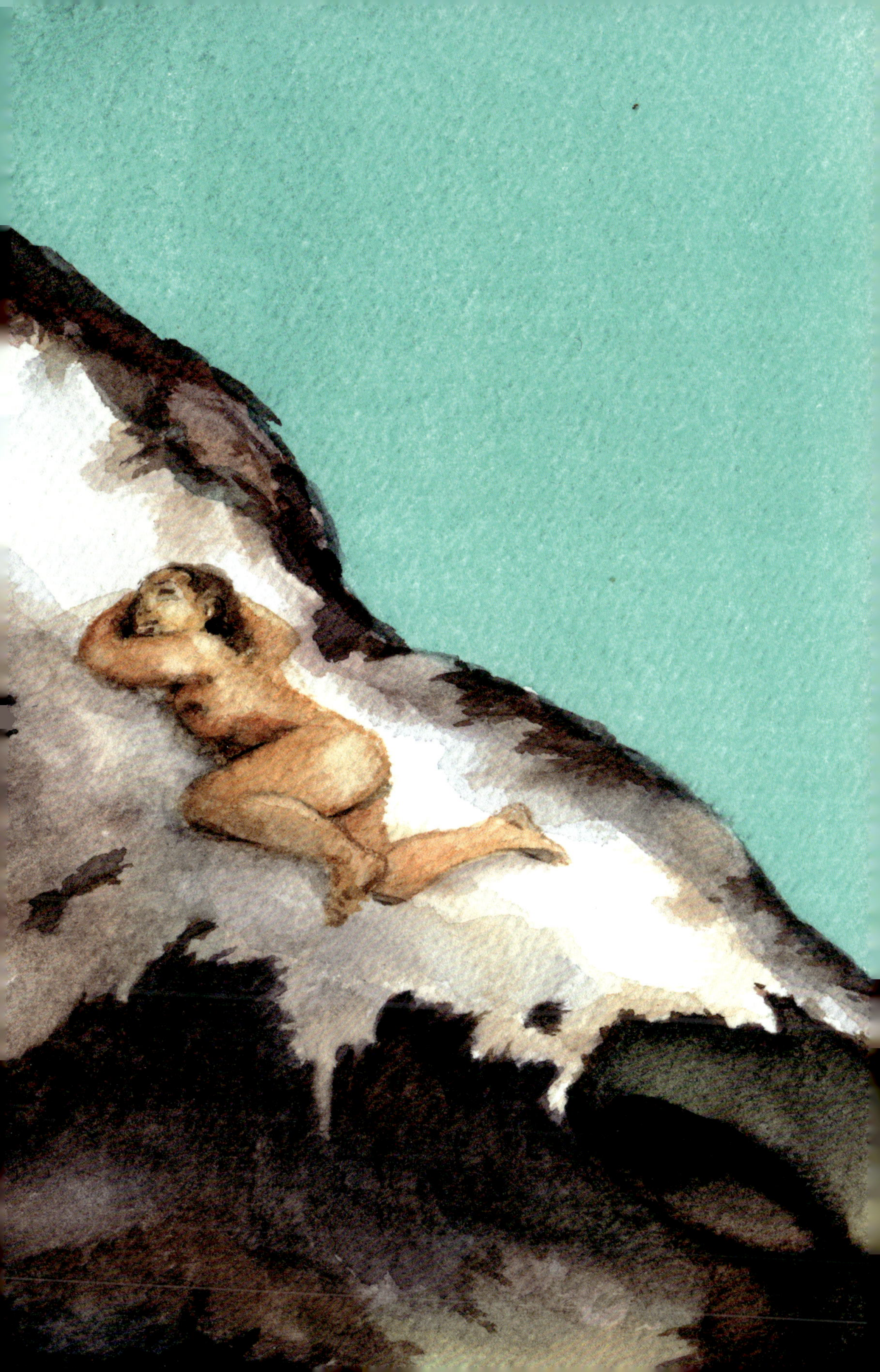

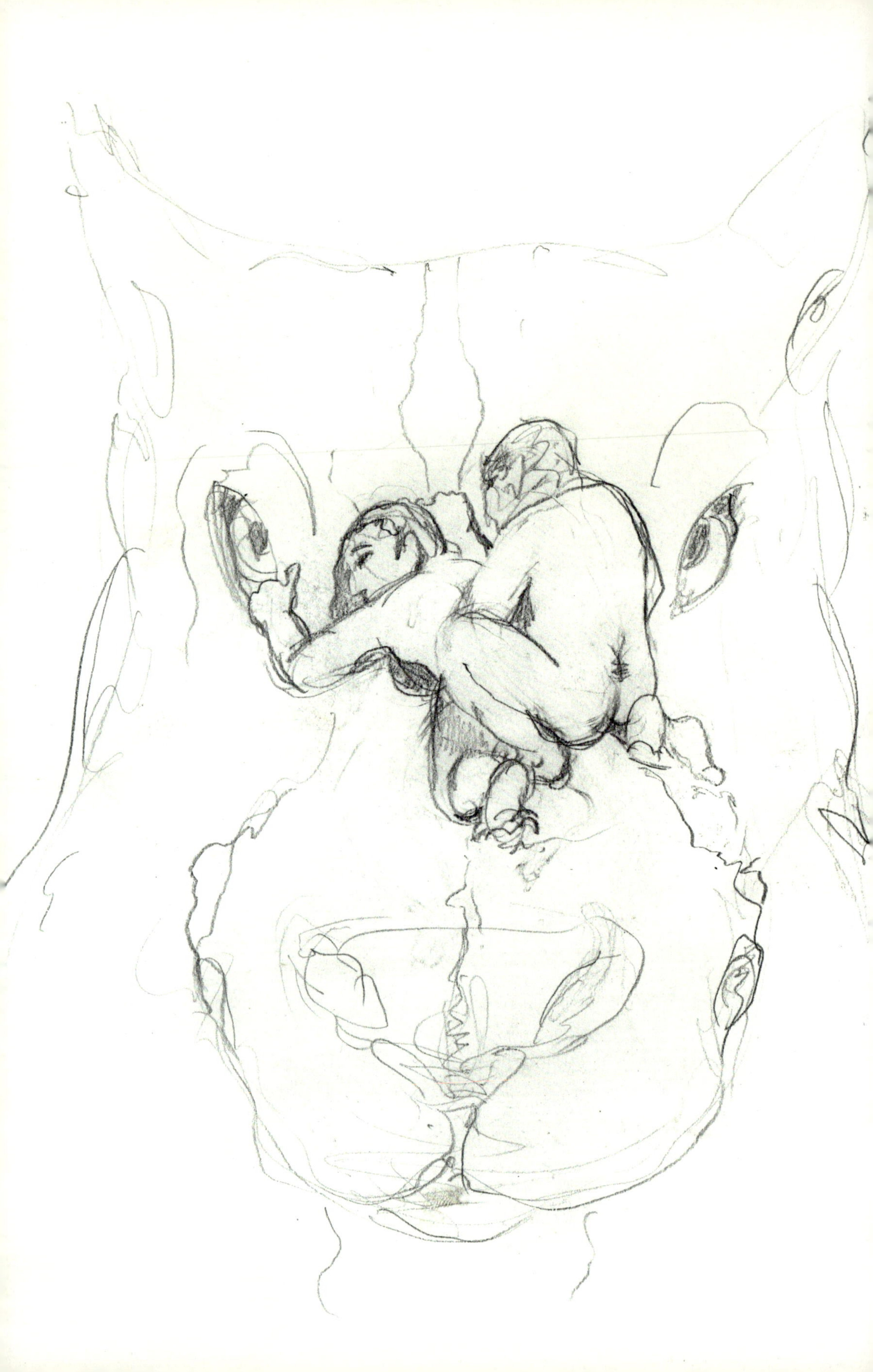

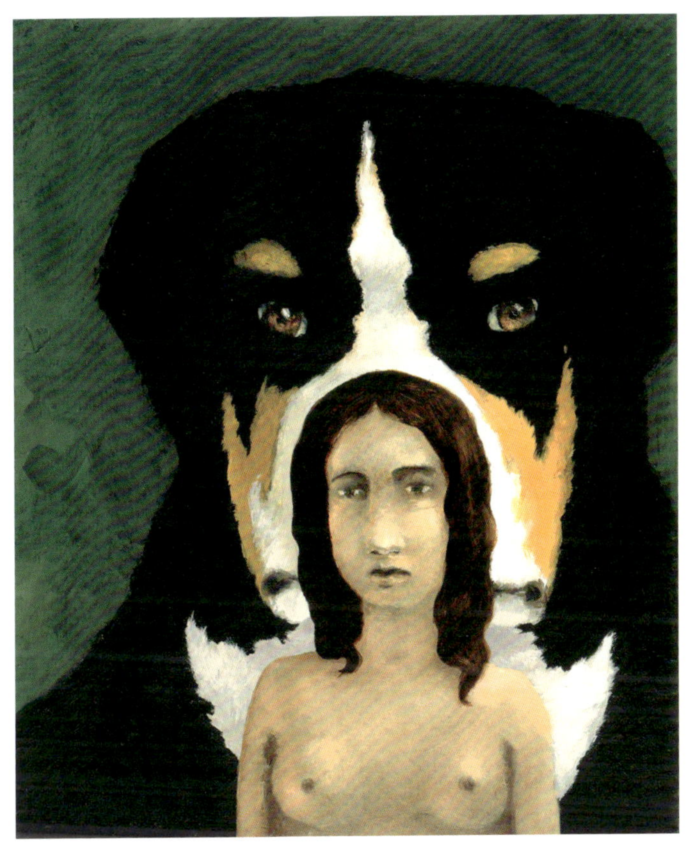

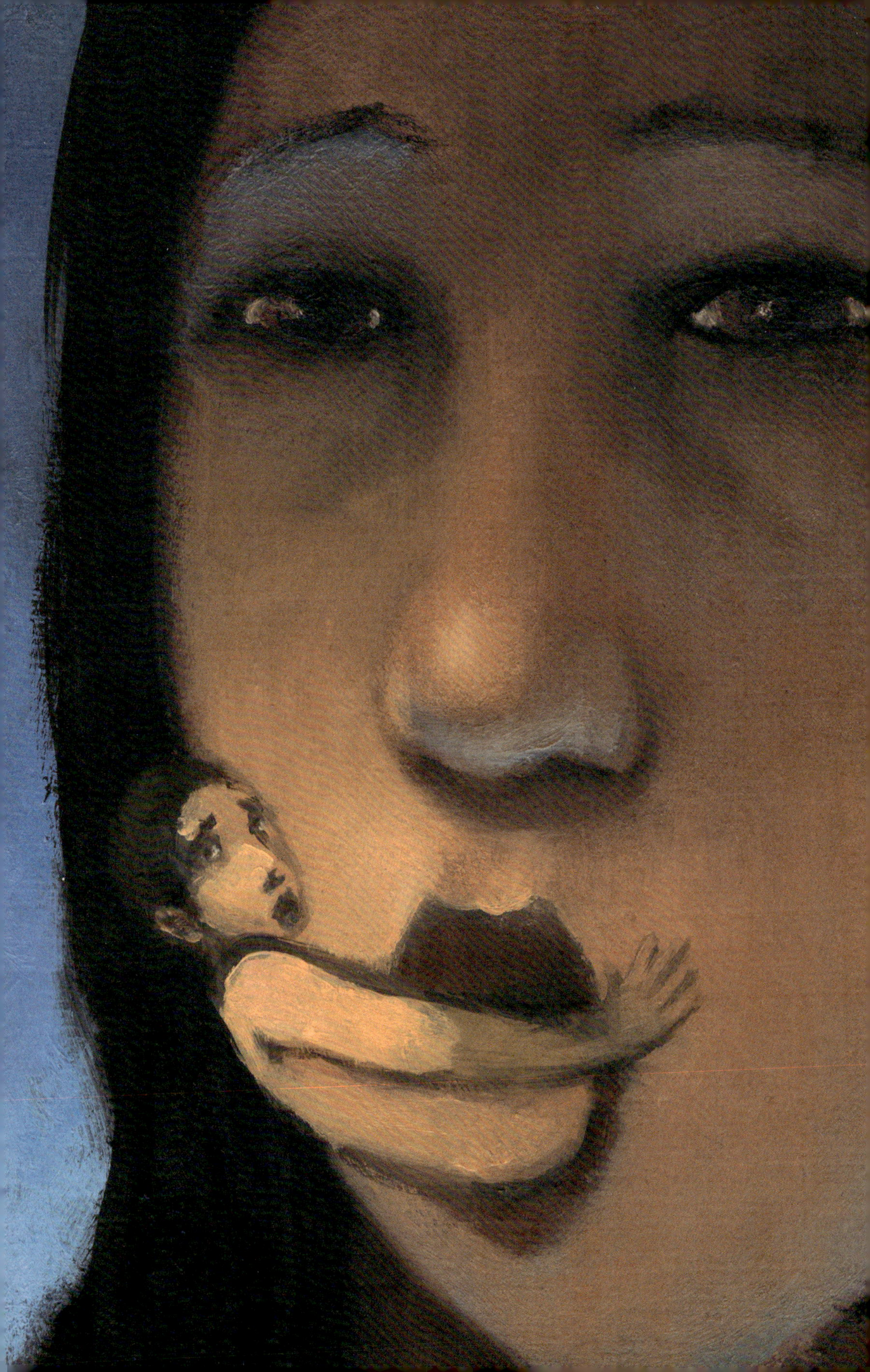

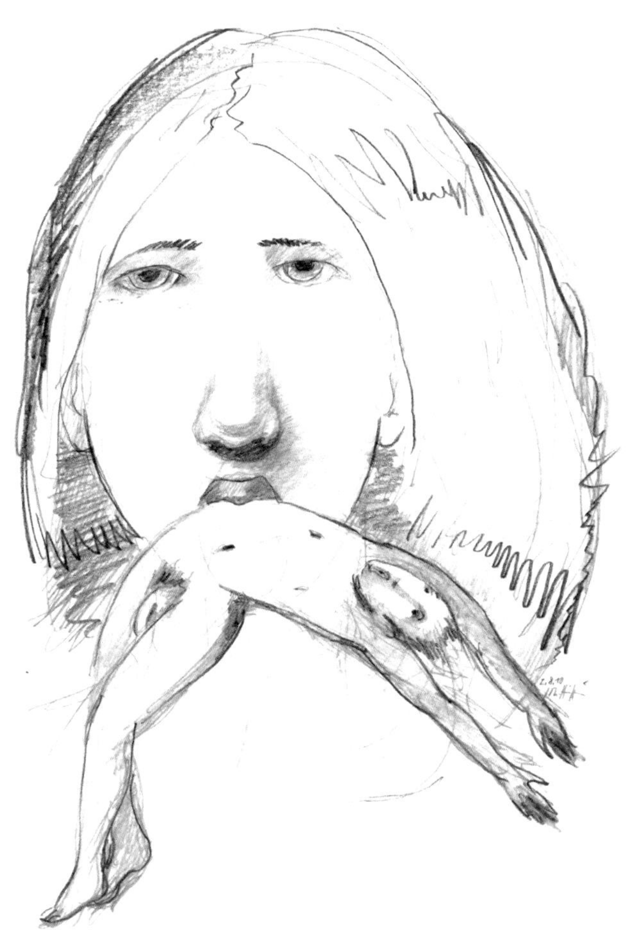

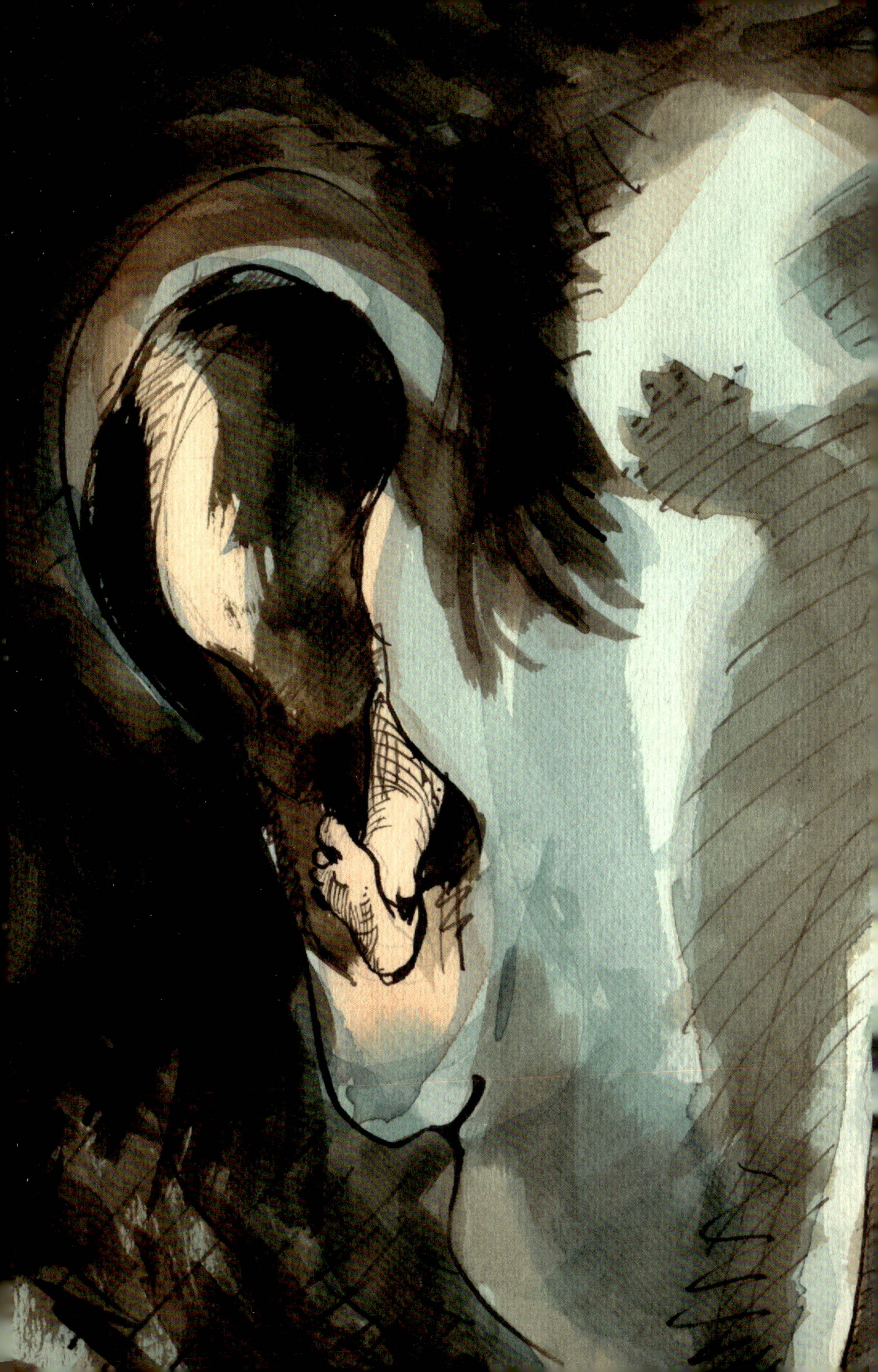

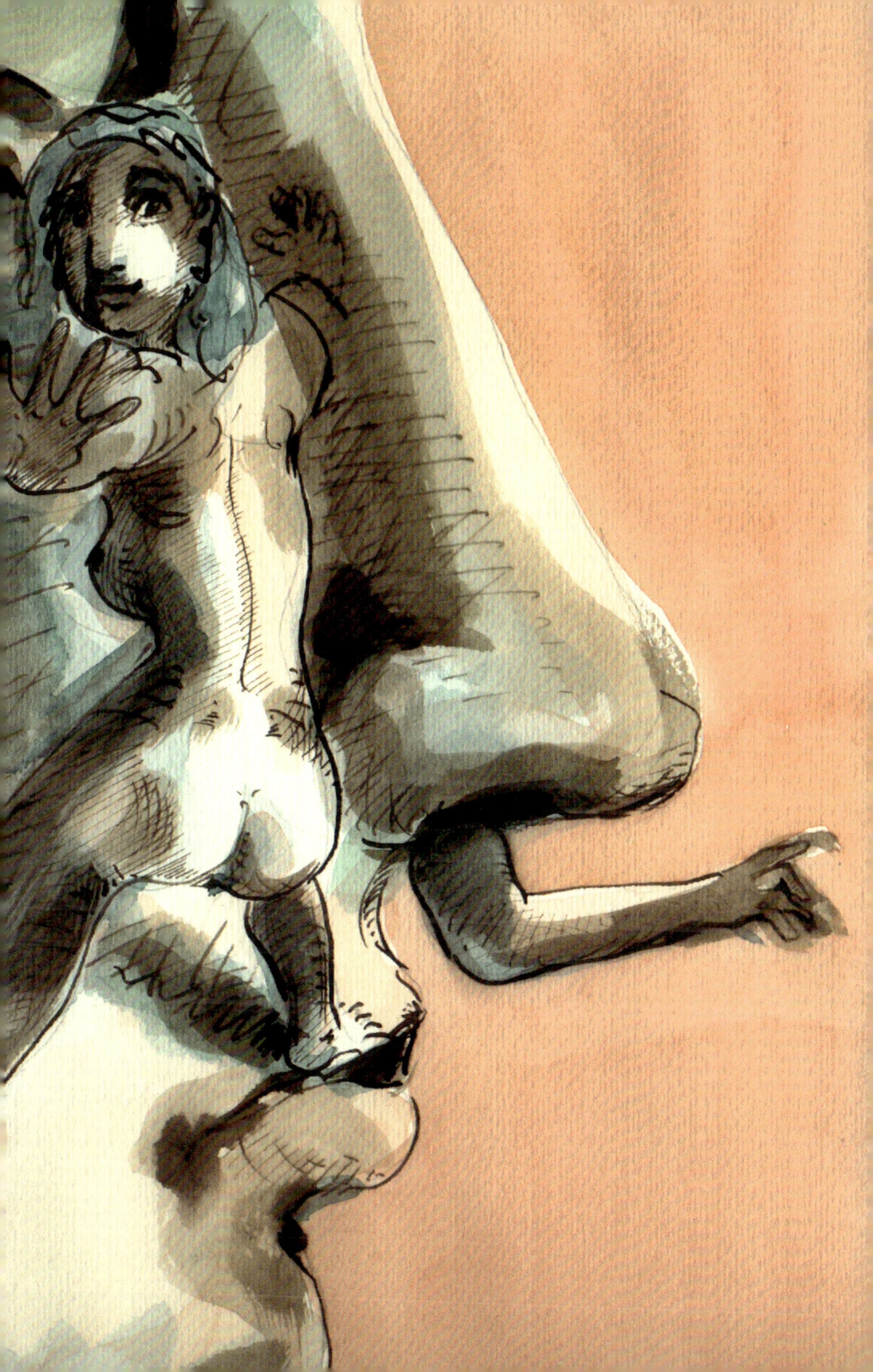

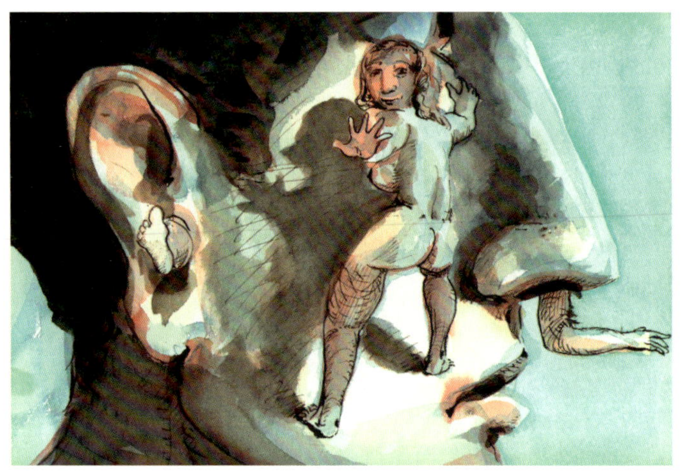

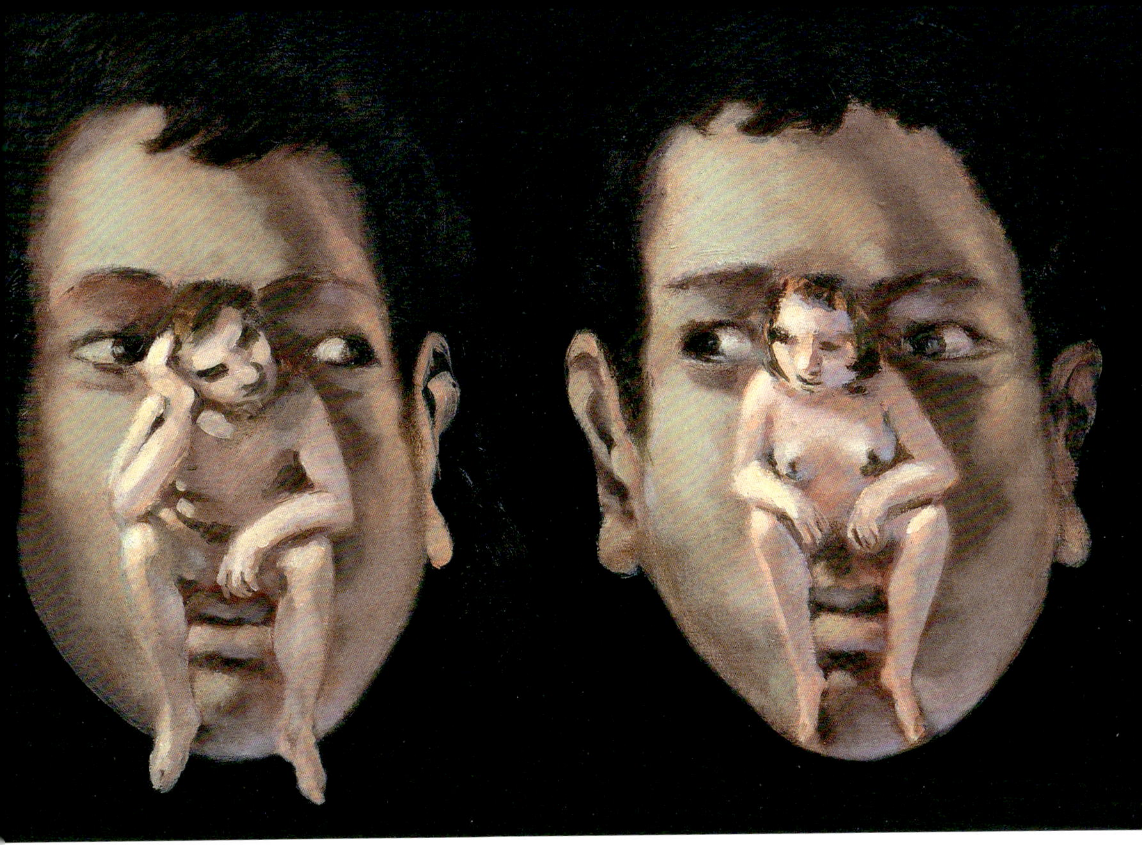

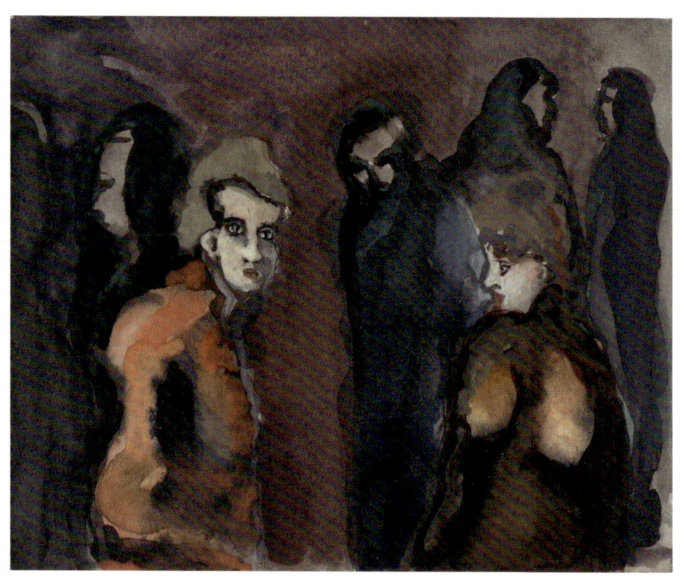

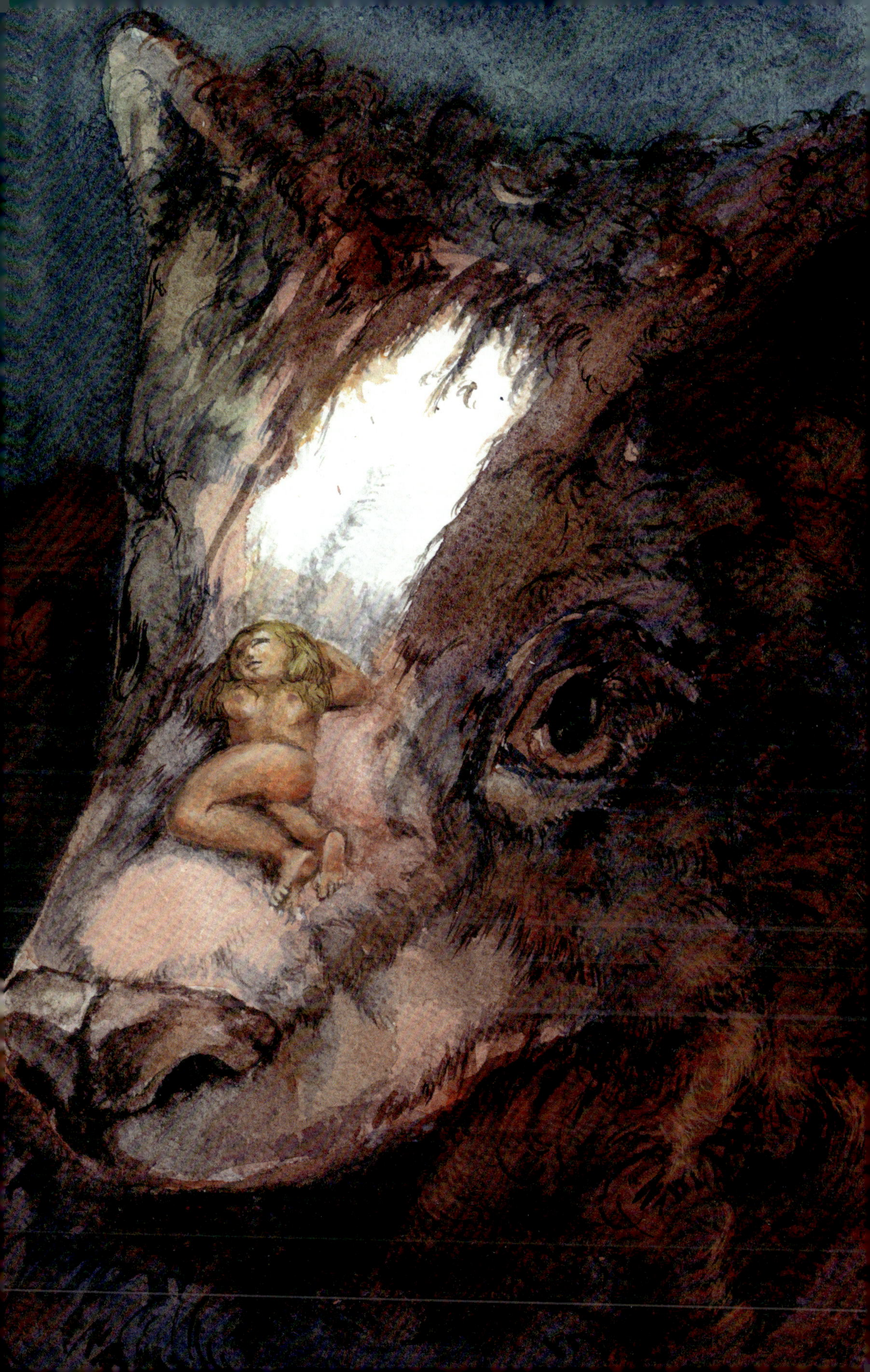

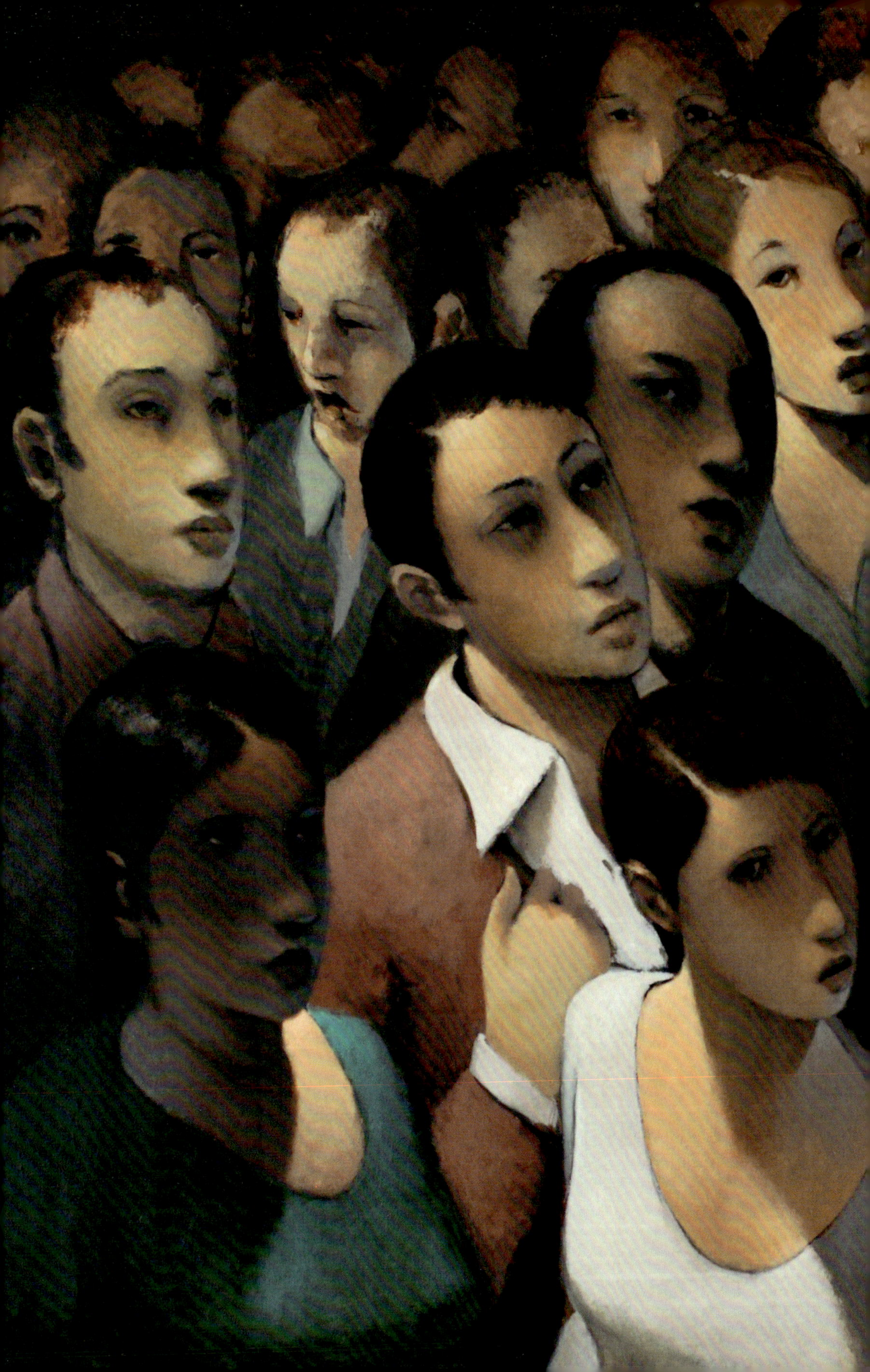

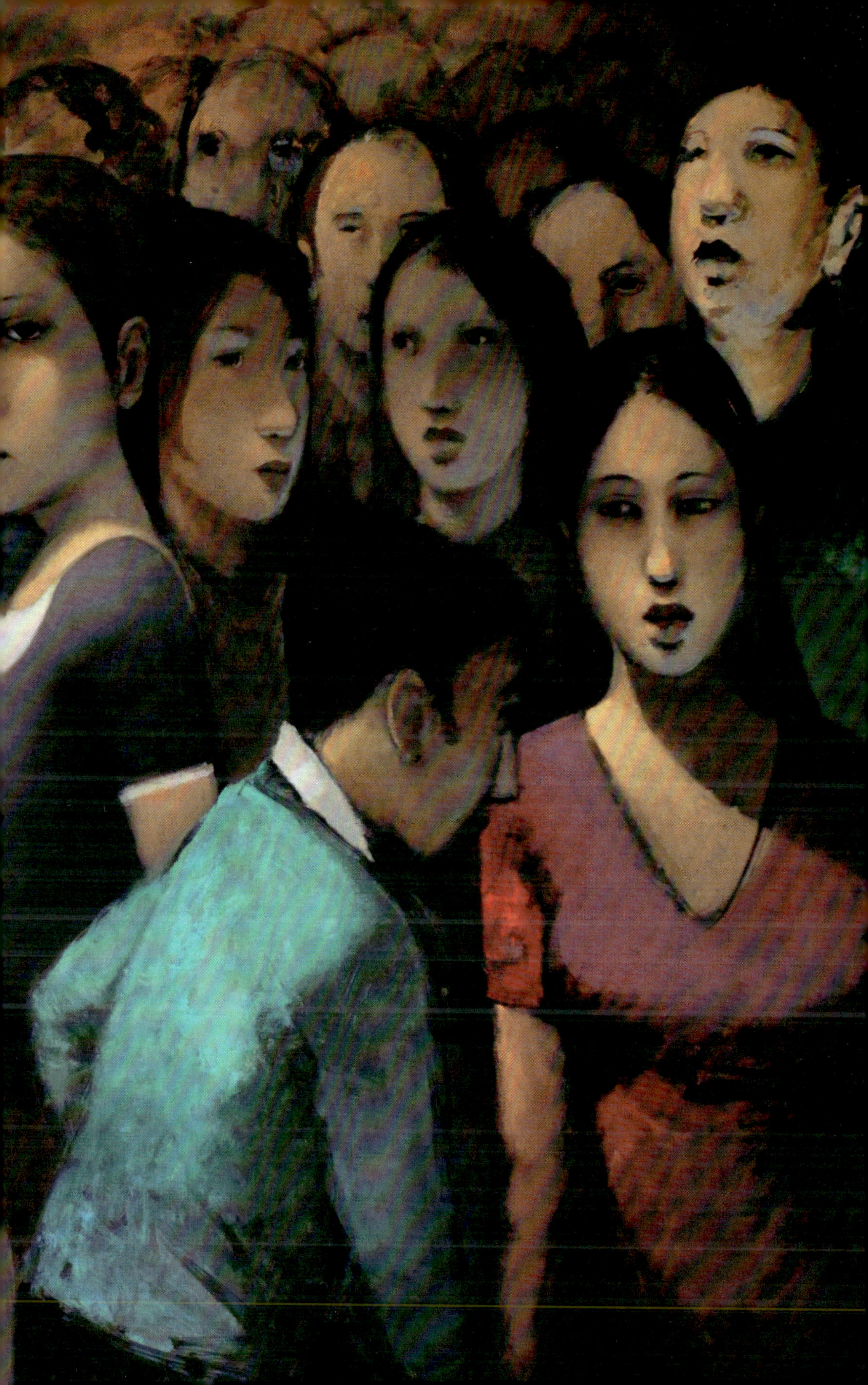

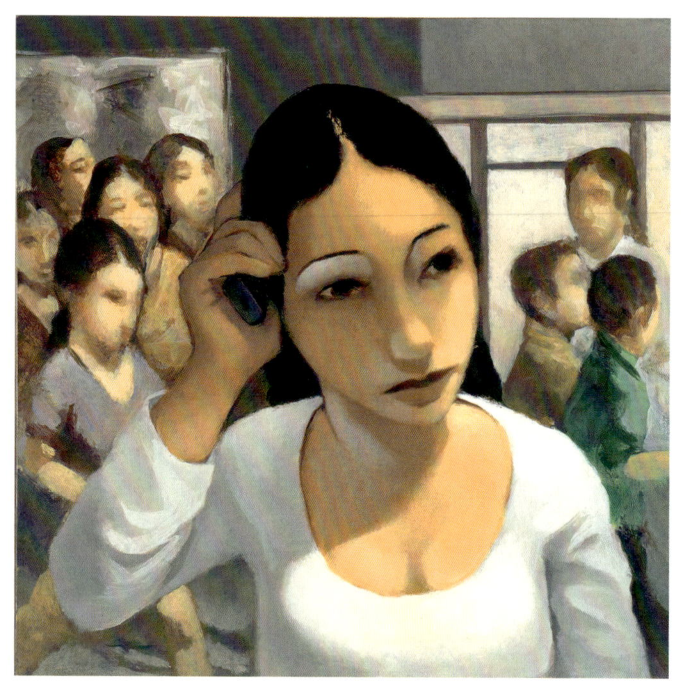

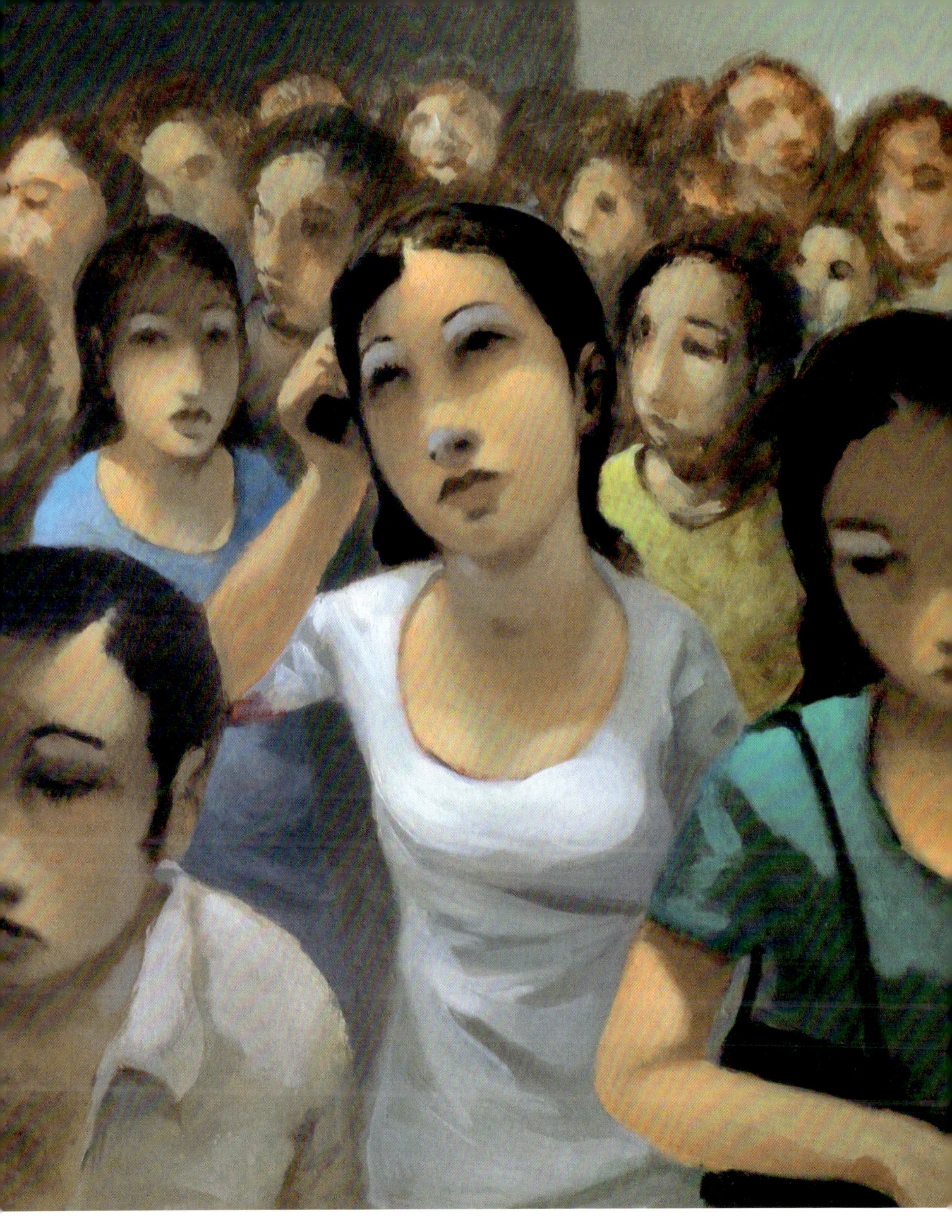

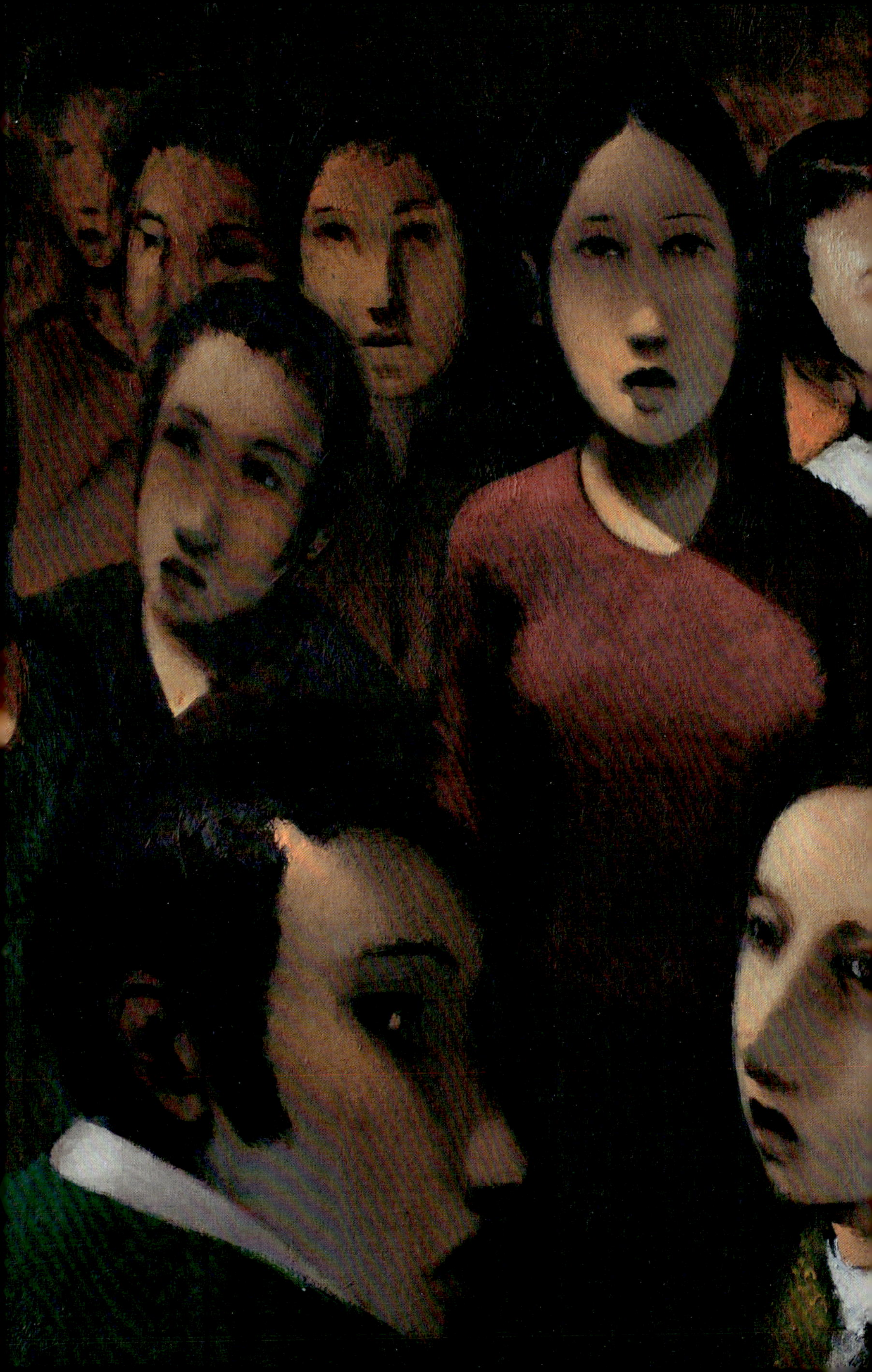

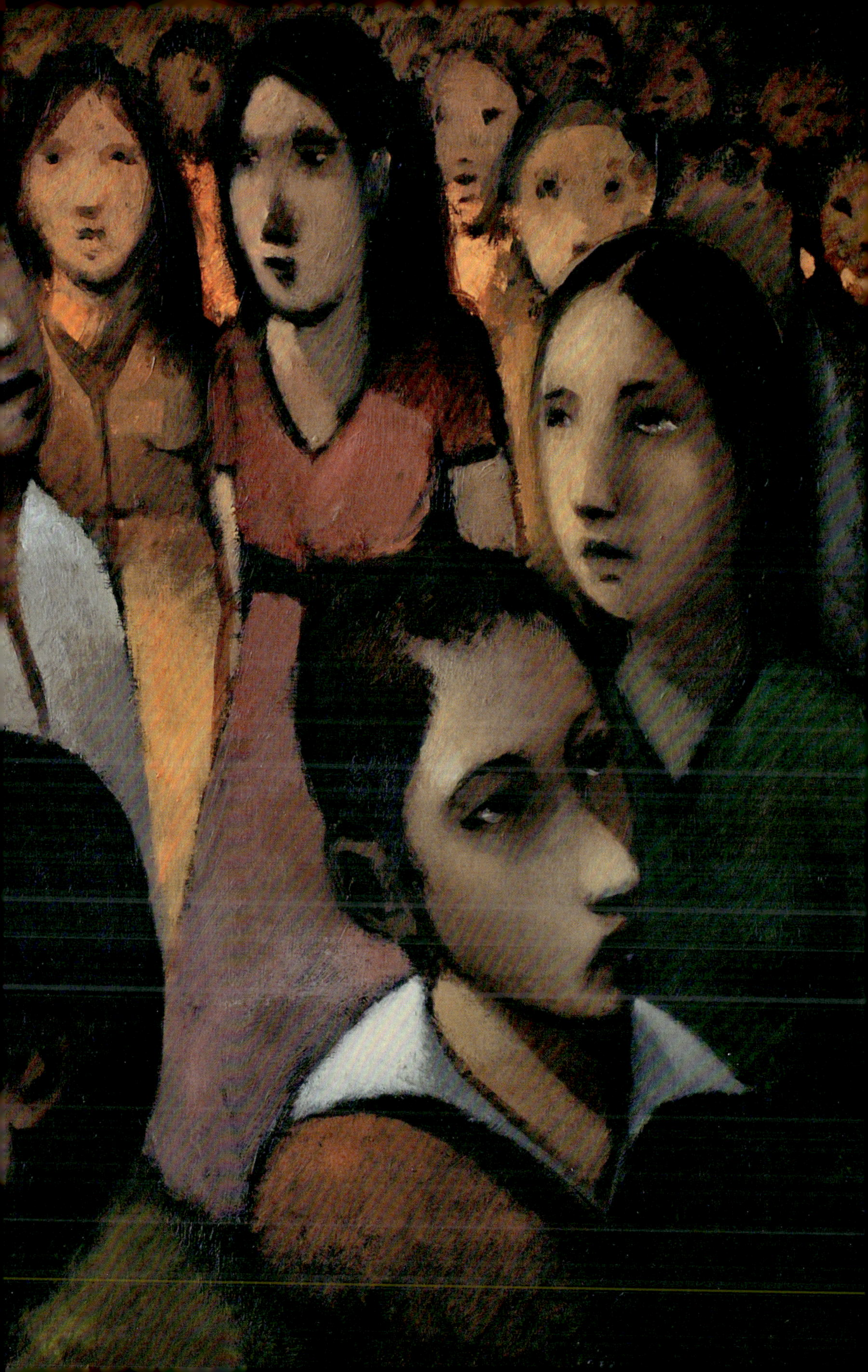

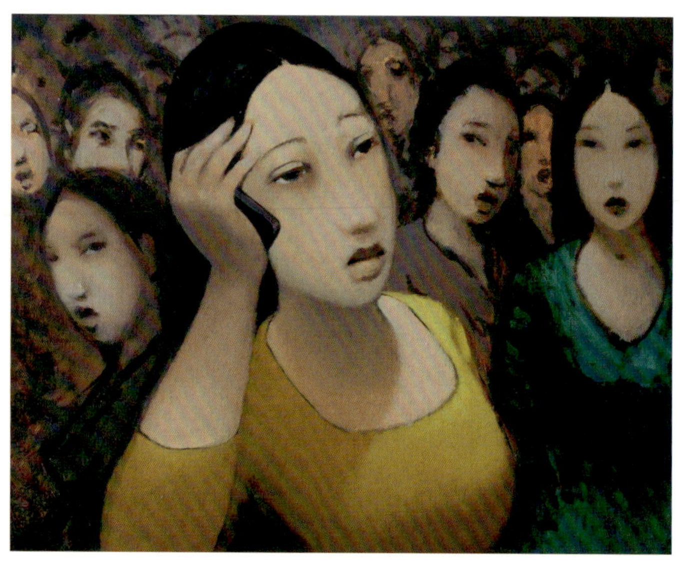

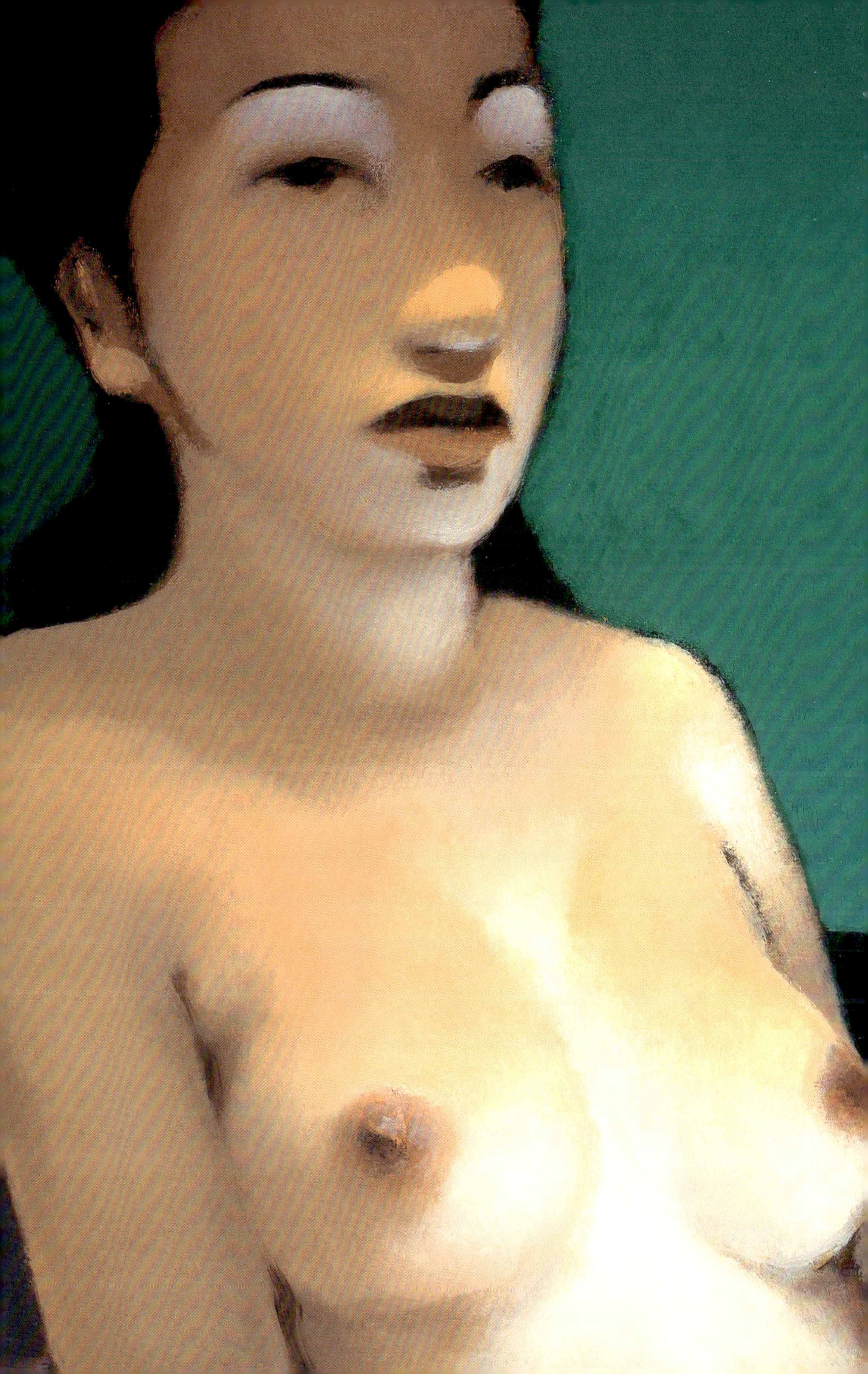

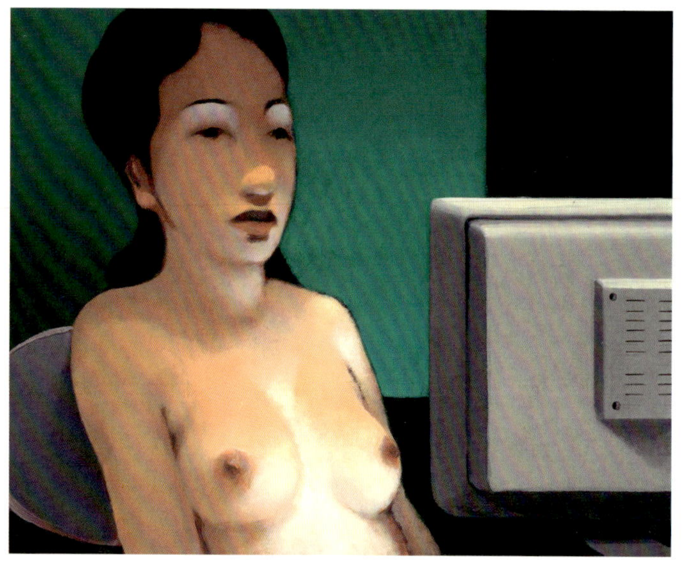

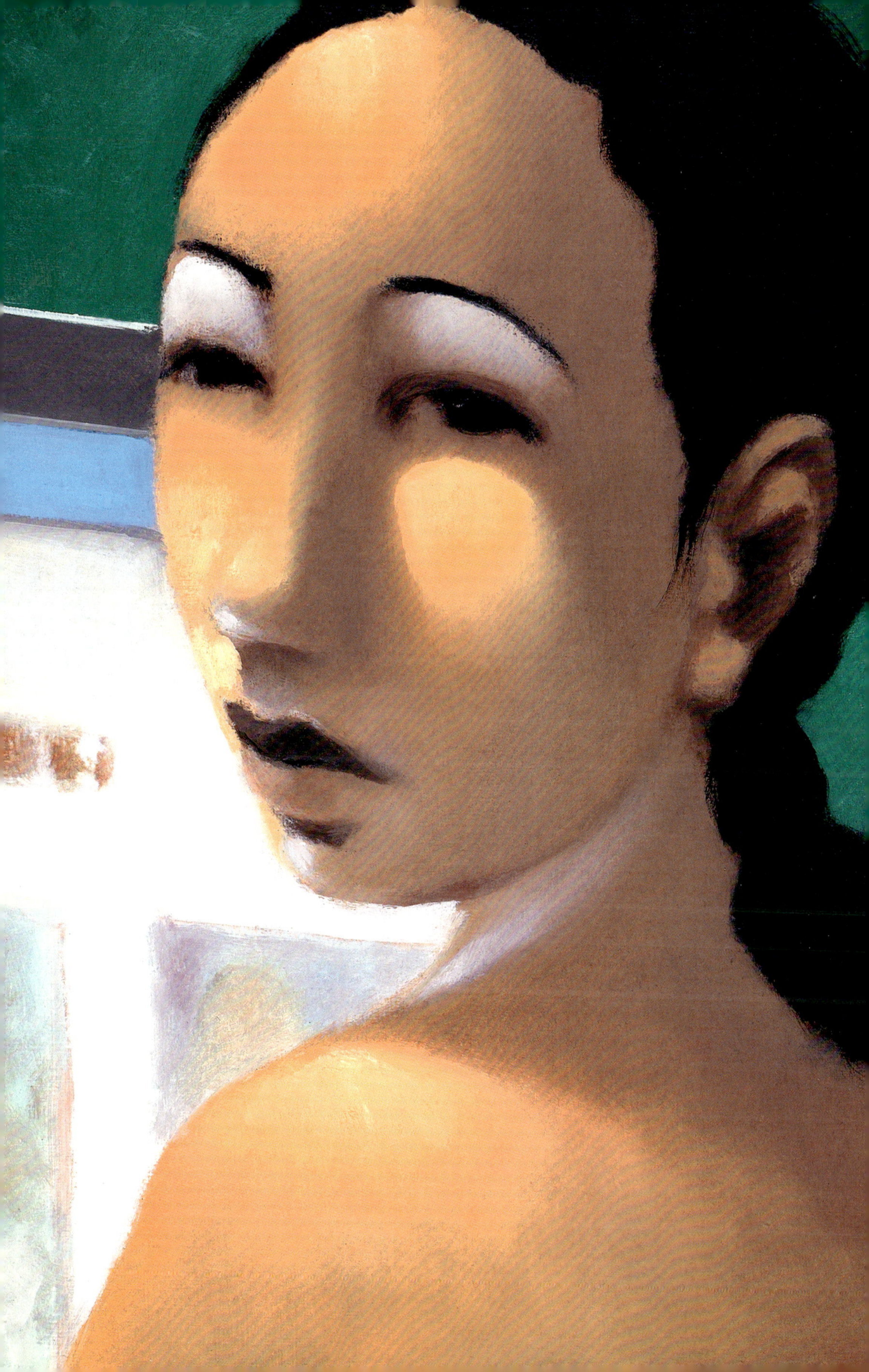

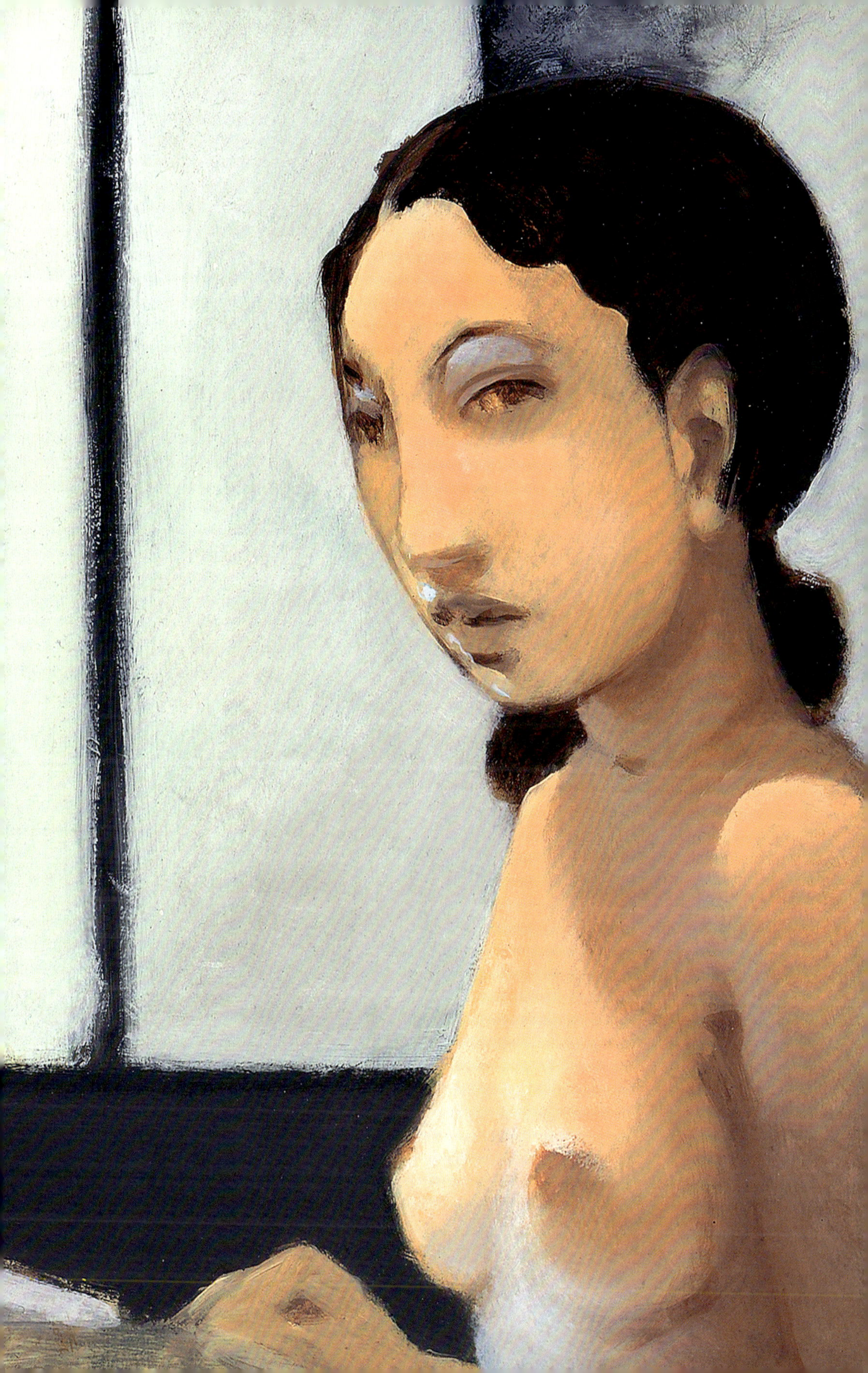

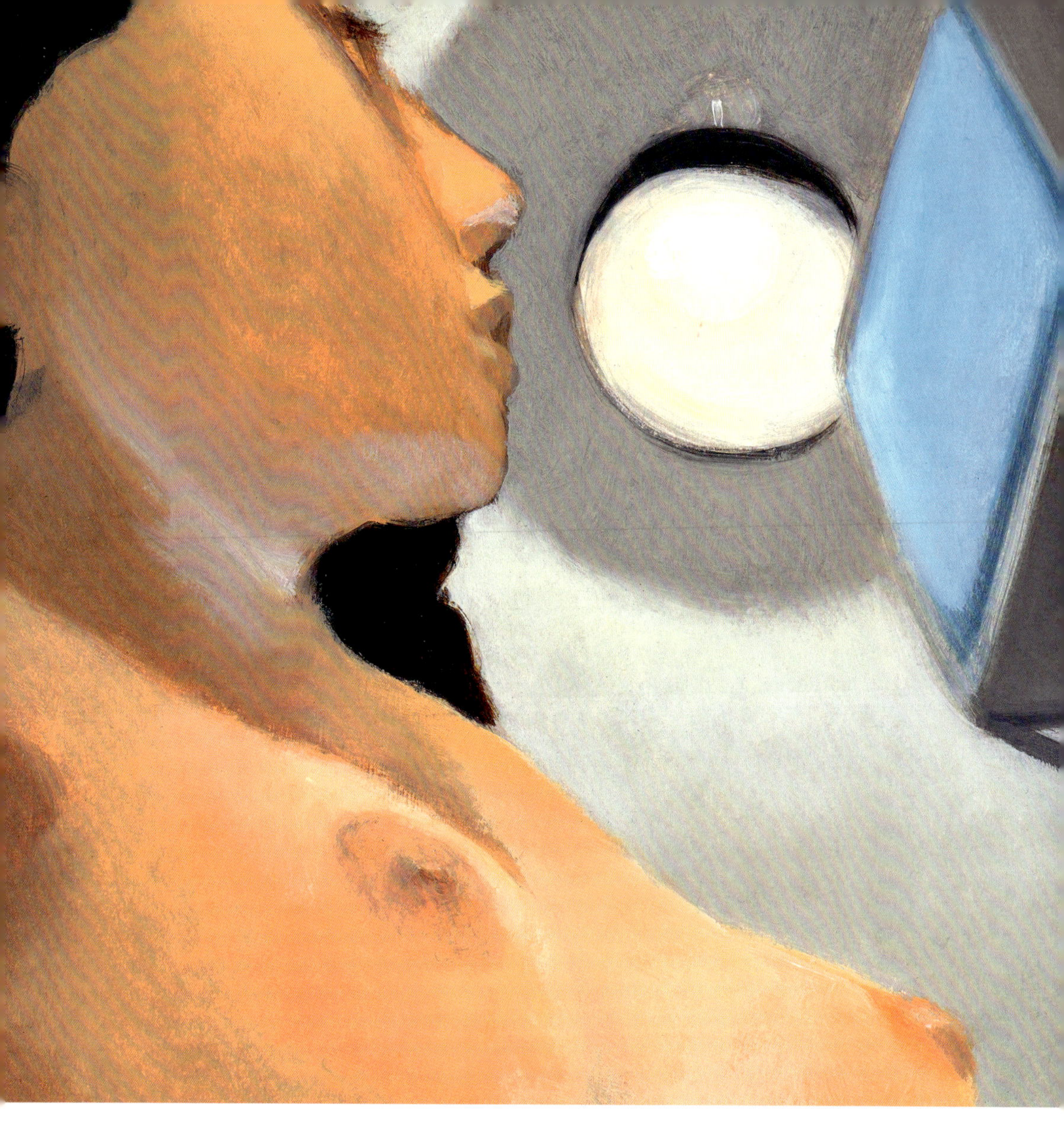

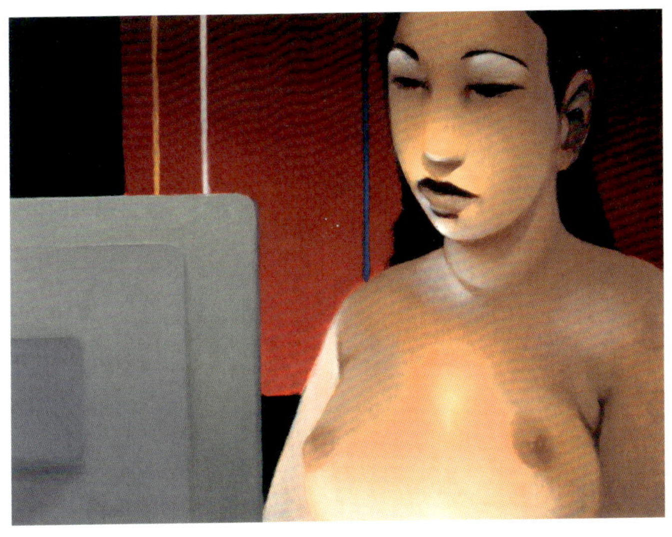

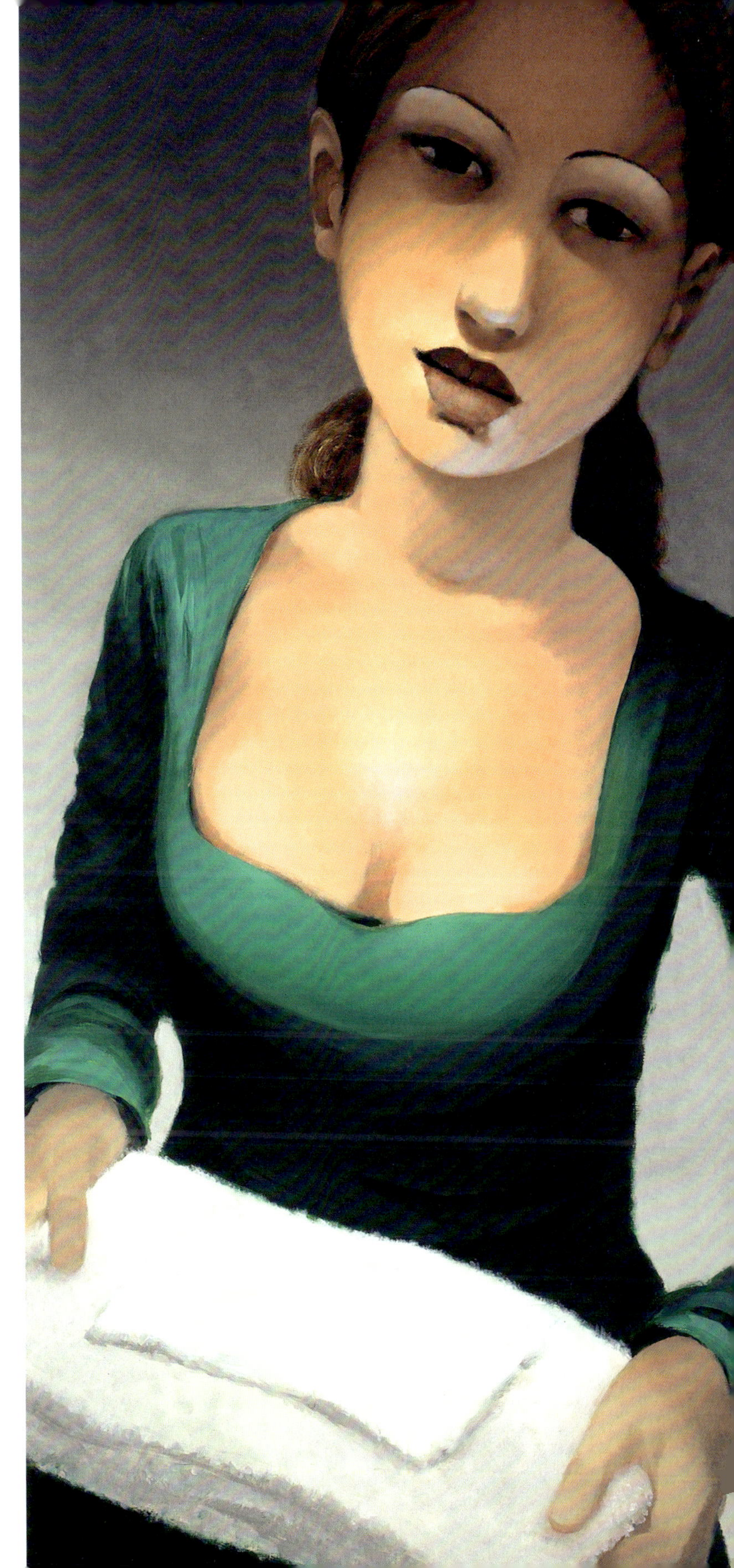

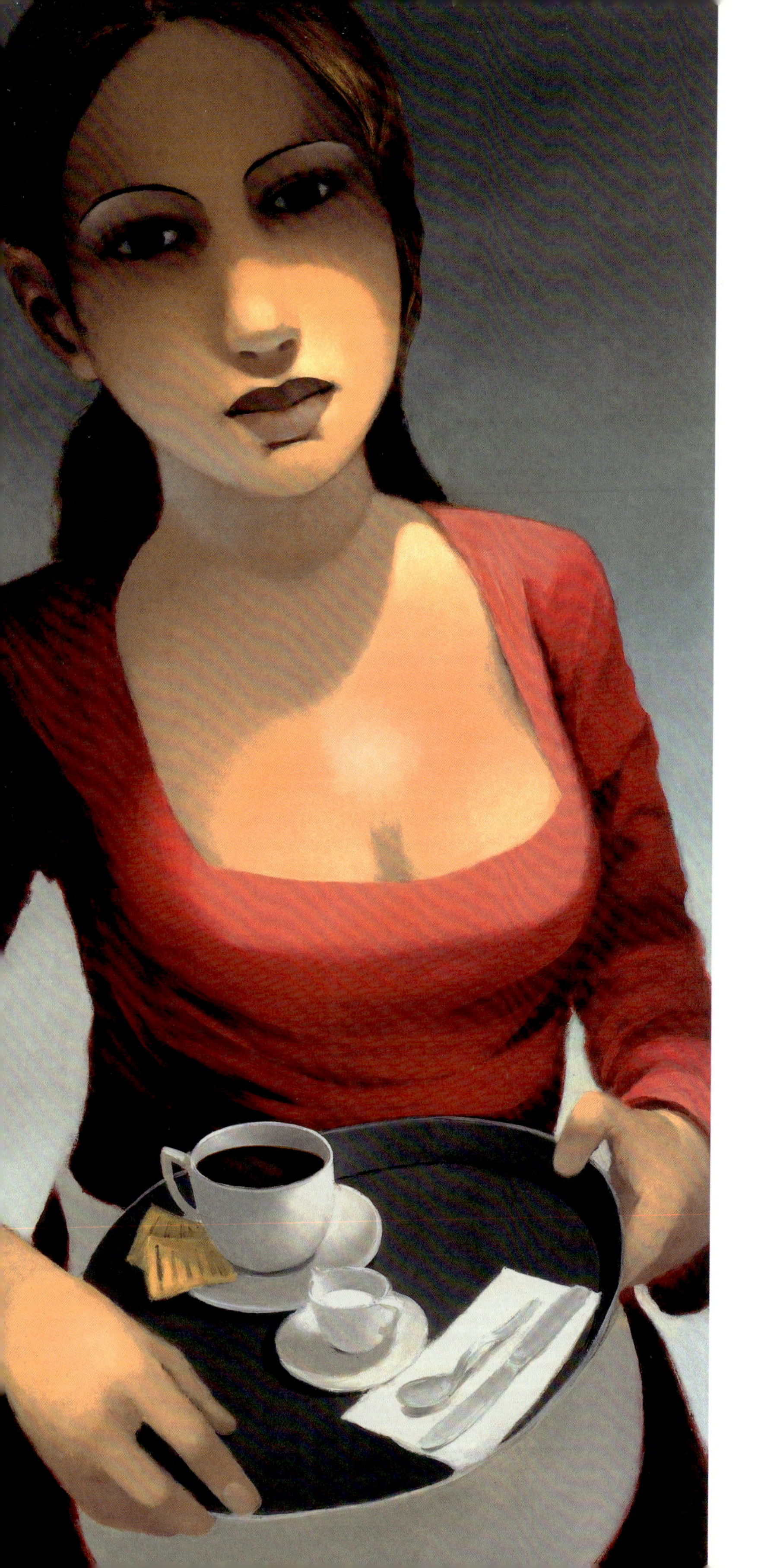

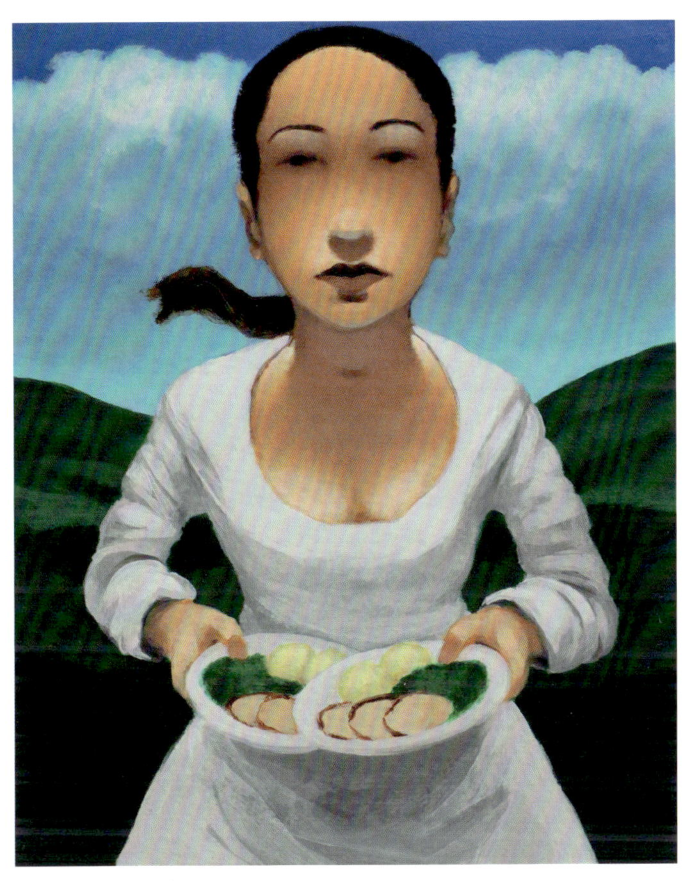

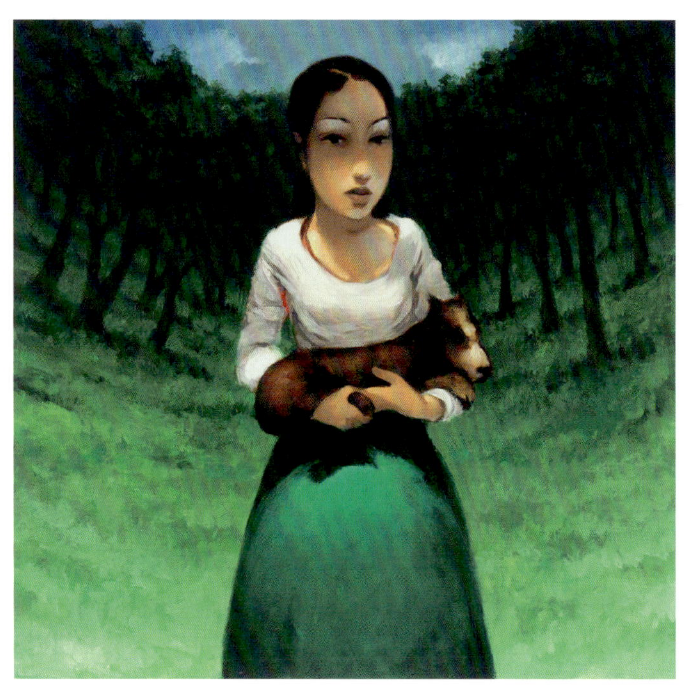

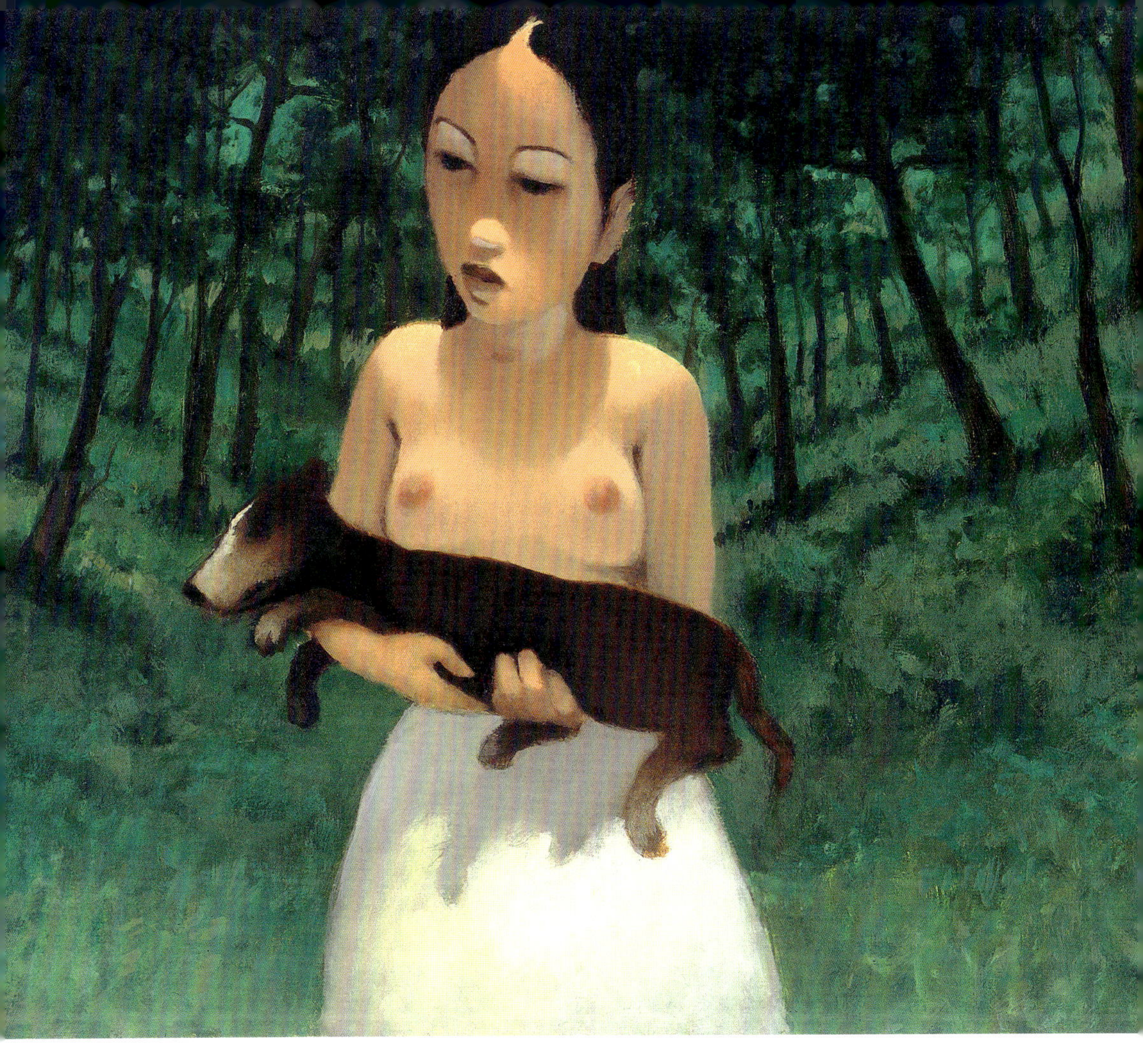

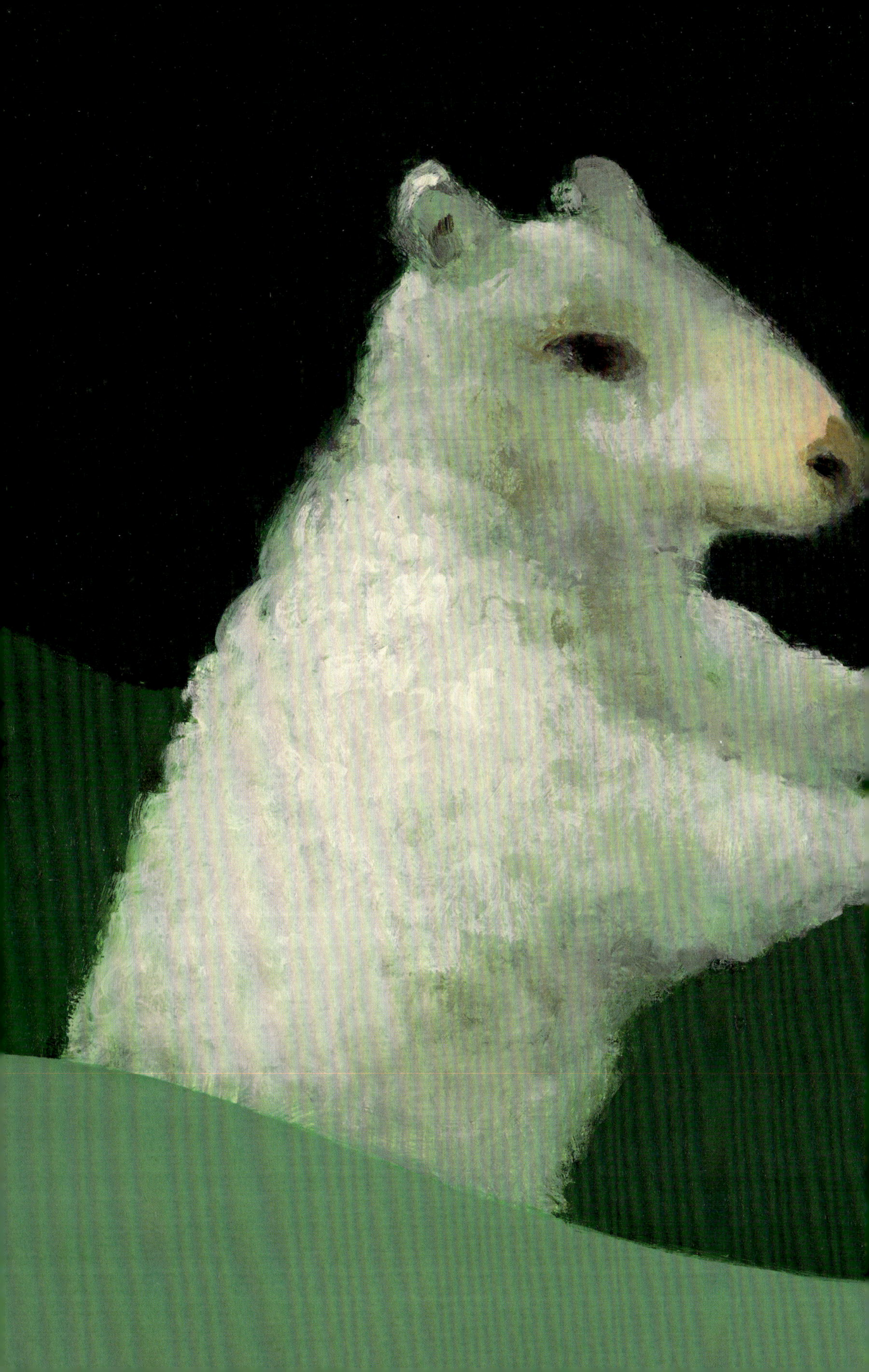

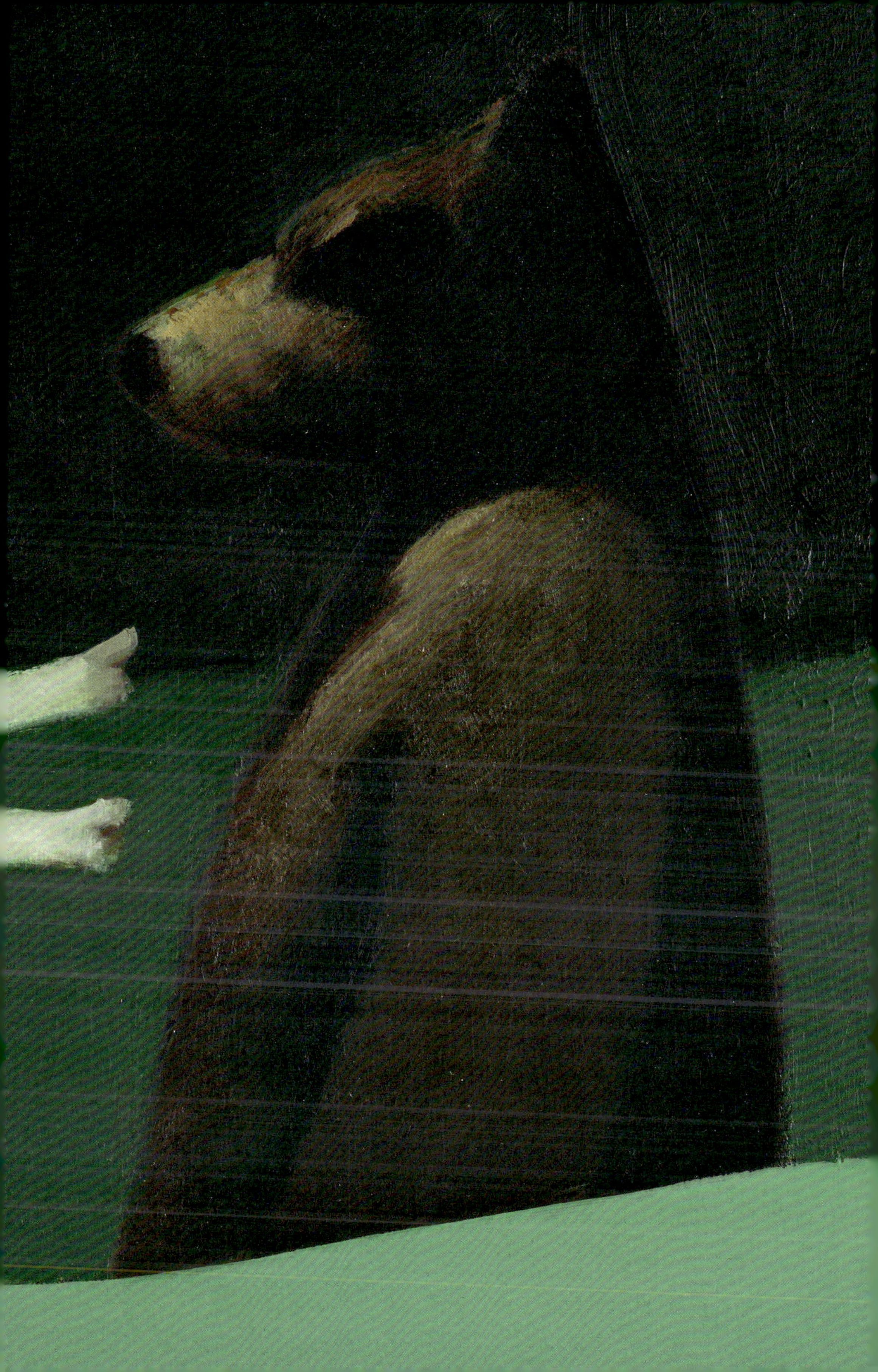

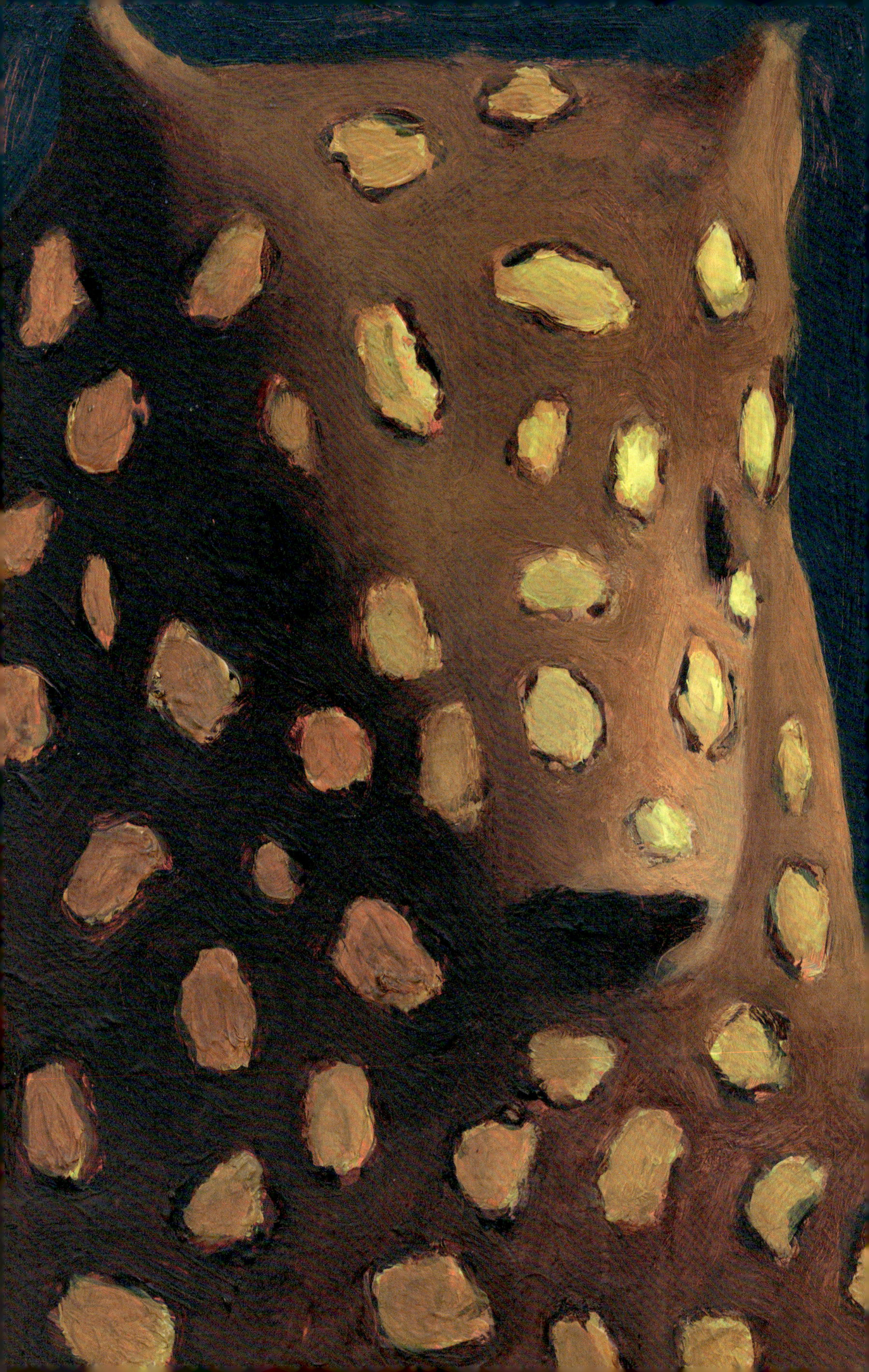

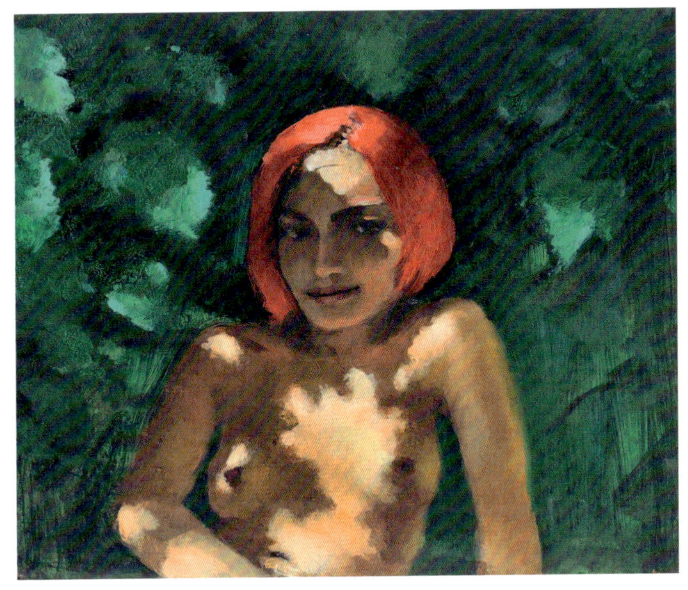

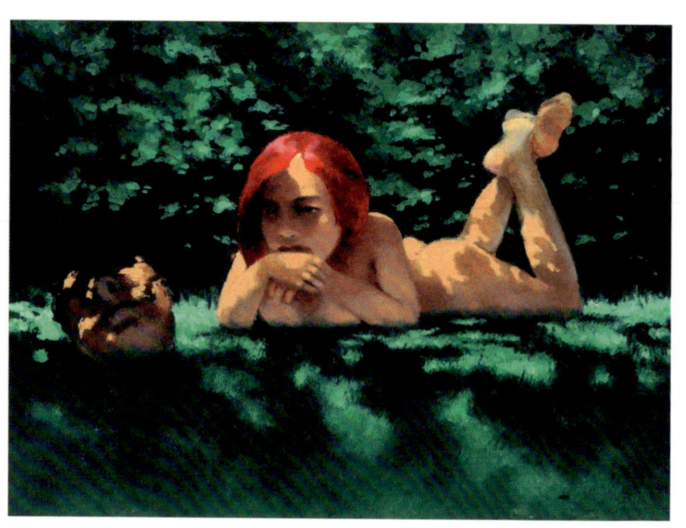

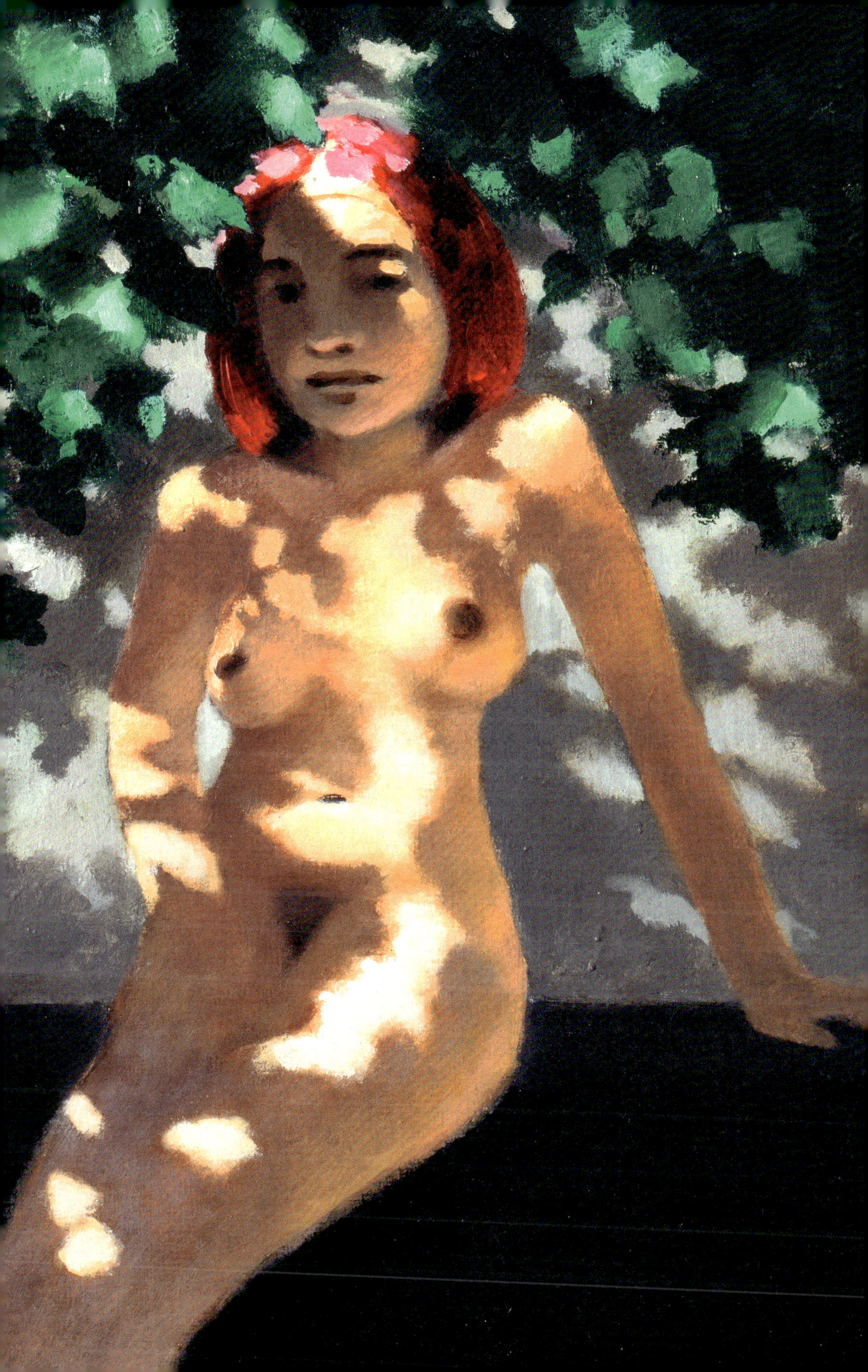

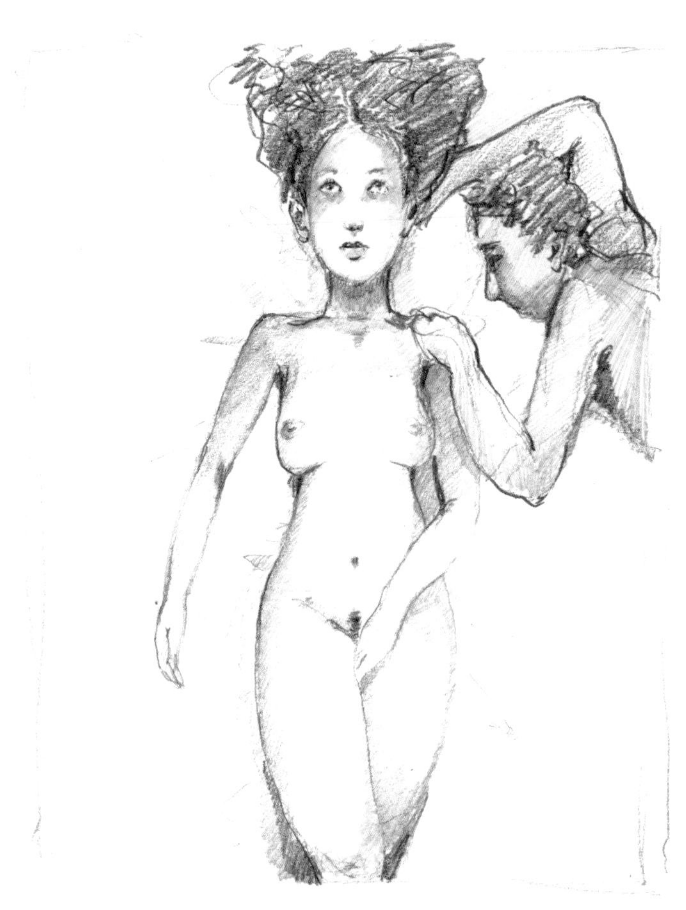

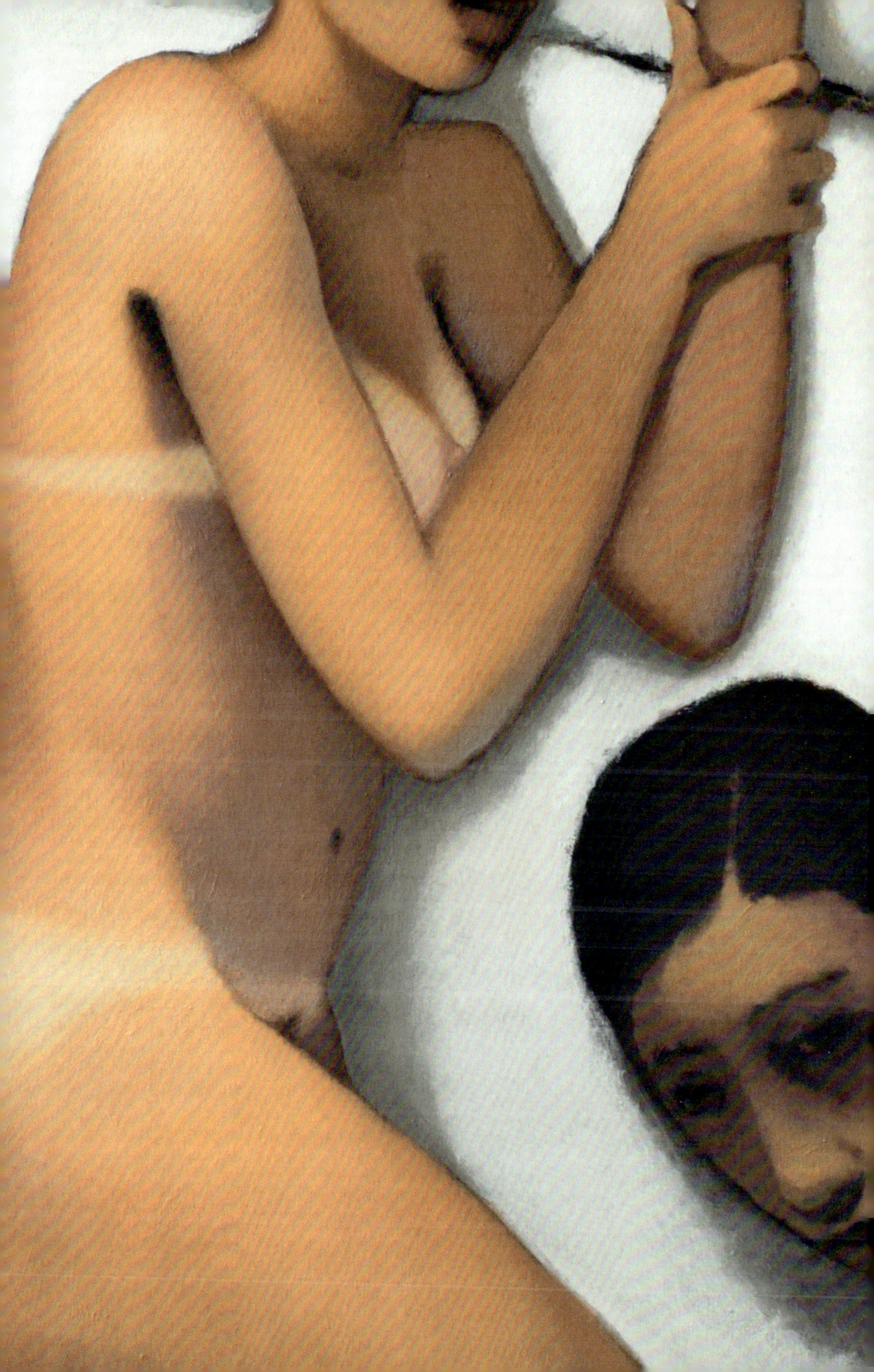

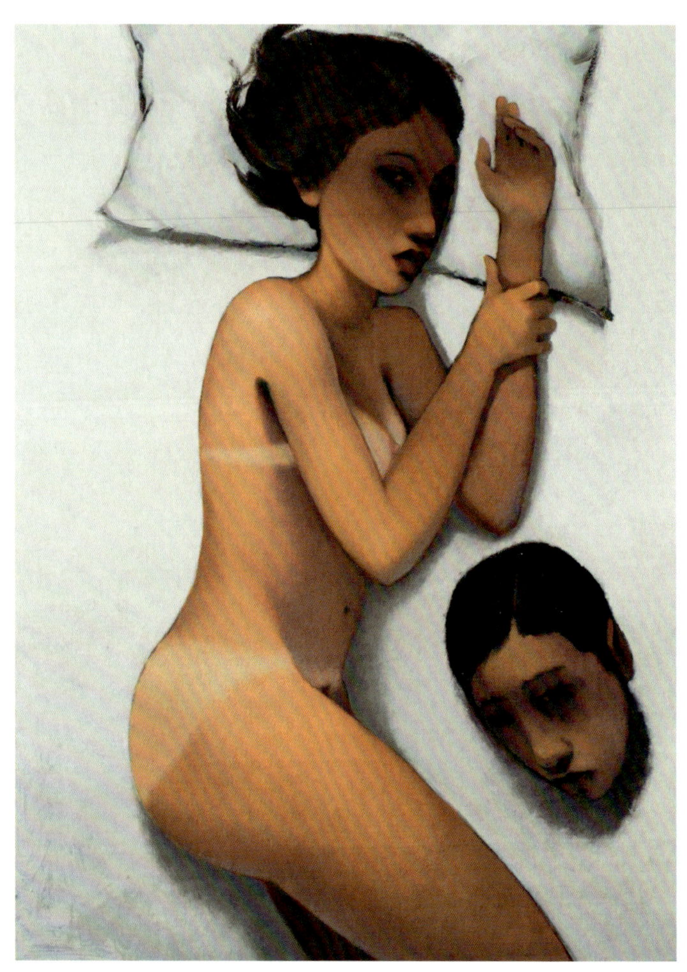

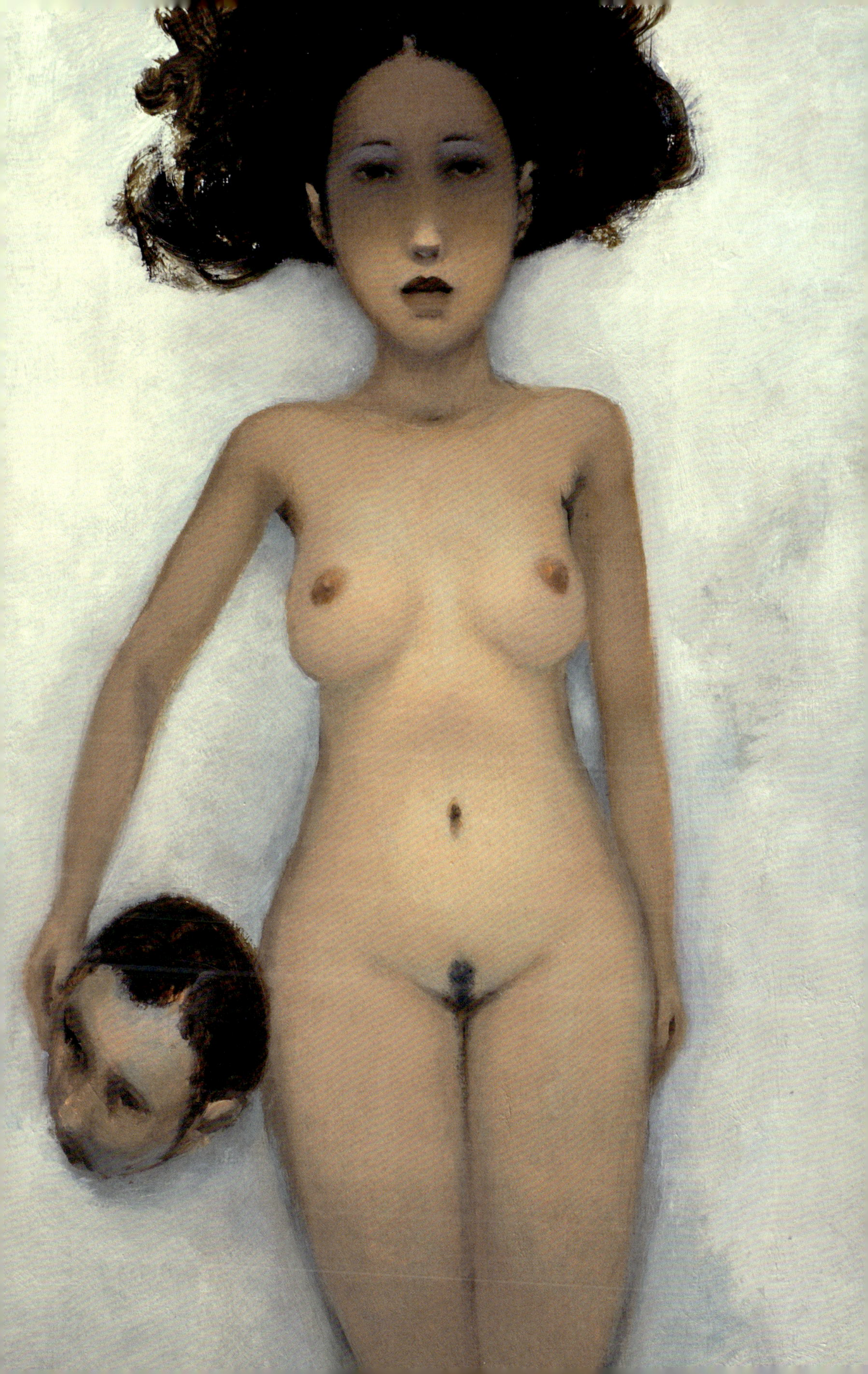

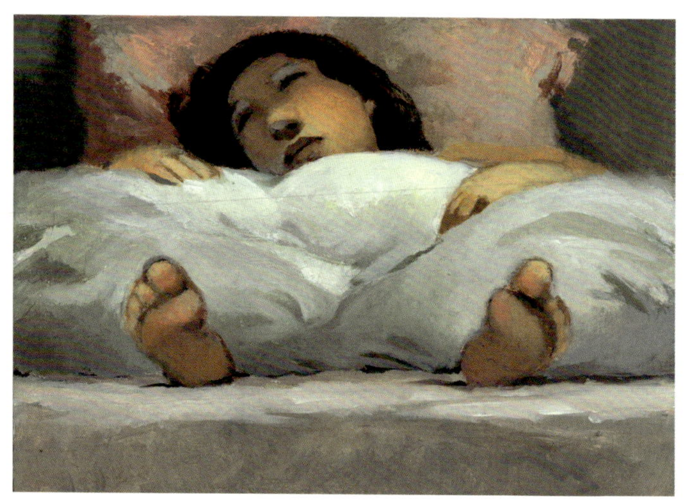

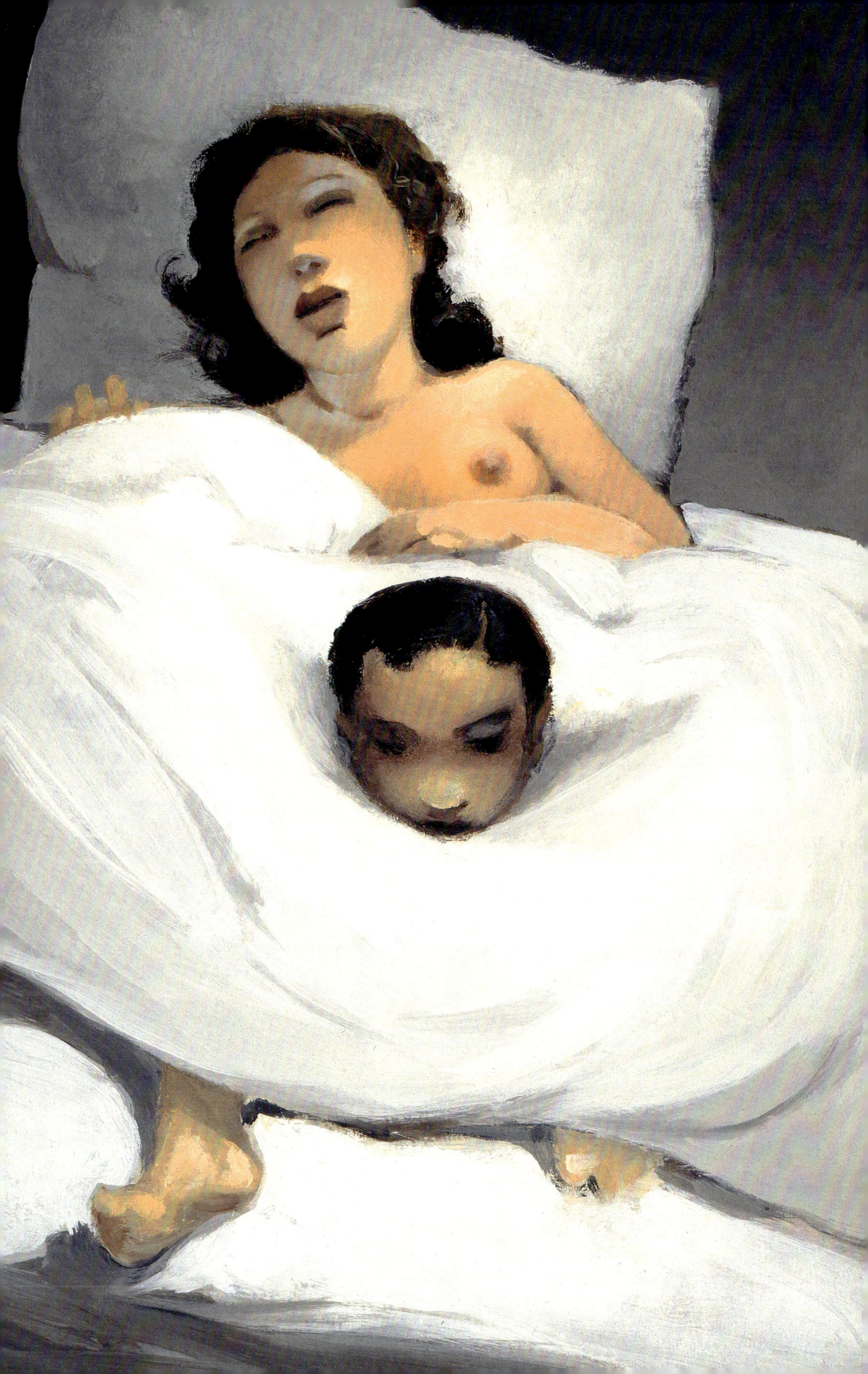

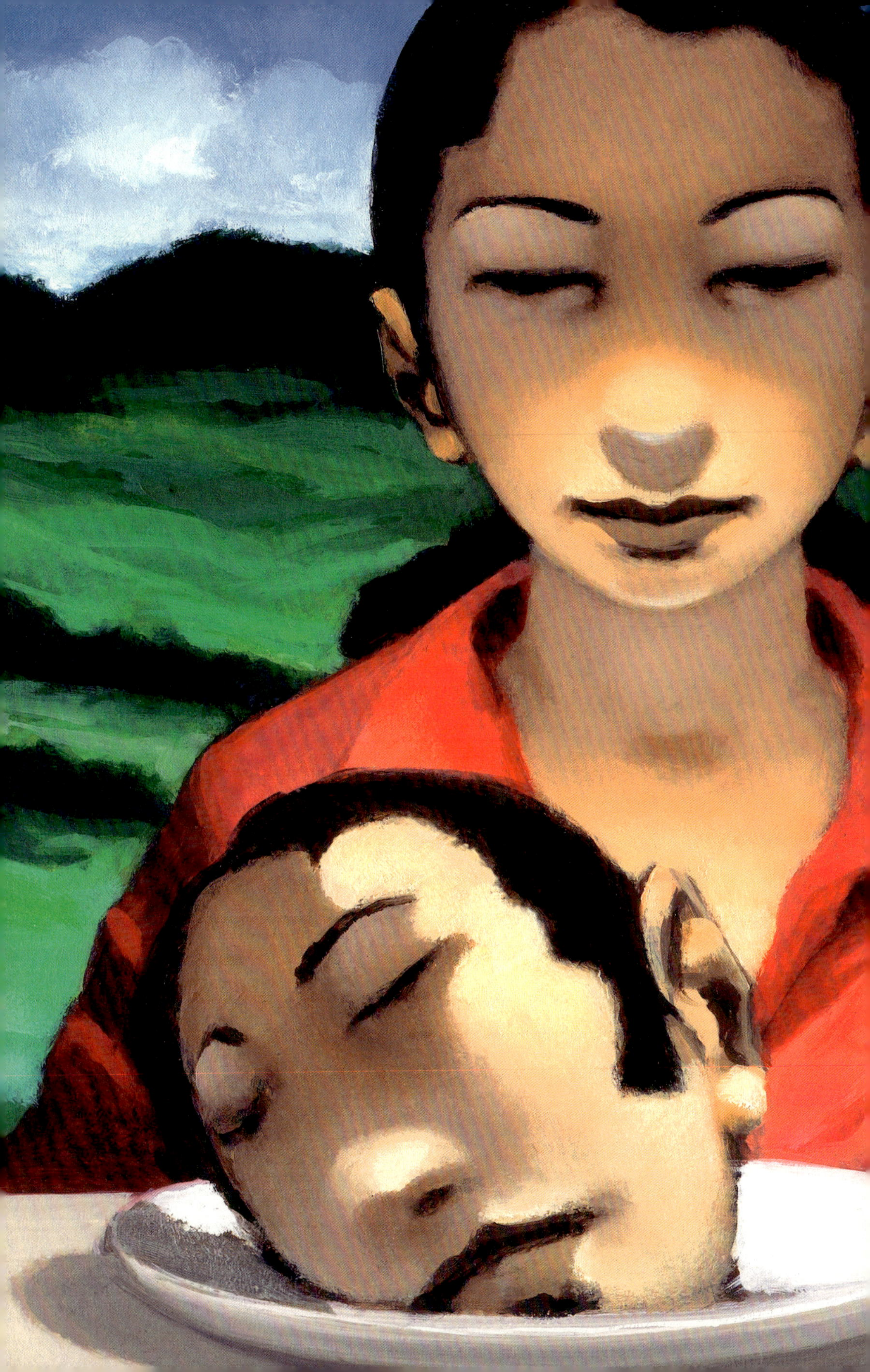

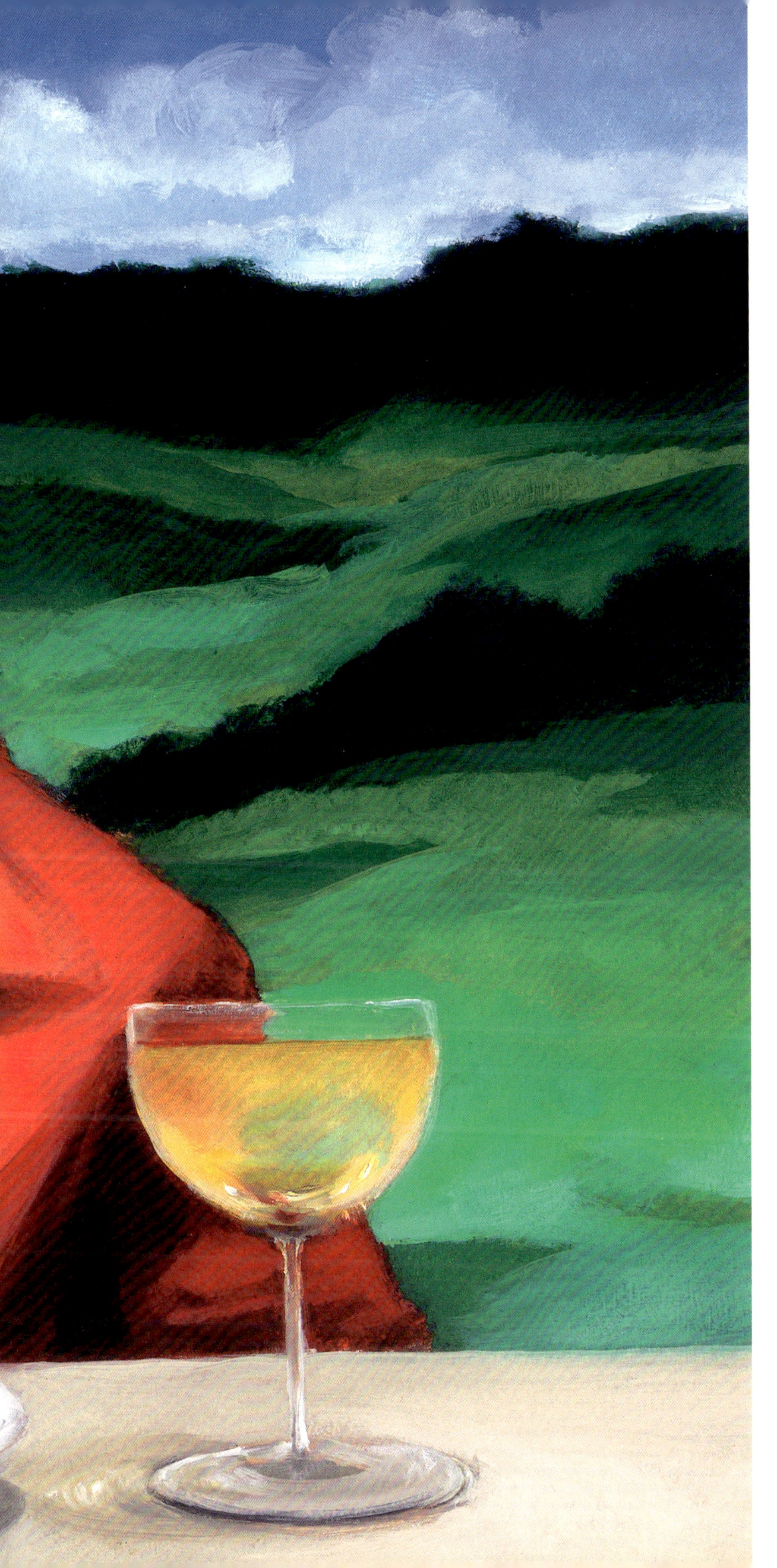

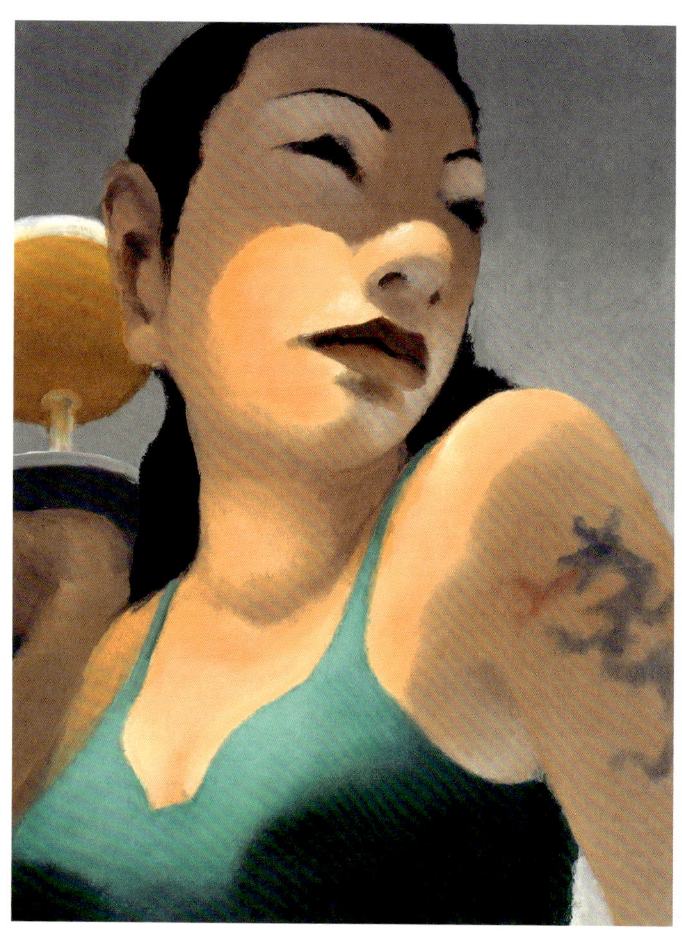

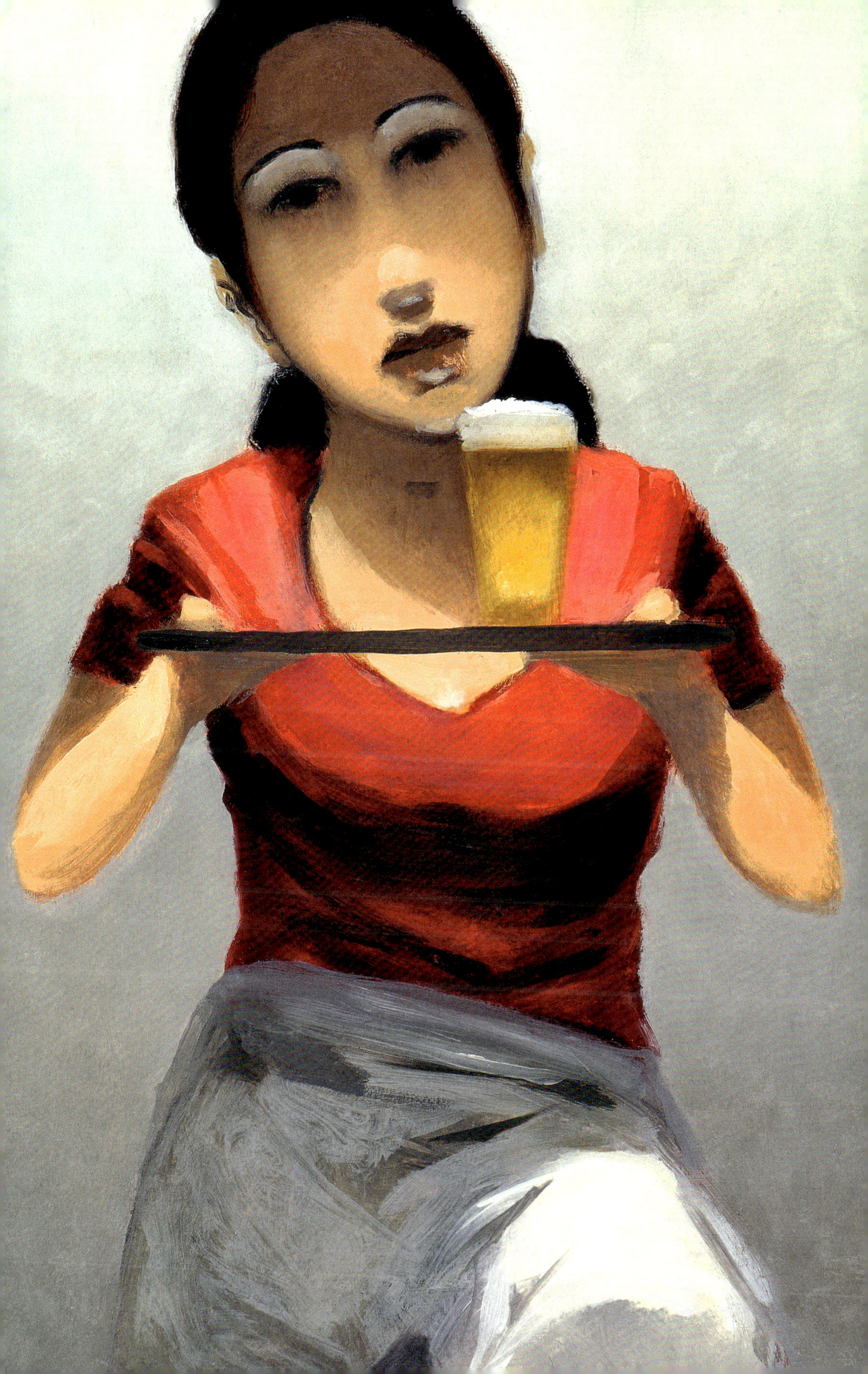

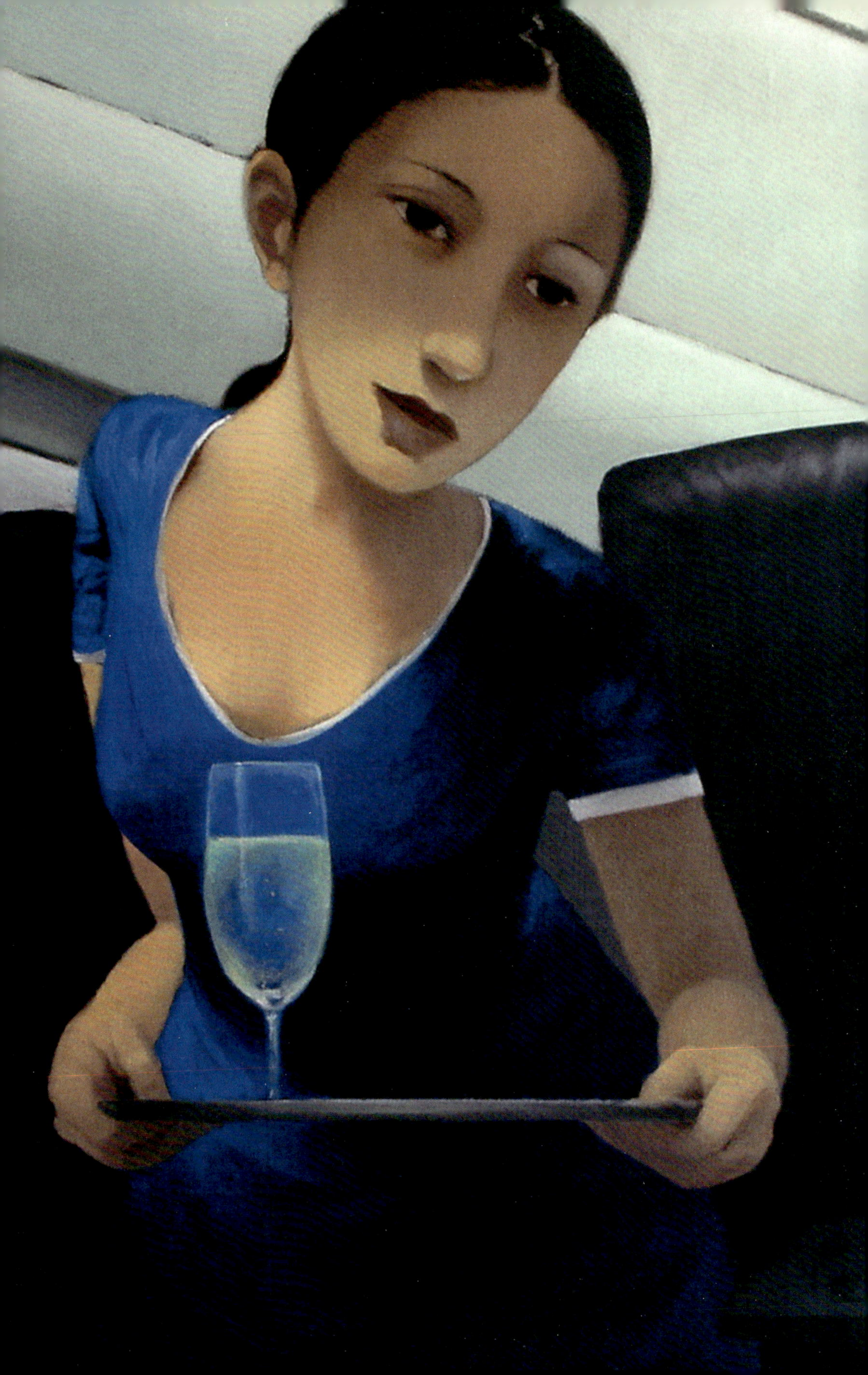

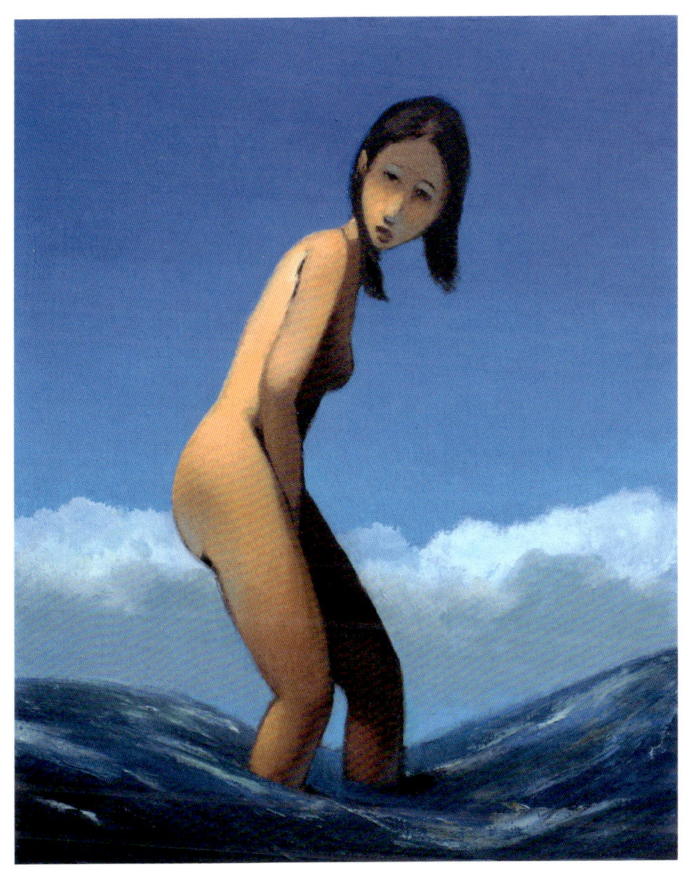

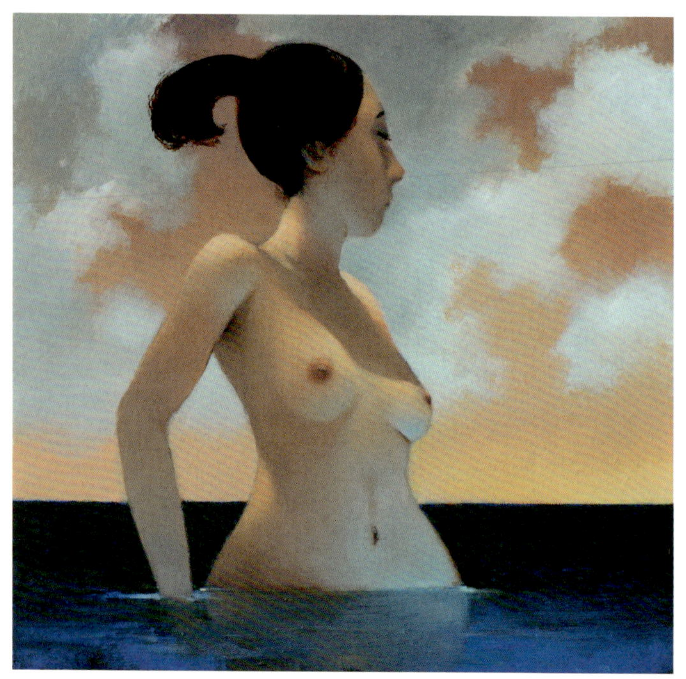

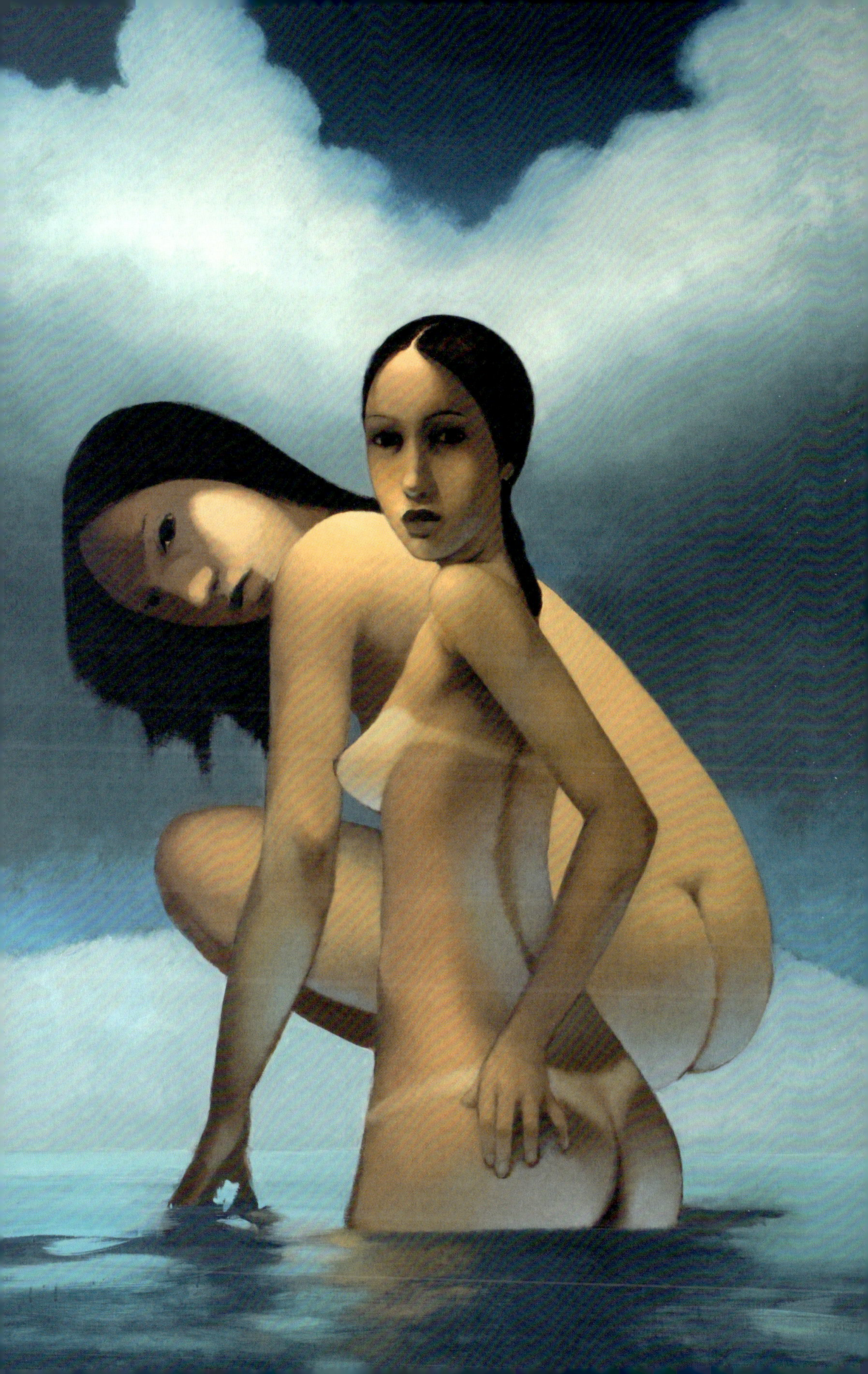

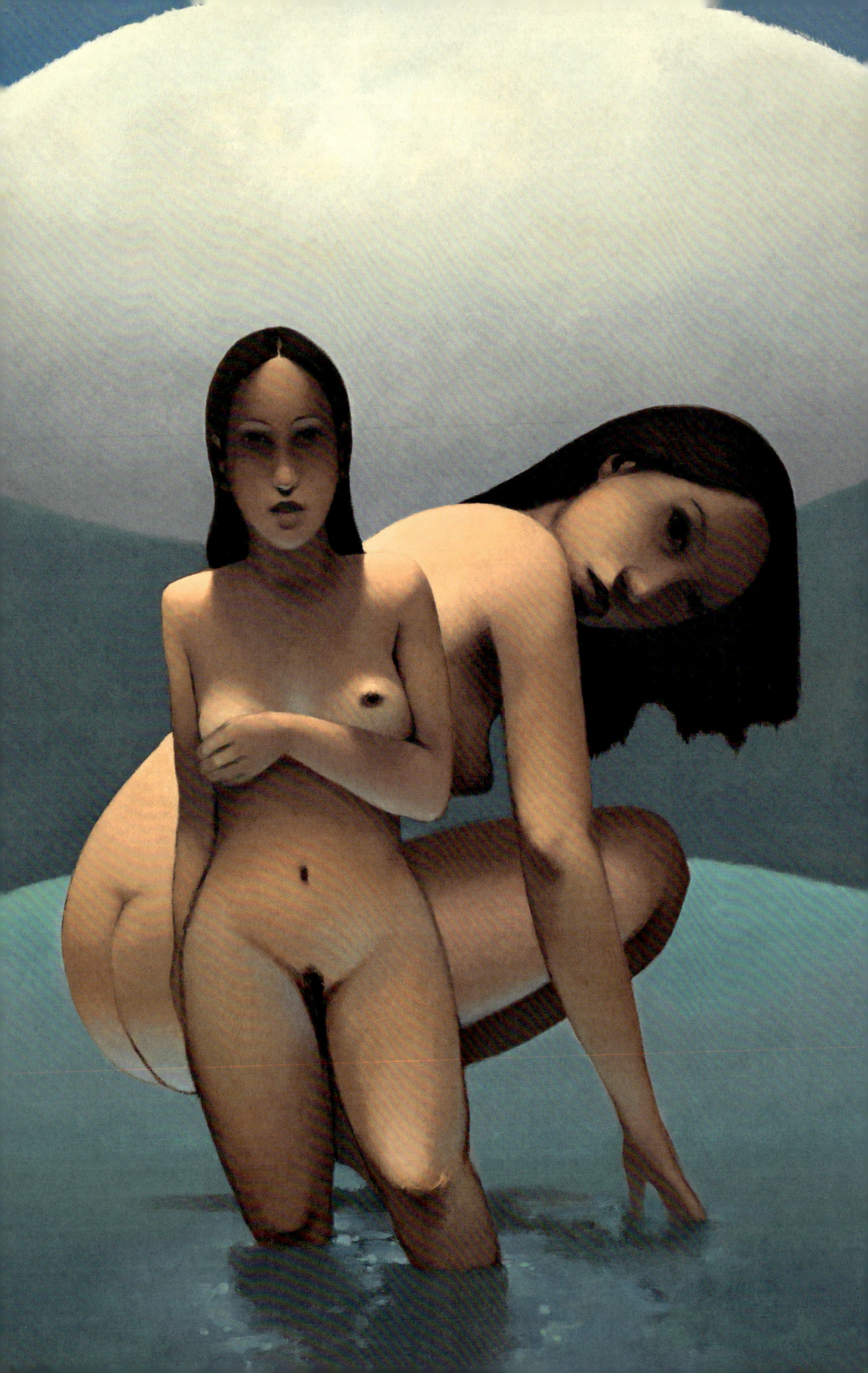

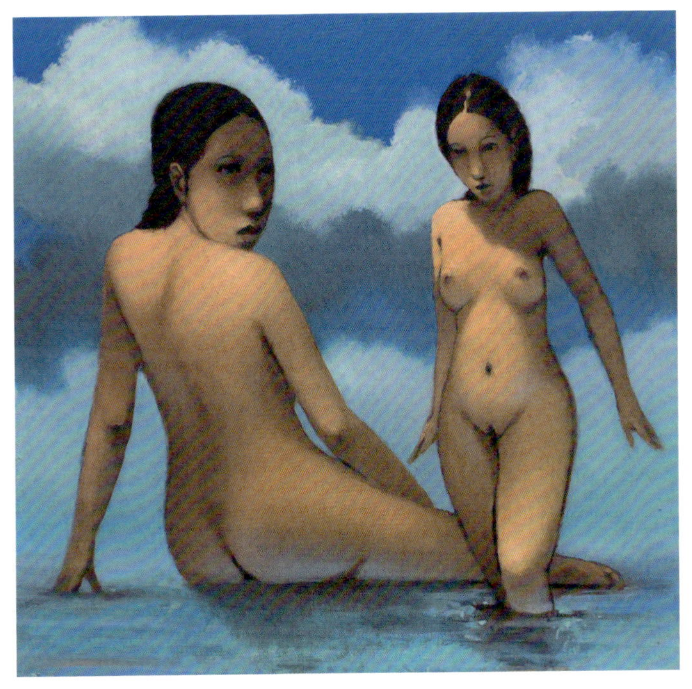

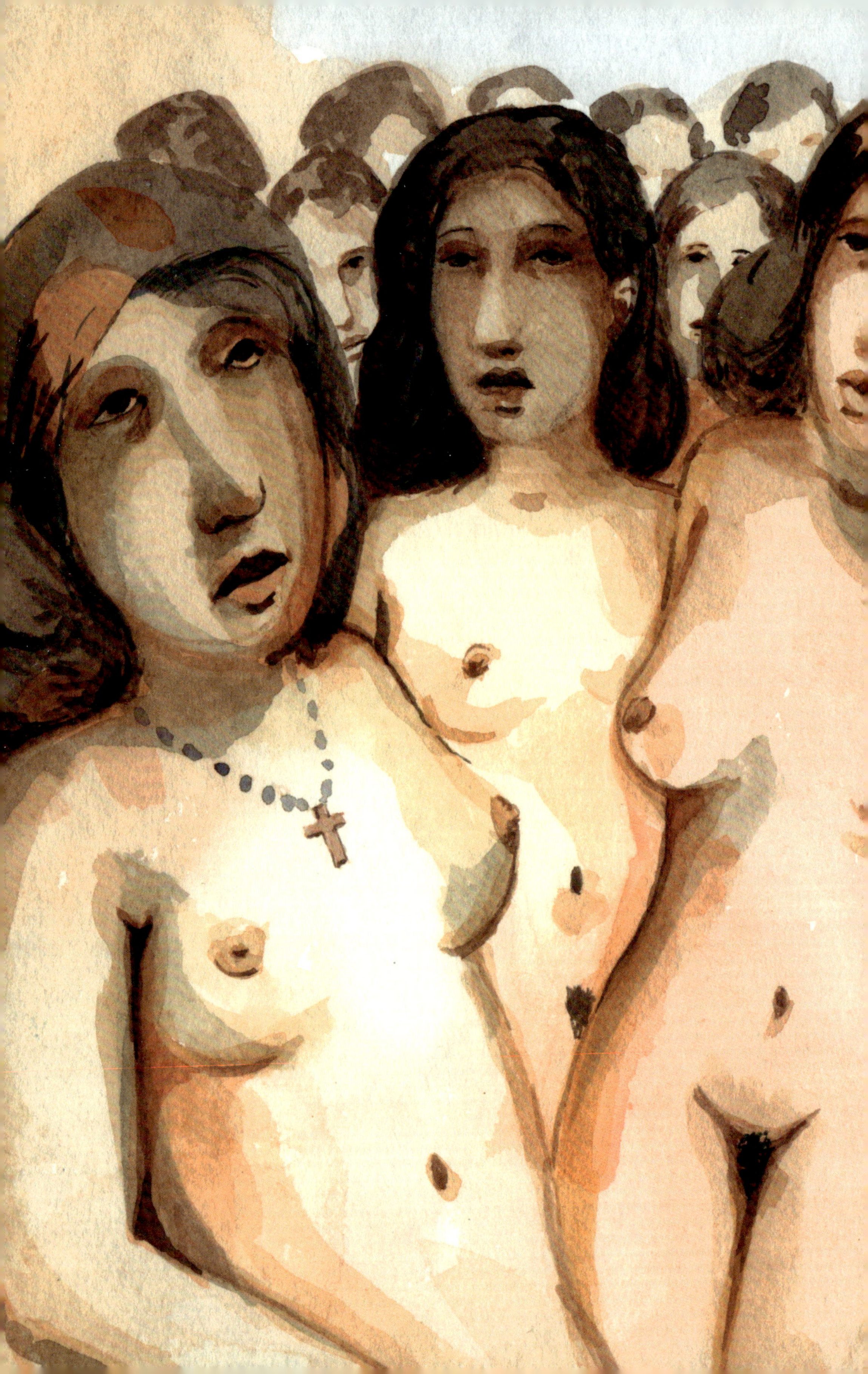

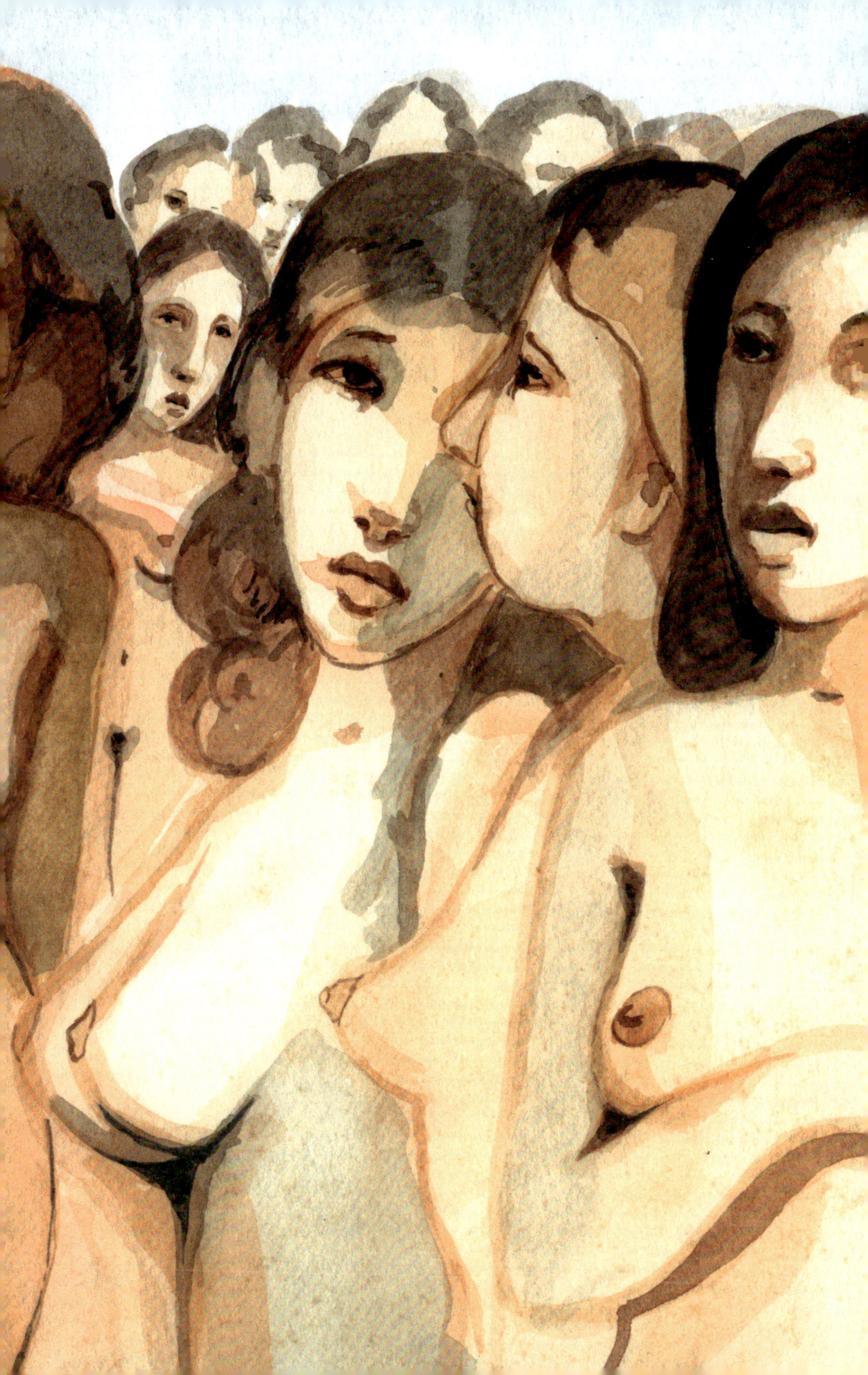

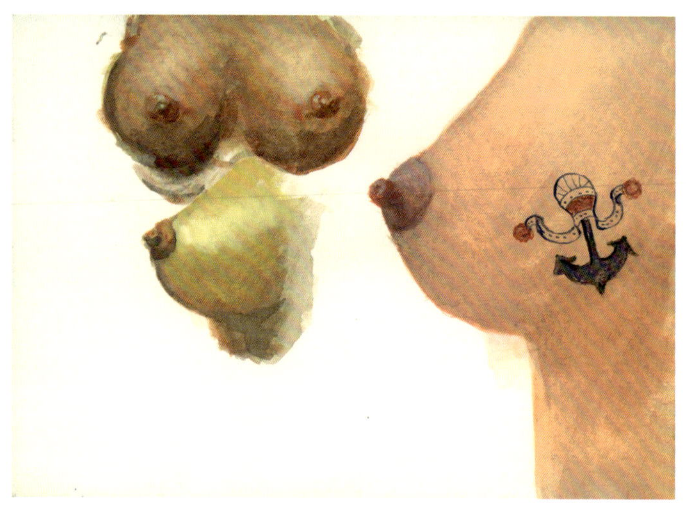

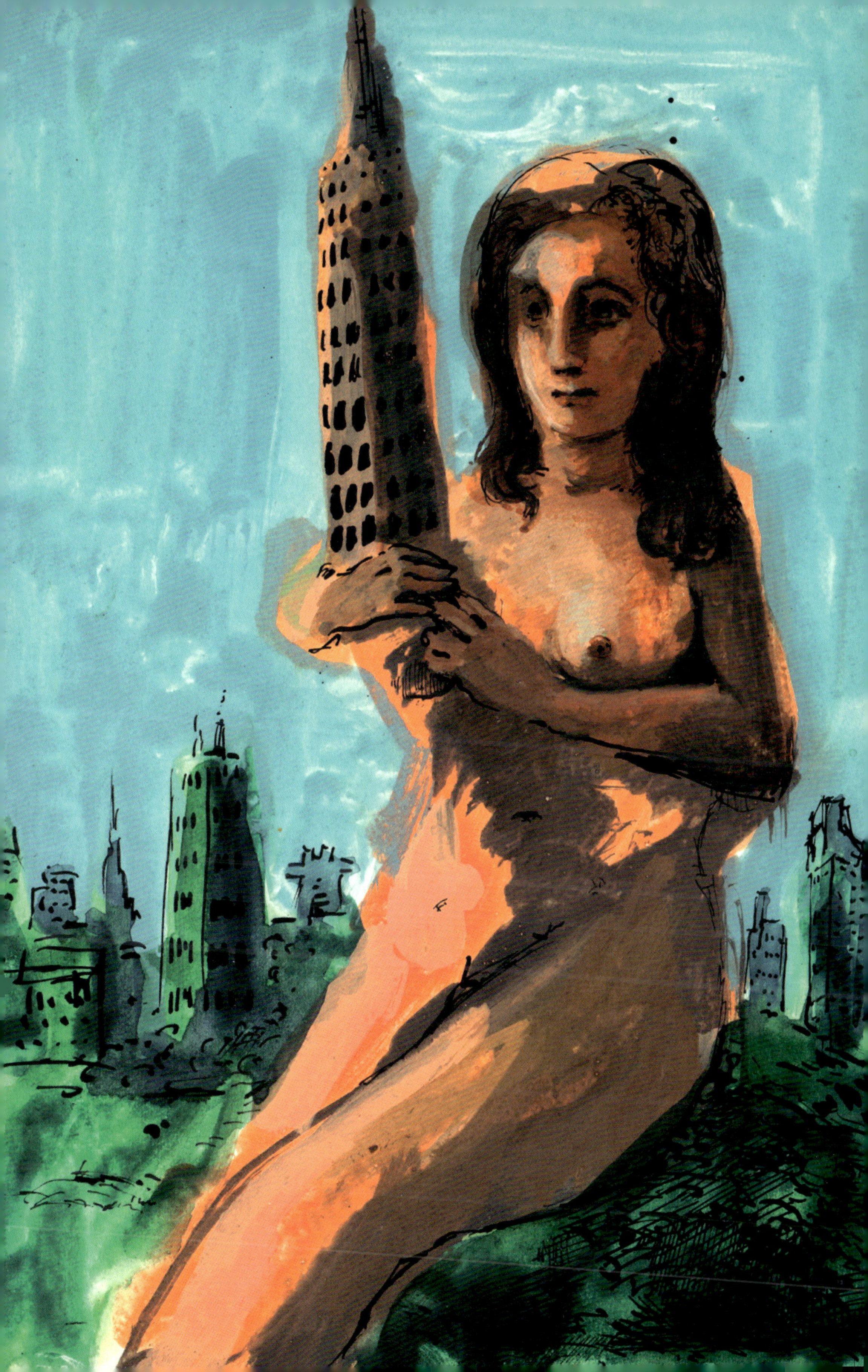

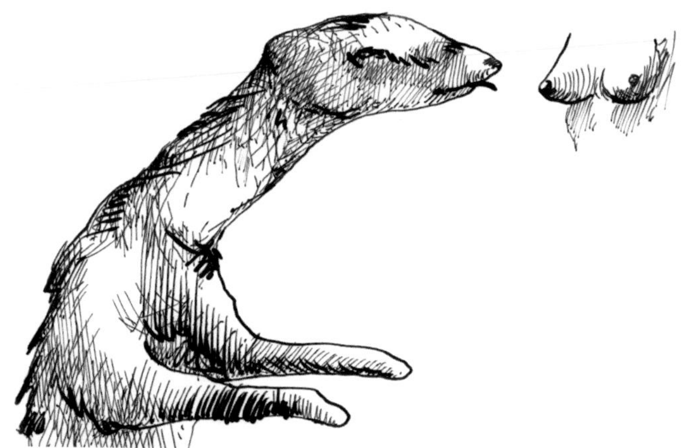

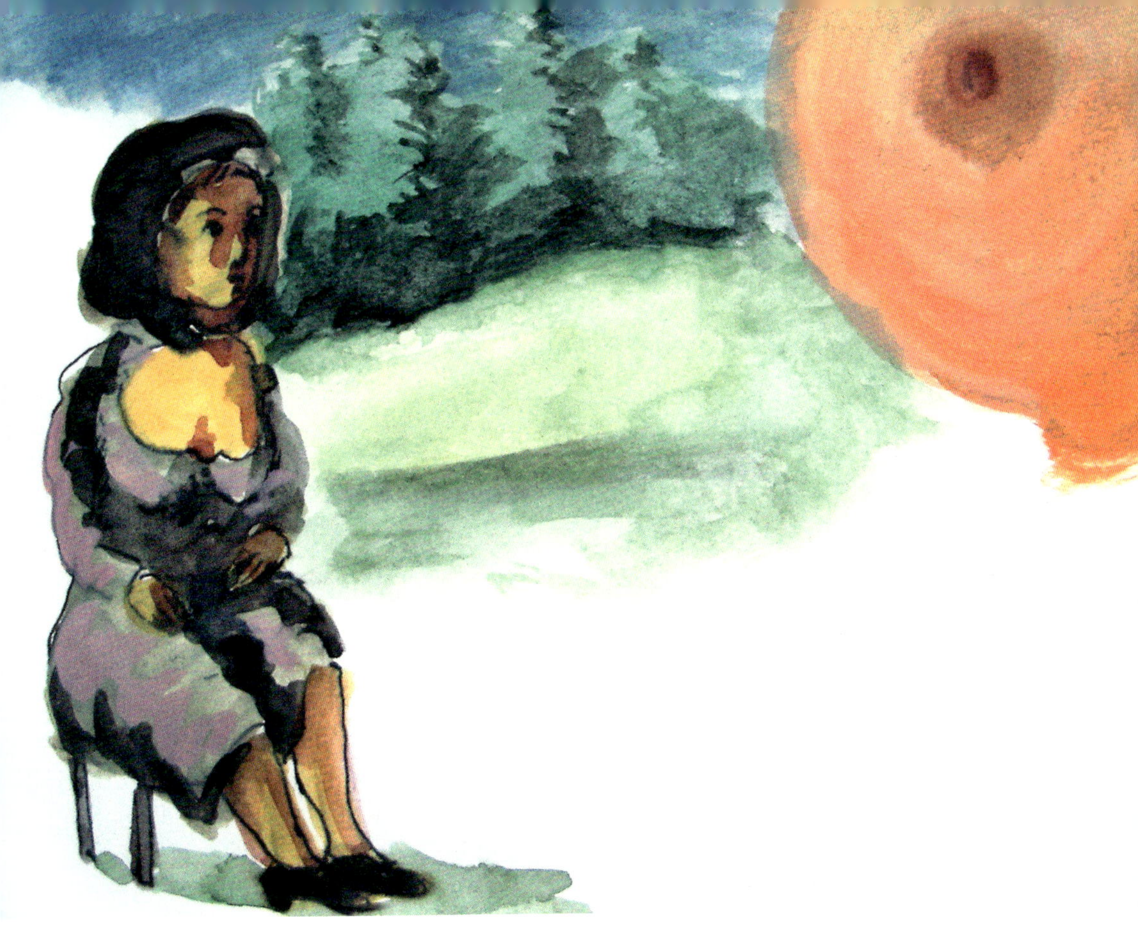

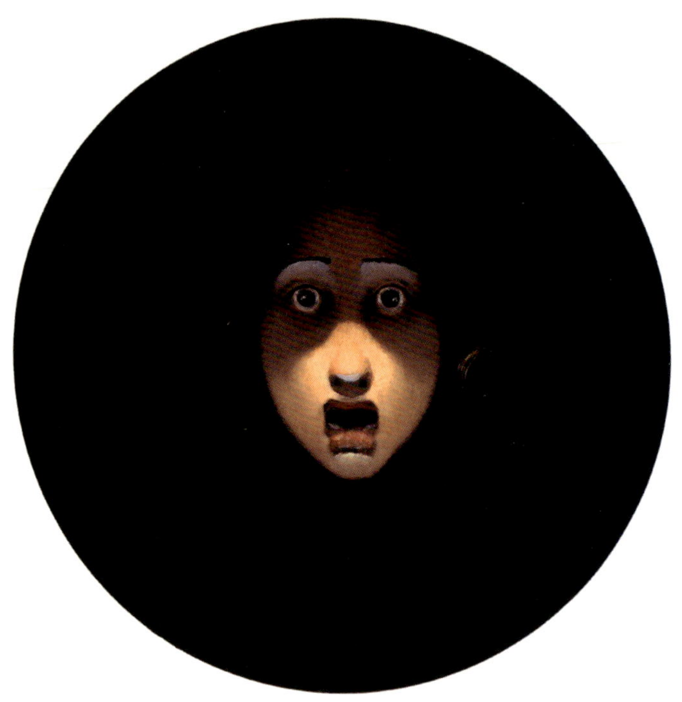

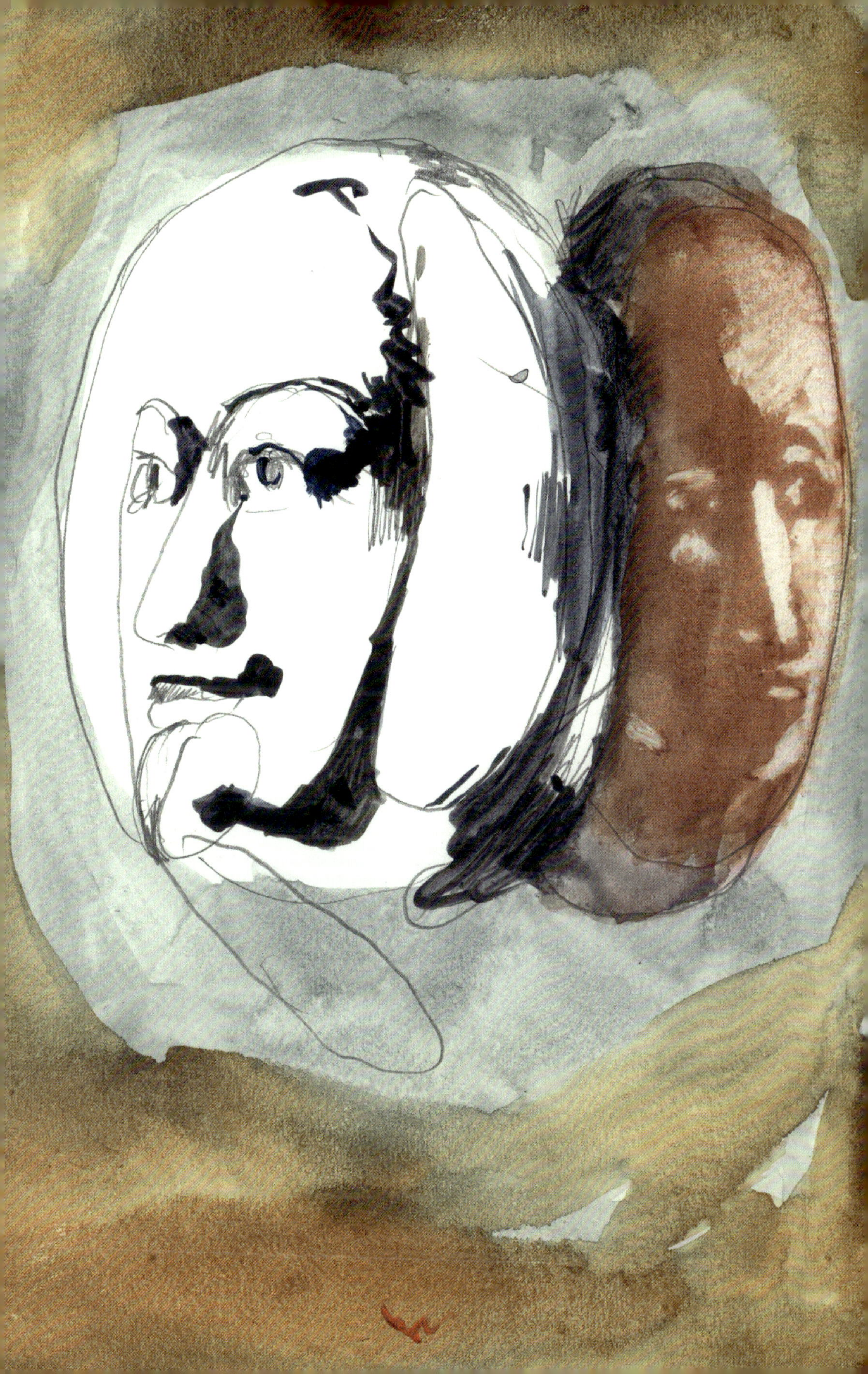

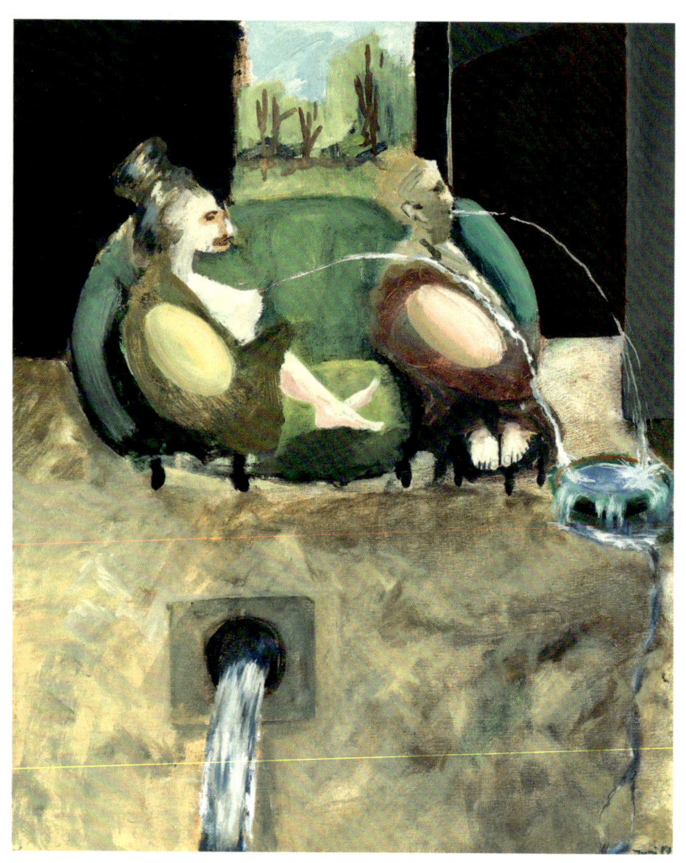

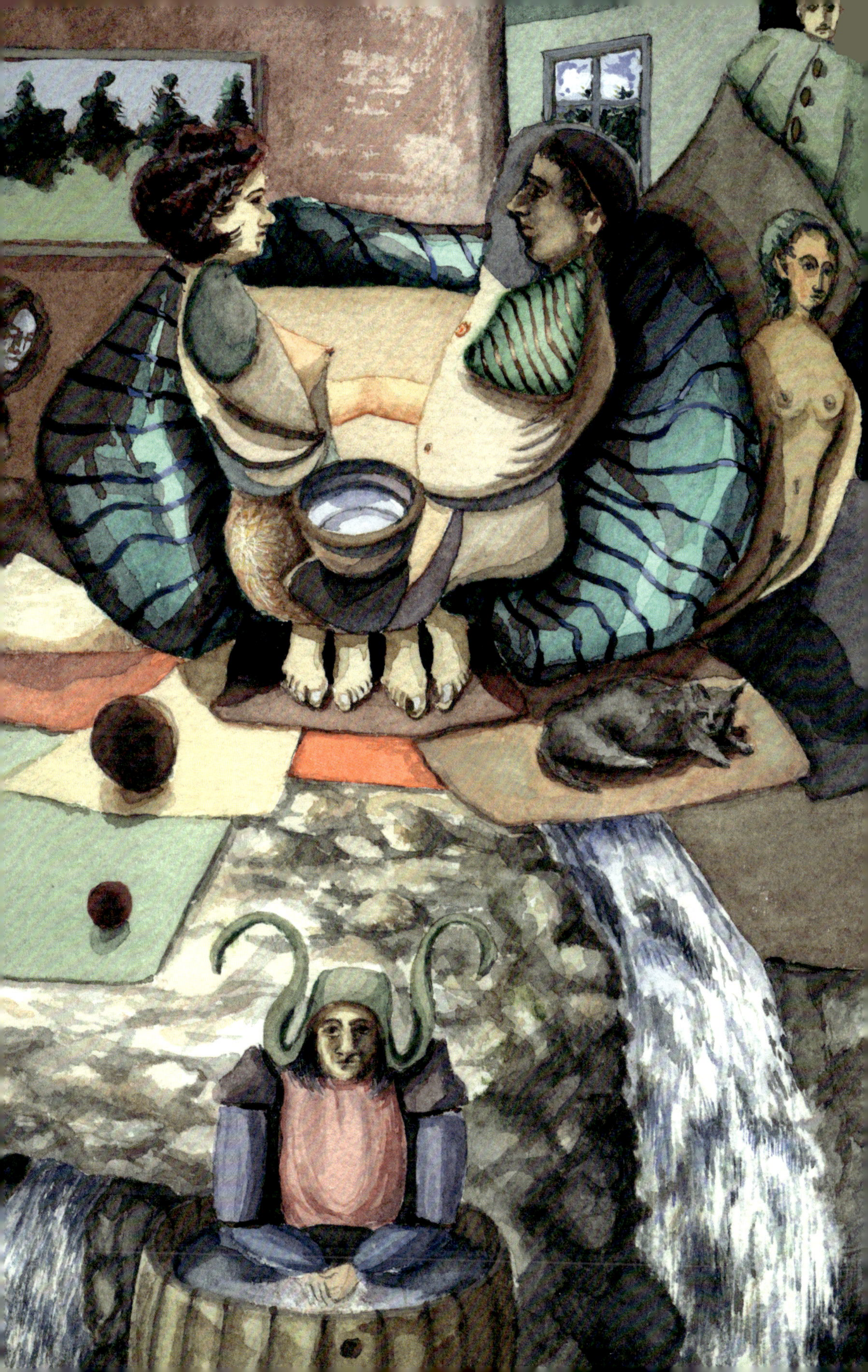

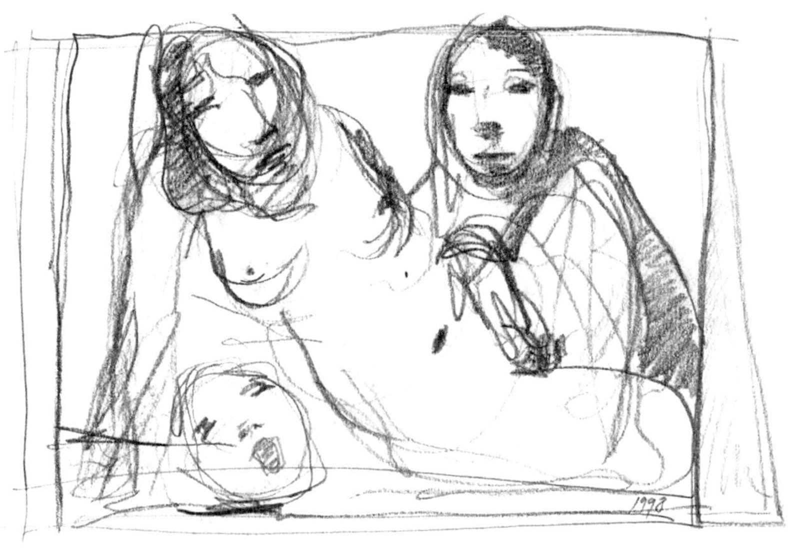

120

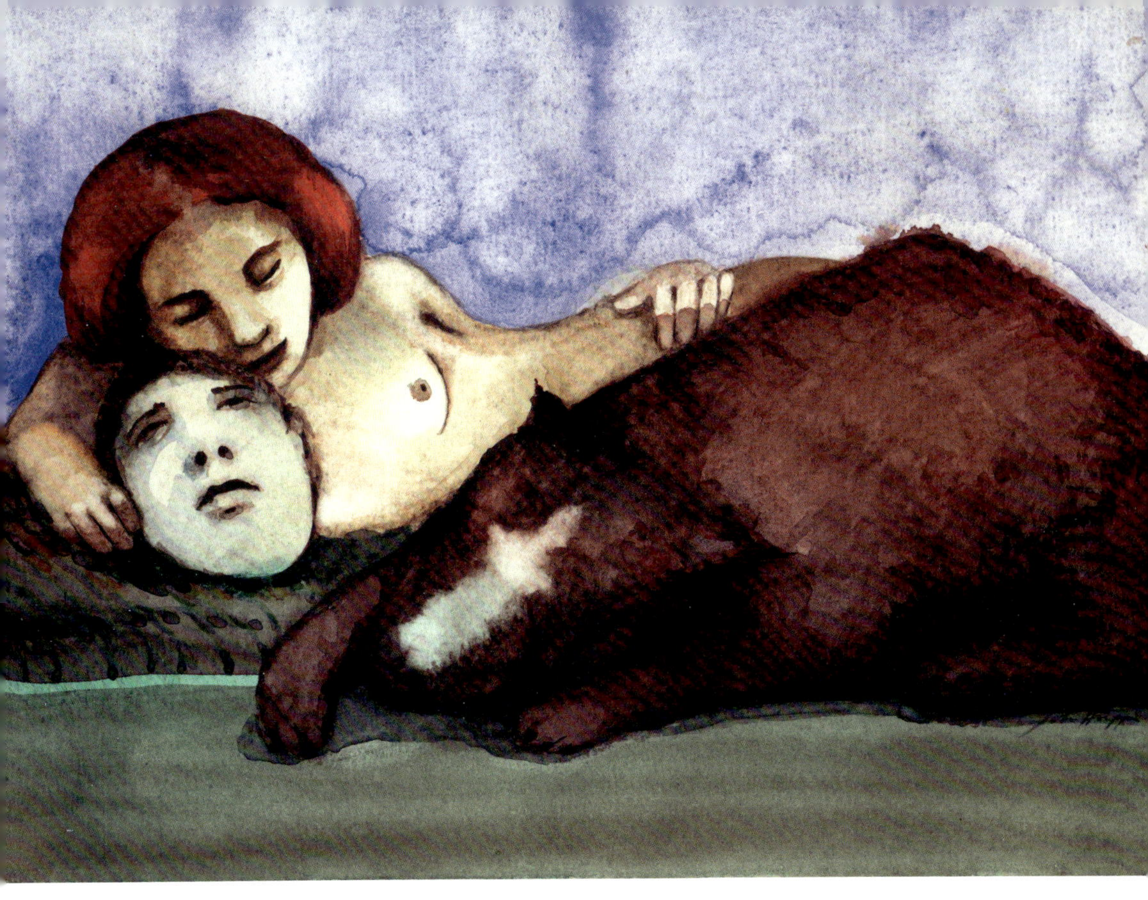

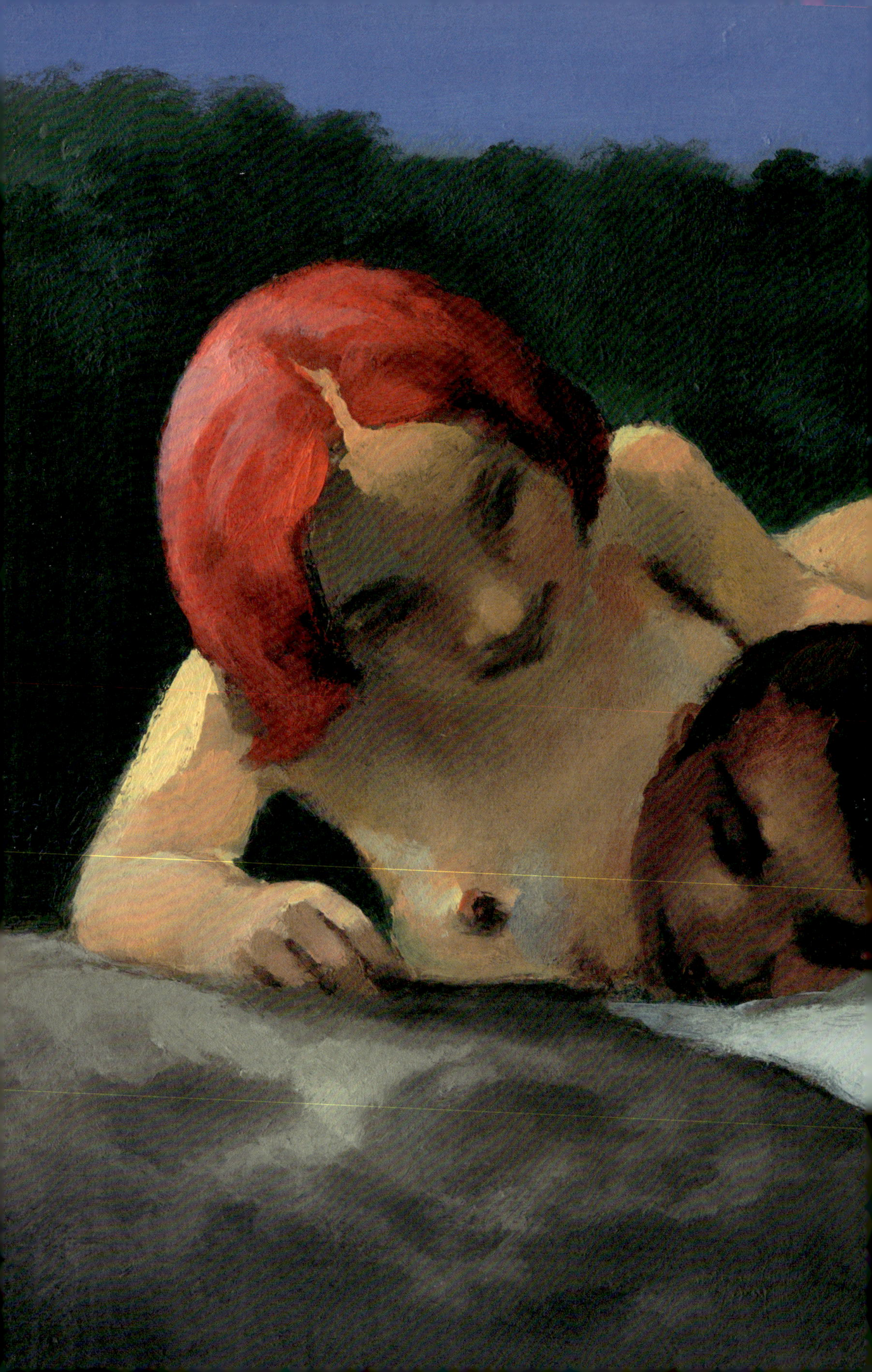

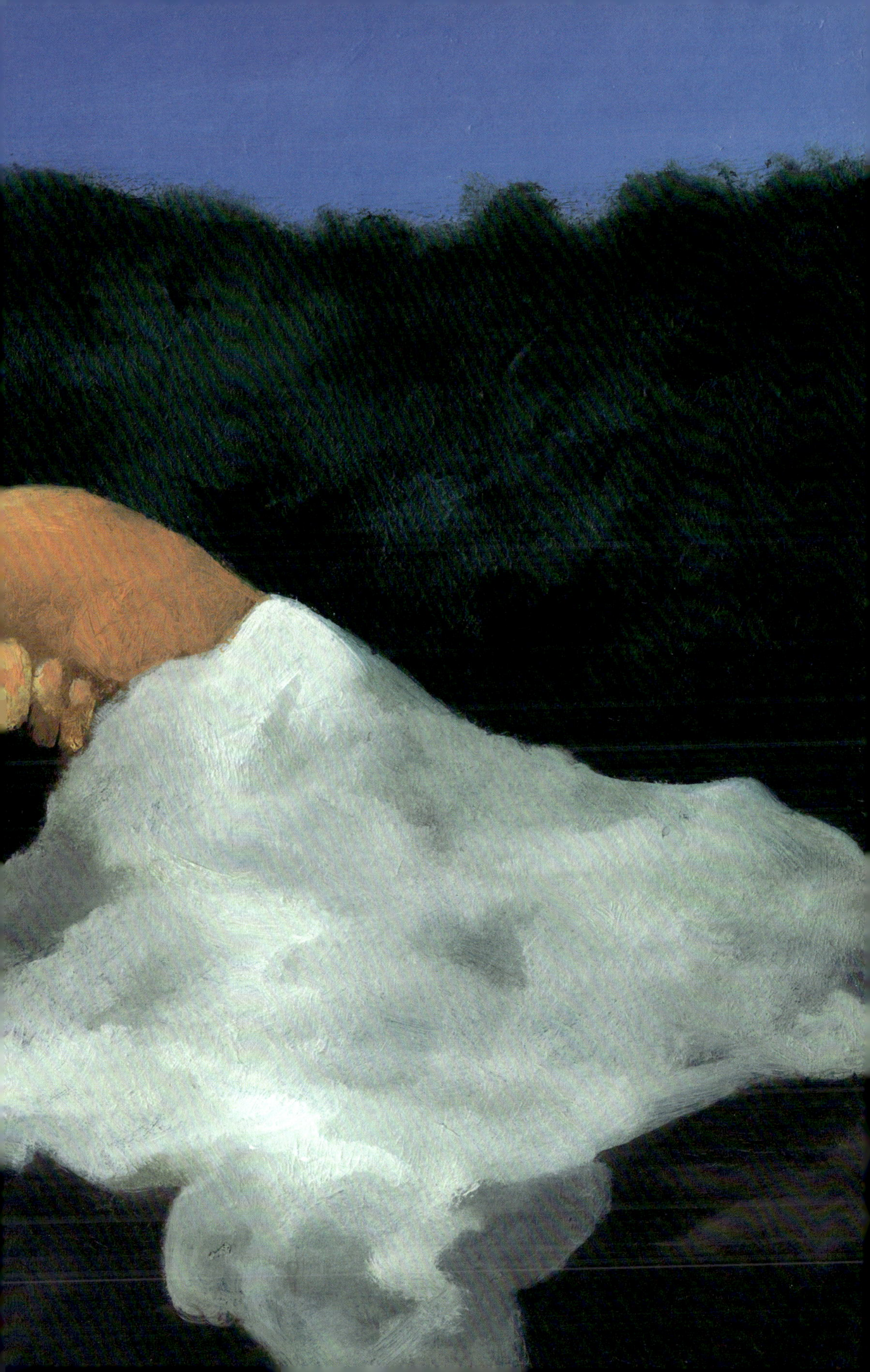

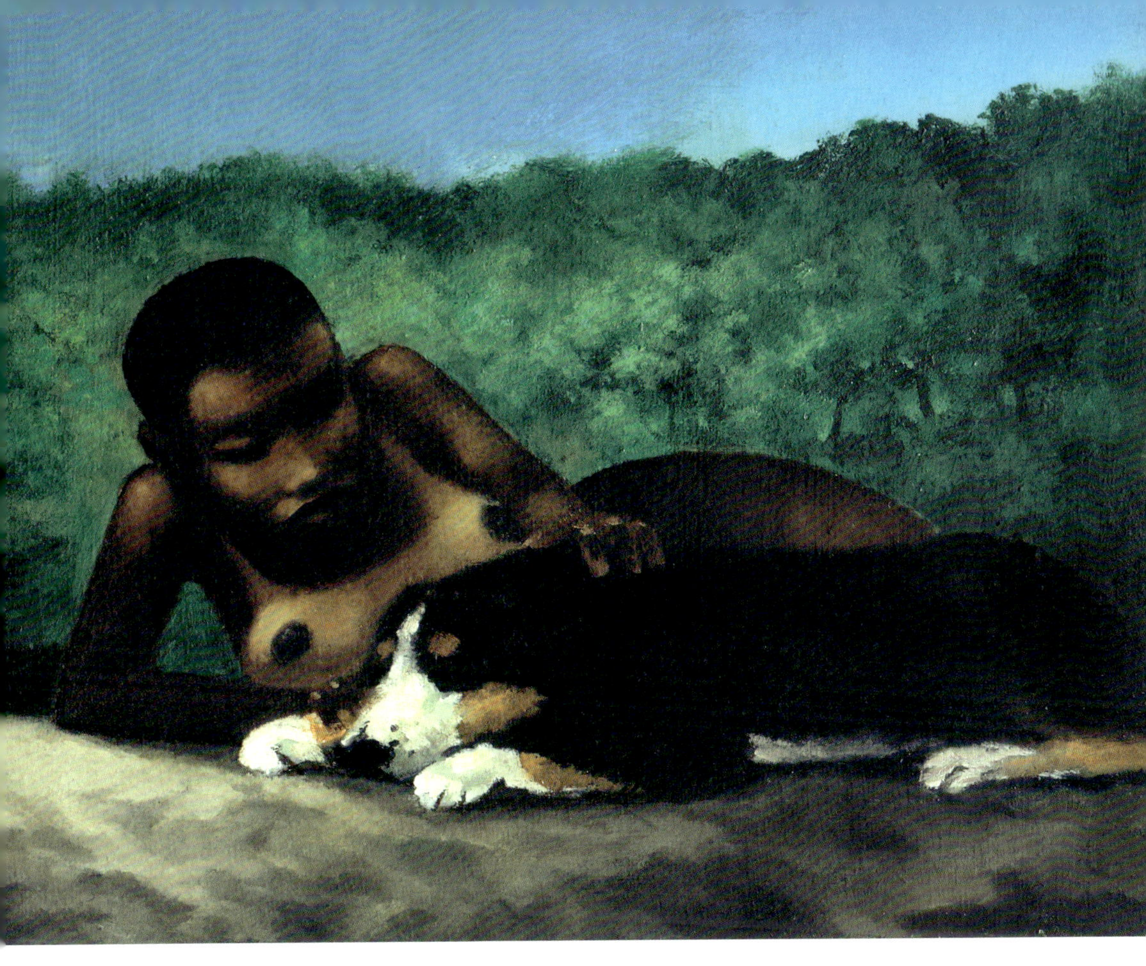

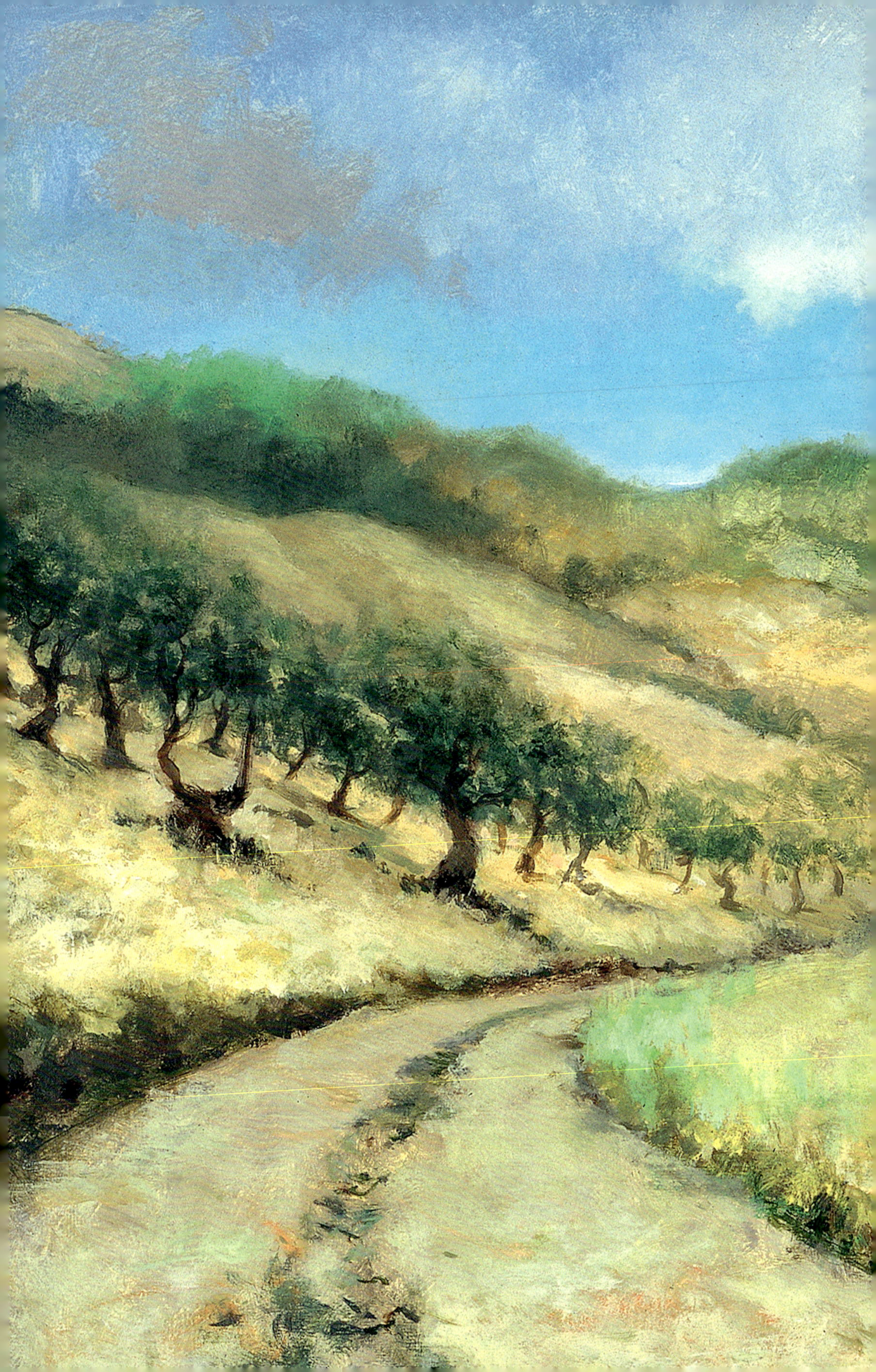

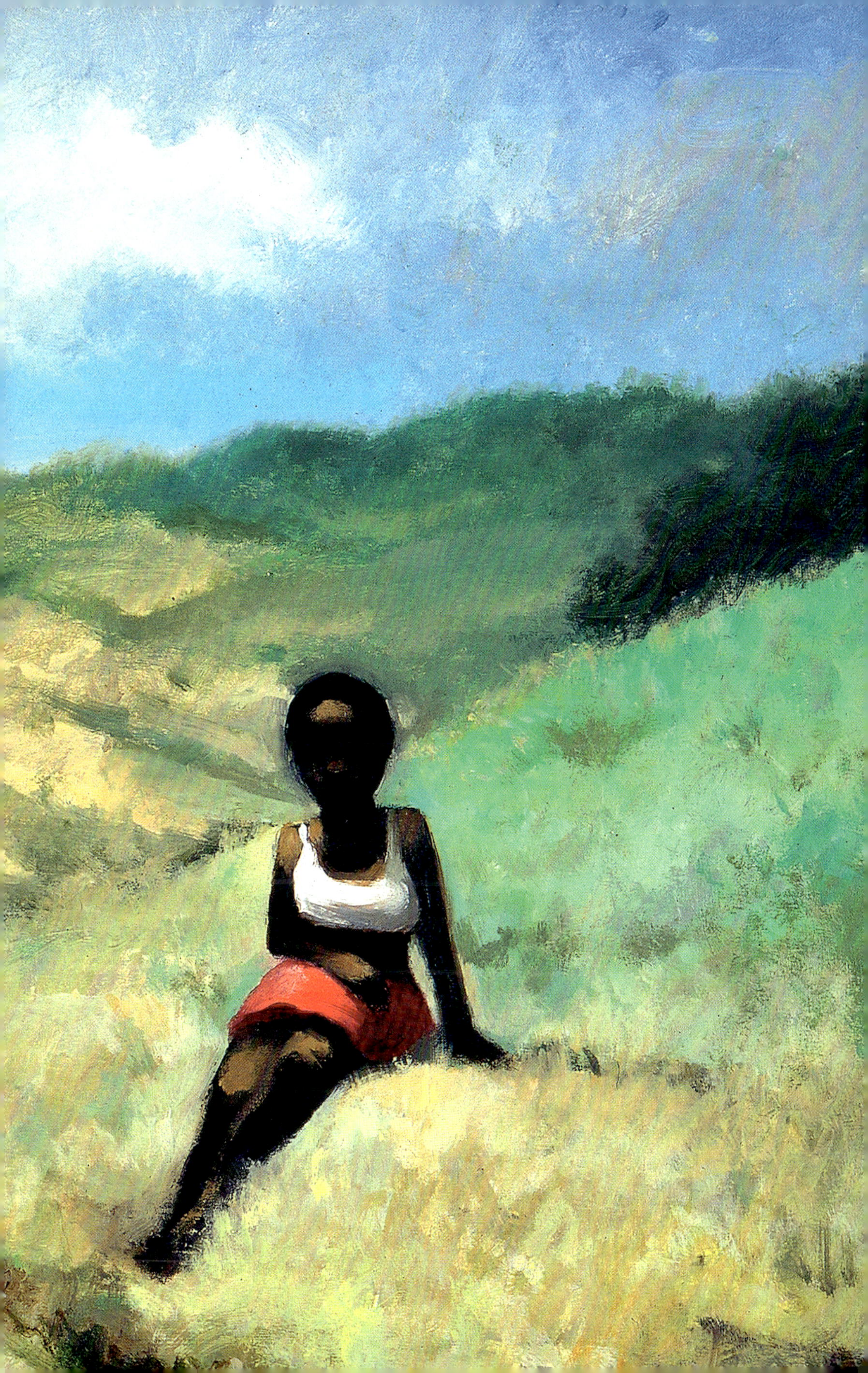

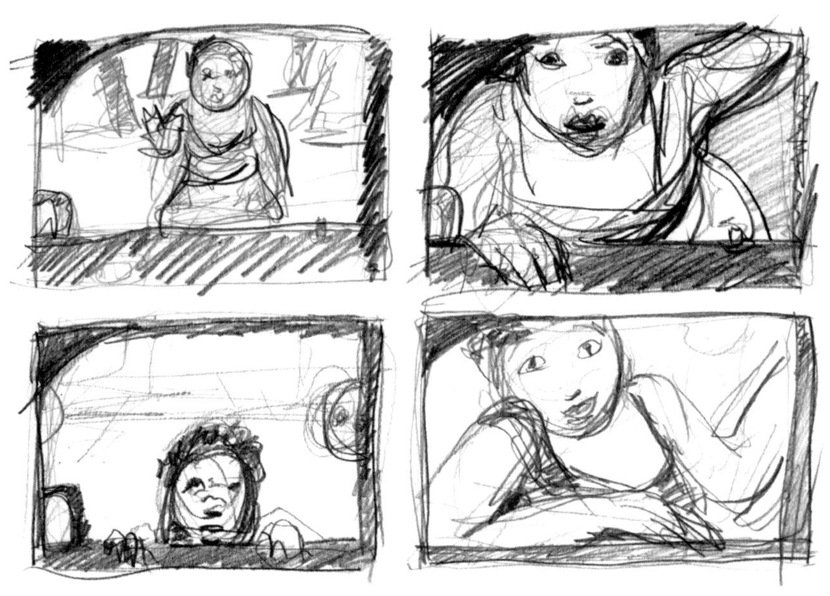

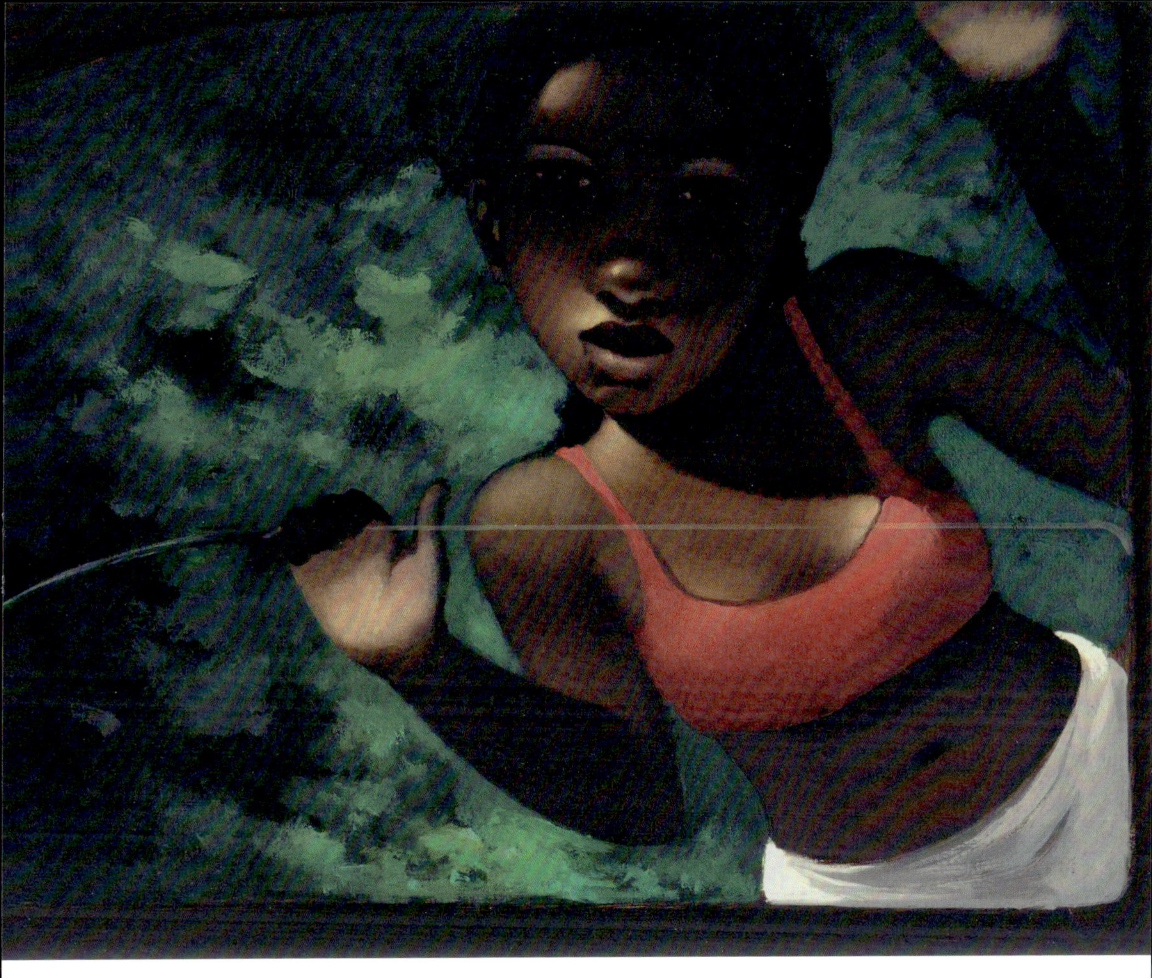

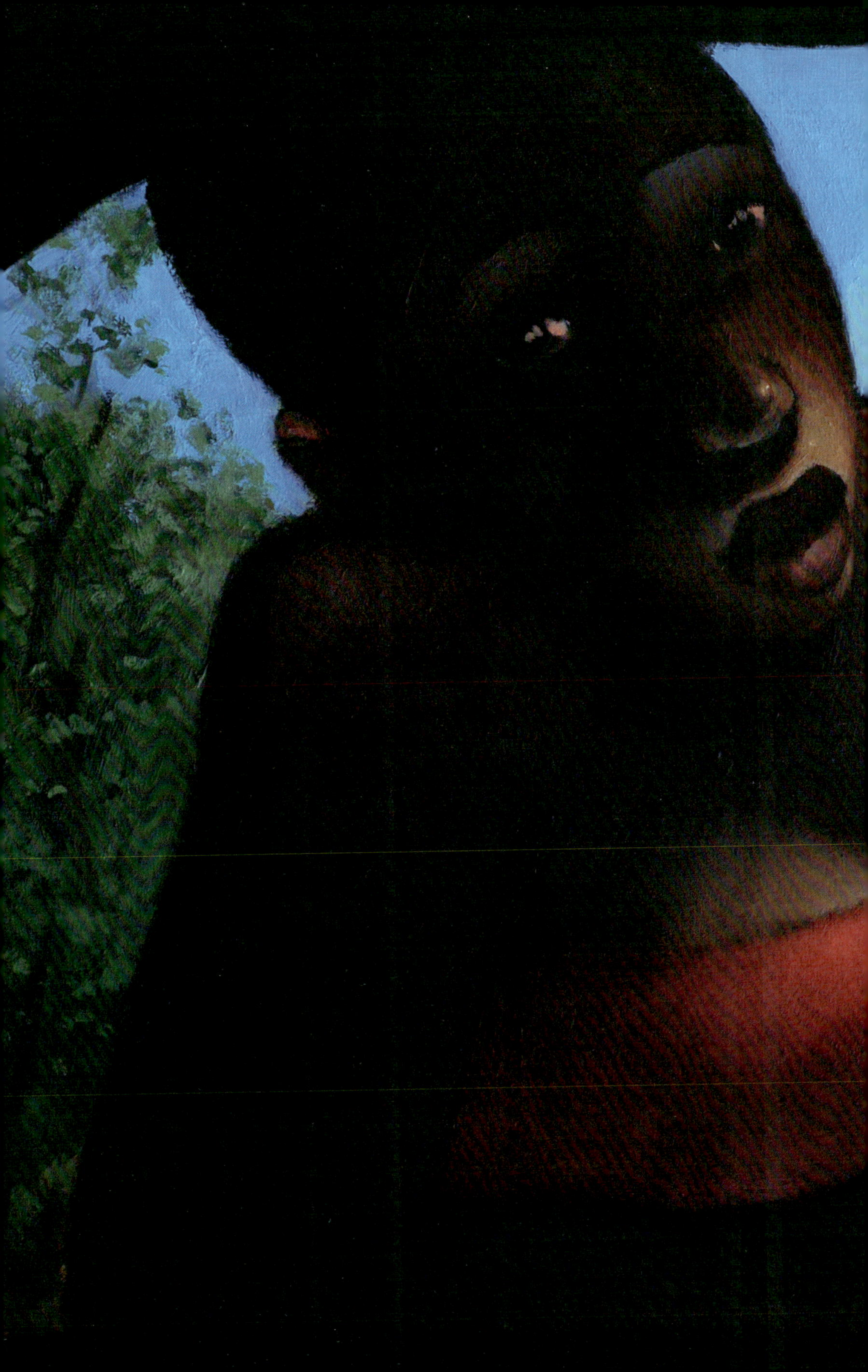

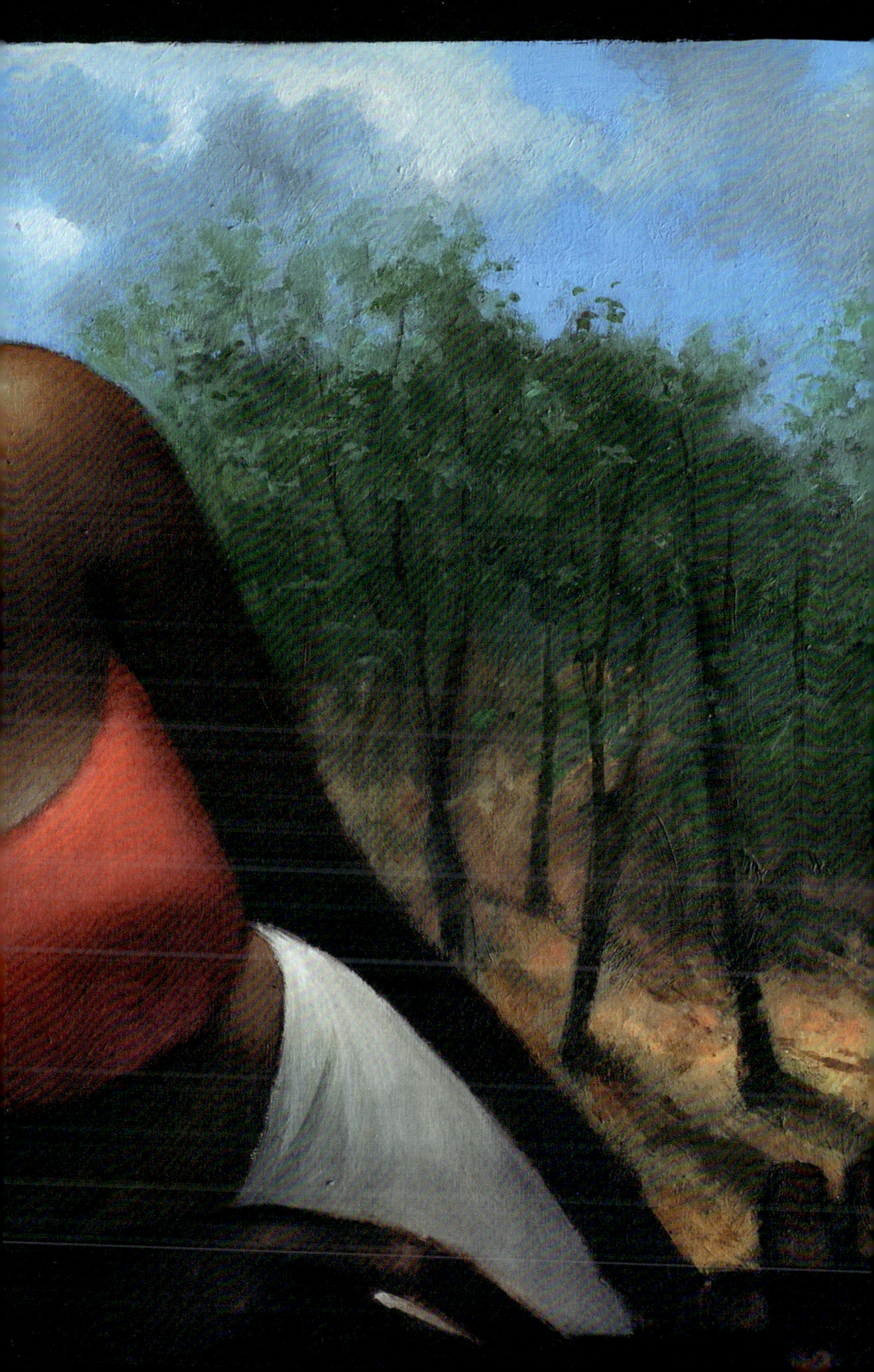

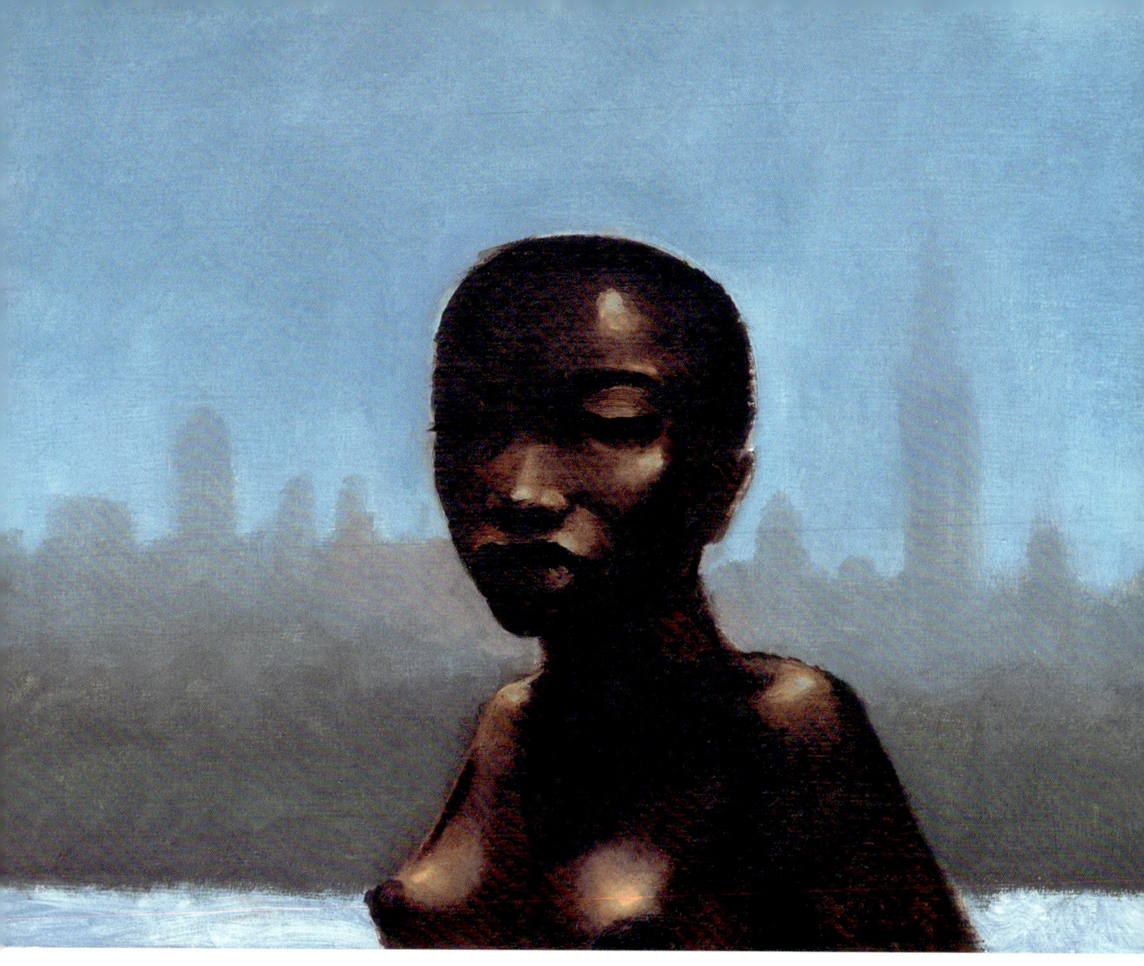

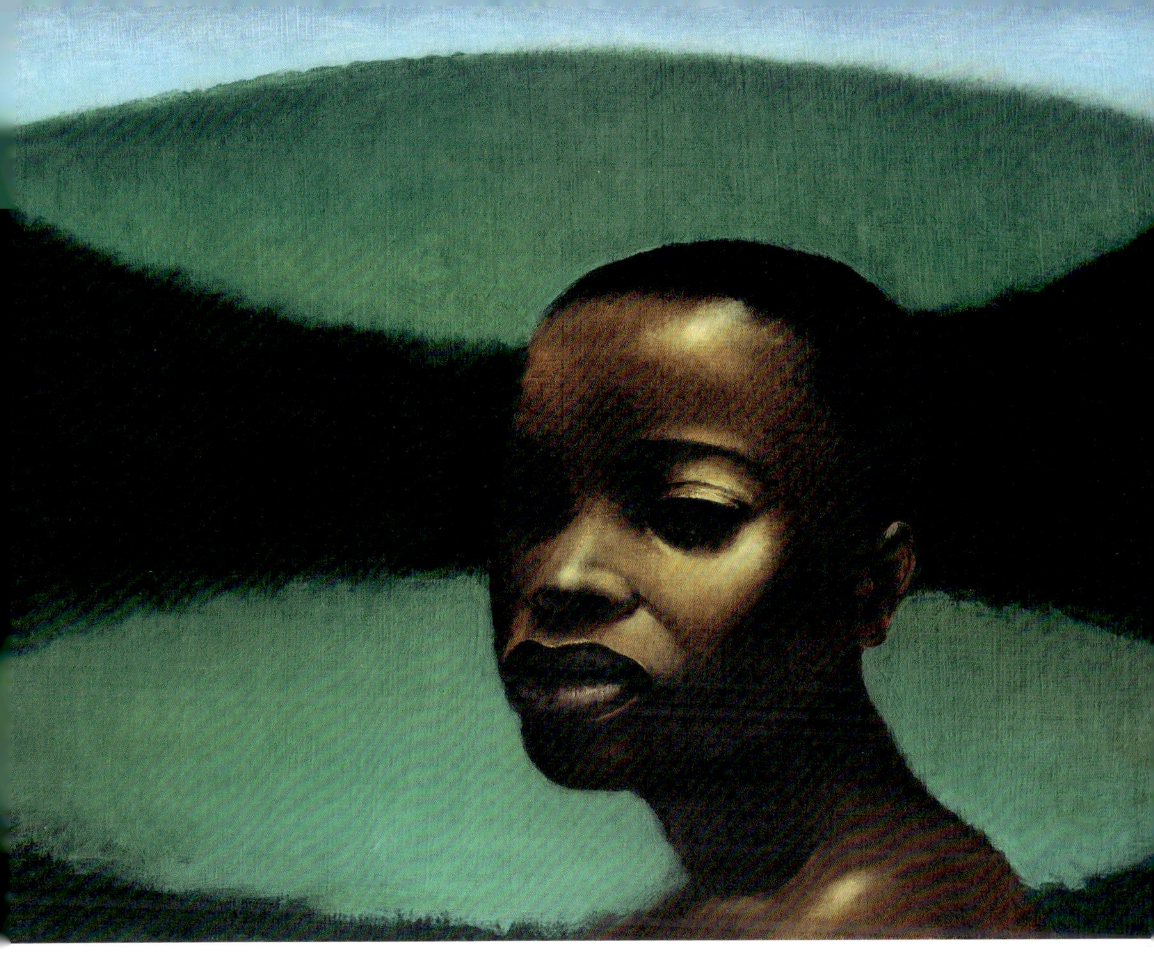

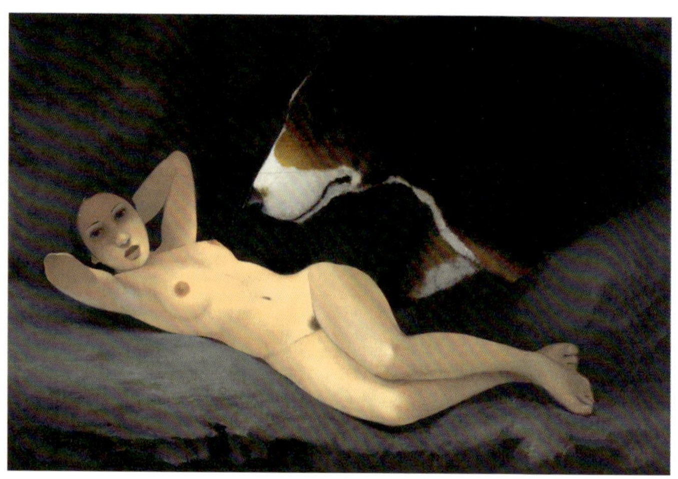

o.T. / Untitled,
Öl auf Holz / oil on wood
83,5 × 123,5 cm, 2005

(...)

Ich habe früh für das Museum für Moderne Kunst in Frankfurt am Main Arbeiten von Johannes Hüppi erworben. 1998 haben wir sie gezeigt. Zwei Aquarelle hängen bei mir zu Hause. Schaue ich sie an, gerate ich ins Träumen.

Vor nicht allzu langer Zeit habe ich in der Sammlung von Frieder Burda die zweite Version eines Frauenaktes mit Hund gesehen. Das Bild, auf Holz gemalt, misst 83,5 × 123,5 cm. Es ist 2005 enstanden. Ich musste natürlich sofort an Felix Vallotton denken, an sein grandioses Gemälde aus dem Jahr 1913 mit dem Titel *La Blanche et la Noire* (Die Weiße und die Schwarze). Es ist auf Leinwand gemalt, misst 147 × 114 cm und gehört der Hahnloser/Jäggli-Siftung in Winterthur (Villa Flora). Das Bild zeigt eine nackte, attraktive, junge Frau, schlafend, mit Ponyfrisur. Am Bettende sitzt eine schwarze Frau, die Arme (kräftig), die Schultern und der Rücken sind nackt. Sie hat wunderschöne Hände. Auf ihrem Haar trägt sie ein orangefarbenes Stoffgebilde. Der Hintergrund ist durchgehend türkis gemalt. Und jetzt kommt das Unerhörte: Die schwarze Frau raucht. Sie hat eine Zigarette im Mund. So, als gelte es, den selbstbewussten Status einer Bediensteten zu unterstreichen. Vallottons Bild ist eine provokante Antwort auf Manets *Olympia*. Und Manet wiederum reagierte auf viele Vorbilder aus früheren Jahrhunderten. 1913 ist dieses Bild entstanden. Das war die Zeit des Kubismus.

2005 malt Johannes Hüppi die *Maja desnuda* von Francisco de Goya. Ein überdimensionierter Berner Sennenhund bewacht sie. Sie ist schön und sinnlich, diese Maja. Vielleicht atmet der Hund sie begehrlich ein. Es ist ein dunkles, mystisches Bild. Das Anlitz in dem hellen Körper zeigt einen präsenten, erwartungsvollen Ausdruck.

Erinnern wir uns, dass man in den neunziger Jahren, als Johannes Hüppi zu malen begann, vor lauter Videos die Kunst aus den Augen verlor, und die Fotografie wie ein Flächenbrand um sich griff. Was ich sagen will: Während die Moderne im 20. Jahrhundert in Zehnjahresschritten – sprich: Avantgarden – das Tempo diktierte, gab es Künstler, die früh erkannten, dass es nichts gibt, was es nicht schon gegeben hätte. Picasso, der Verräter am Kubismus, gehört zu ihnen. Mit seinen großartigen Figurenbildern, von 1920/21 betrat er wieder den Boden der Realität. Im Vordergrund stand der Mensch: Das Menschsein.

Kritiker beklagen, dass es das Neue in der Kunst nicht mehr gibt, sie sind der Meinung, dass Kultur heute als »Ablenkung, Unterhaltung, Reiz aufzufassen sei« (Henning Ritter »Behagen in der Kultur«, Frankfurter Allgemeine Zeitung, 6. Mai 2006). Sie beziehen jedoch dieses Neue auf die stilgeschichtlichen Phänomene des 20. Jahrhunderts. Wenn es in der Tat dieses Neue nach dem Ende der historischen Avantgarden vor dreißig Jahren nicht mehr gibt – »fugit irreparabile tempus« (es flieht unwiederbringlich die Zeit) – dann zählt nur noch *Intensität* und *Authentizität*. Das genau zeichnet Vallotton aus in dem erwähnten Gemälde von 1913. Und das genau zeichnet Johannes Hüppi aus. Die malerische, emotionale Hingabe wischt die kunstgeschichtlichen Verweise vom Tisch.

Zwei Punkte. Erstens: Die Aussage, dass es nichts gibt, was es nicht schon gegeben hätte, schließt das innovative Moment keineswegs aus. Denn jeder Künstler muss zuerst den Weg schaffen, den er beschreitet. Zweitens: Jede Kunst kommt aus der Erinnerung. Aber ein Künstler geht nicht in die Vergangenheit zurück. Er holt sie sich in die Gegenwart. In der Erforschung des Selbst aus einem Bewusstsein und Denken von Gegenwart wird vergegenwärtigte Vergangenheit zur Blaupause für das Begehren der Kunst und der Malerei im Besonderen.

Die Bilder von Johannes Hüppi drücken eben nicht Begehren aus. Sie *sind* Form und Farbe gewordenes Begehren in einer Verdichtung, die wir nur körperlich erfahren können. Ein Begehren, das auch immer wieder in eine immense Zärtlichkeit mutiert. Stets ist es die Frau, in deren Obhut sich der Mann begibt. Als wäre es eine Mantelmadonna. Jedoch: unbefleckt ist sie nicht! Die Serviererinnen bringen das Bier oder das Essen, so wie die weiblichen Figuren die Tiere auf ihren Armen tragen. Die Serviererinnen bringen aber auch das »Haupt des Johannes« auf einem Teller, zusammen mit einem Glas Rot- oder Weisswein. – Die Macht des Weiblichen ist wie der Resonanzraum in uns, die wir Männer sind. Es ist eine Melancholie, die fähig ist, sich selbst zu unterminieren. Um es auf eine Kurzformel zu bringen: Für uns Männer sind die Mütter die Erdung und die Frauen unser Schicksal.

Ein letztes Wort: Häufig stellt sich die Frage, ob es heute möglich sei zu unterscheiden, ob ein Werk von einem Künstler oder einer Künstlerin stamme. Das ist in der Tat manchmal schwierig. Im Fall von Johannes Hüppi ist der Befund klar: Es kann nur ein Künstler sein. Nicht der weiblichen Thematik wegen, sondern weil die Hingabe an das Weibliche eben nur von einem Liebenden stammen kann.

JEAN-CHRISTOPHE AMMANN

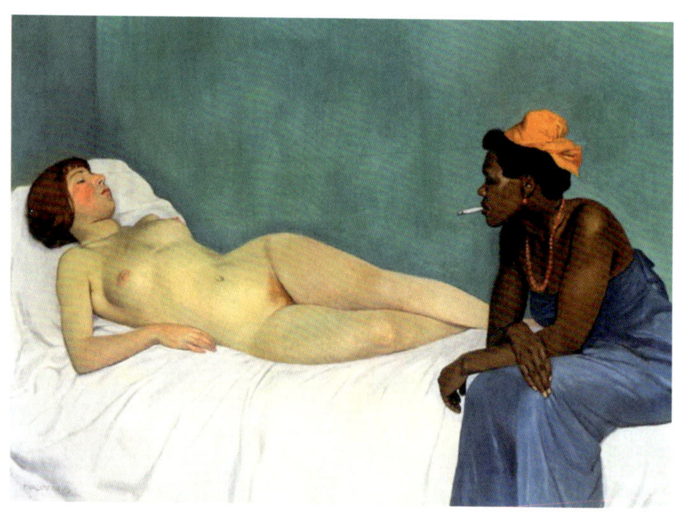

Félix Vallotton, *La Blanche et la Noire*, 1913
Öl auf Leinwand / oil on canvas, 114 × 147 cm
Hahnloser / Jäggli Stiftung, Villa Flora Winterthur
Foto / Photo: Reto Pedrini, Zürich

(...)

Already at an early point, I acquired works by Johannes Hüppi for the Museum of Modern Art in Frankfurt/Main. We exhibited these works in 1998. I myself own two watercolors, which are on display in my home. Looking at them, I start dreaming. Not too long ago, I saw the second version of a female nude accompanied by a dog in the Frieder Burda Collection. The artist produced this picture, which is painted on wood and measures 83,5 × 123,3 centimeters, in 2005. Of course, I immediately had to think of Félix Vallotton's grandiose painting from the year 1913 entitled *La Blanche et la Noire* (The White and the Black Woman). Painted on canvas and measuring 114 × 147 centimeters, it is in the possession of the Hahnloser/Jäggli Foundation in Winterthur (Villa Flora). The painting depicts a young attractive nude woman with bangs, asleep in a reclining position. A black woman is sitting at the foot of the bed. Her arms are robust; her shoulders and back are naked. She has beautiful hands. An orange fabric adornment is crowning her hair. The background is consistently painted in a turquoise hue. And here comes the outrageous detail: the black woman is smoking. She has a cigarette in her mouth. As if emphasizing the self-confident position of a servant. Valloton's painting was a provocative answer to Manet's *Olympia*. And Manet, in turn, was reacting to many precursors from earlier centuries. This painting was created in 1913. It was the era of Cubism.

In 2005, Johannes Hüppi painted Francisco de Goya's *La Maja Desnuda*. An oversized Bernese mountain dog is guarding her. This Maja is beautiful and sensual. Perhaps the dog is desirously inhaling her. It is a dark, mystical image. The face upon the luminous body expresses acuteness and expectance.

Let us recall how in the 1990's, when Johannes Hüppi began painting, one completely lost sight of art due to the vast amount of videos, while photography was also spreading like wildfire. What I mean to say is that while Modernism dictated the tempo by ten-year degrees— or avant-gardes—there were artists who recognized at an early stage that nothing existed that had not already been there before. Picasso, the betrayer of Cubism, was among these. With his wonderful compositions dedicated to the figure from 1920/21 he came down to earth again and reentered the real world. The human being: human existence took center stage.

Critics claim that there is no longer anything new in art. They believe that today culture "is to be understood as diversion, entertainment, stimulus" (Henning Ritter, "Behagen in der Kultur," Frankfurter Allgemeine Zeitung, May 6, 2006). However, they apply the notion of the "new" to the phenomena of the 20th century with regard to the history of style. If, indeed, after the end of the historical avant-gardes thirty years ago, the new no longer exists—*fugit irreparabile tempus* (time flees irretrievably)—then only *intensity* and *authenticity* still count. It is exactly this, which distinguishes Vallotton's painting from 1913 mentioned above. And it is exactly this, which distinguishes Johannes Hüppi. The emotional dedication as a painter wipes away the art-historical references.

Two aspects. In the first place: the statement that nothing exists, which has not already been there, does not by any means exclude the innovation. Every artist has to first pave the way before venturing forth. In the second place: every work of art arises from memory. Yet an artist does not go back into the past. He brings the latter forth into the present. In the investigation of the self, which is based upon an awareness of and a reflection upon the present, the past that has been rendered current becomes a blueprint for the desire of art and of painting in particular.

In fact, Johannes Hüppi's paintings precisely do not express desire. They *are* desire that has become form and color condensed to such an extent that we are only able to experience it in a physical manner: a form of desire that again and again mutates into an immense tenderness. It is always the woman into whose care the man commits himself. As if she were a Virgin of Mercy. And yet: she is definitely not undefiled! The waitresses serve the beer or the food in the same manner in which the female figures carry the animals in their arms. But the waitresses also present the "head of St. John" on a platter, together with a glass of red or white wine.—The power of femininity is like a resonance chamber within us men. It is a melancholy state, which is capable of undermining itself. Putting it in a brief formula: for us men mothers embody the foundation, and women are our destiny.

A final remark: often the question arises whether it might be possible to distinguish whether or not a work of art has been created by a male or a female artist. This is indeed sometimes difficult. In the case of Johannes Hüppi, however, the result is clear. His work could have only been created by a male artist. Not because of the emphasis on femininity in his subject matter, but because only a man who loves can be dedicated so deeply to femininity.

JEAN-CHRISTOPHE AMMANN

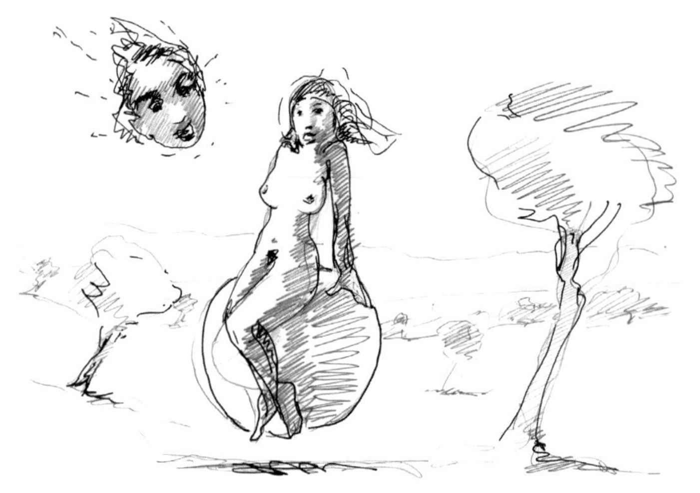

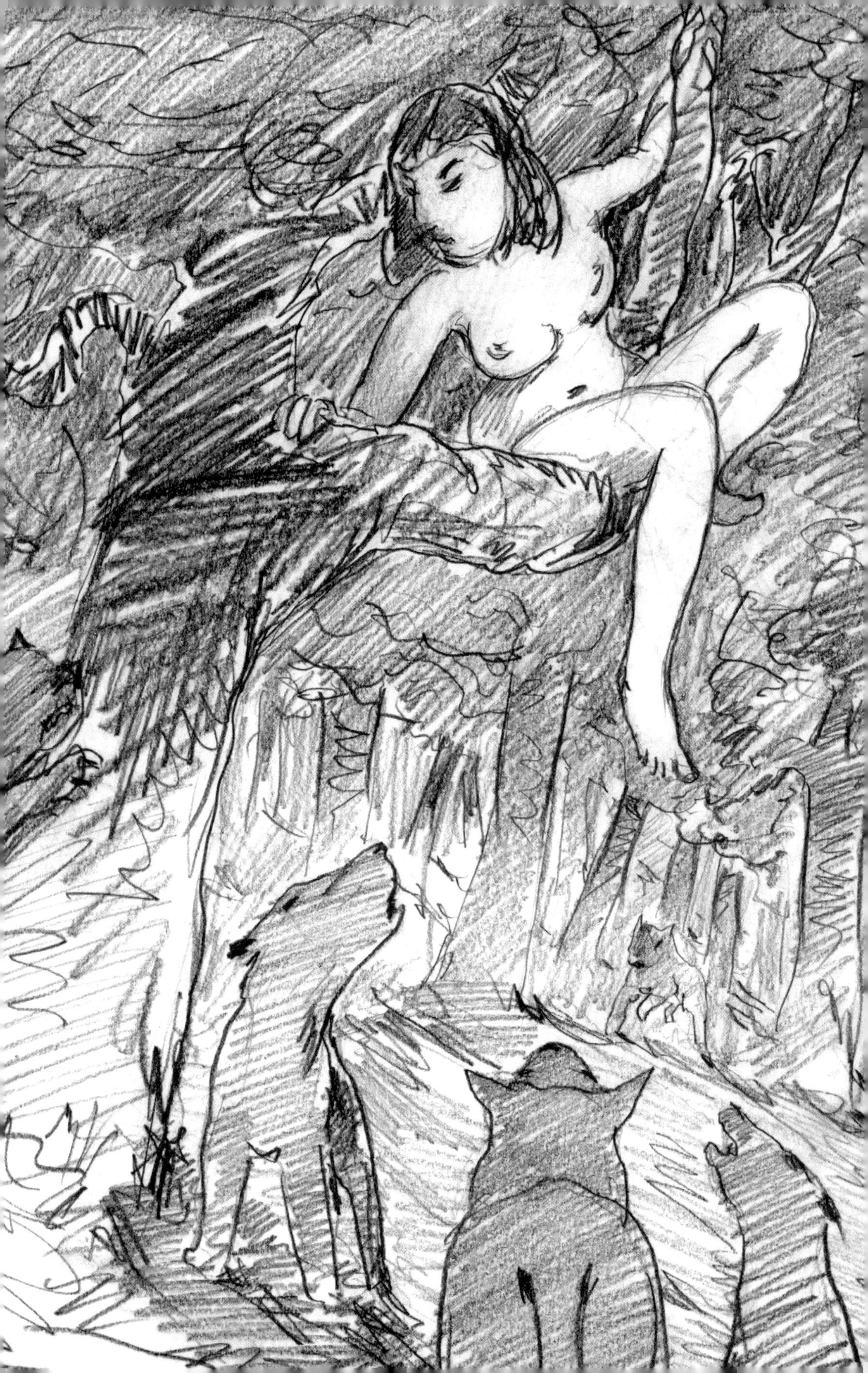

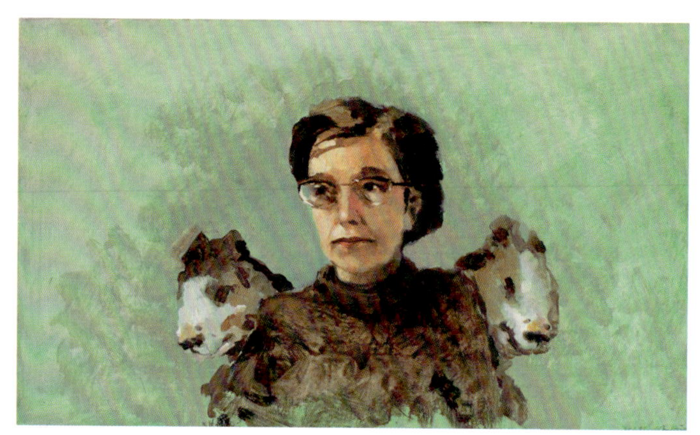

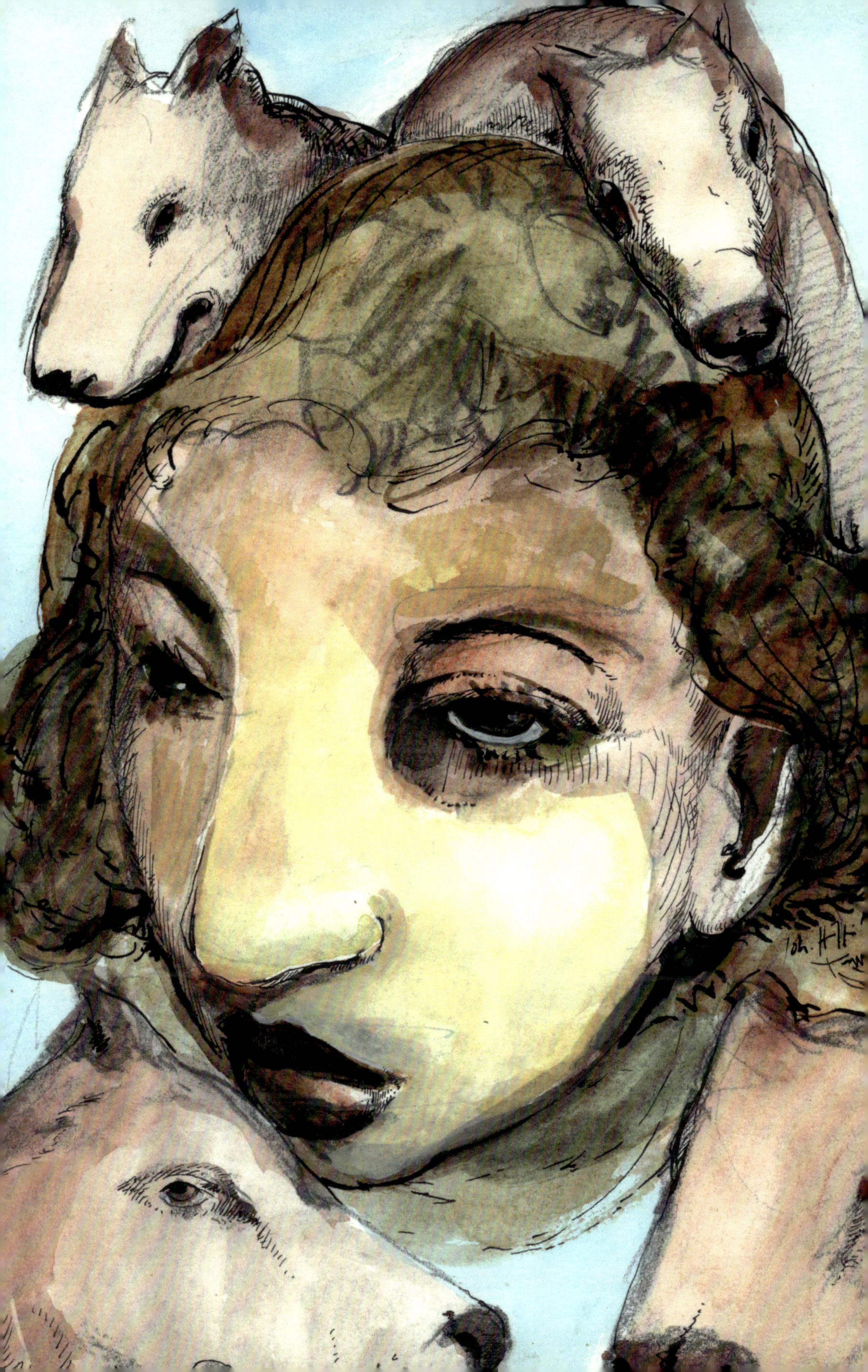

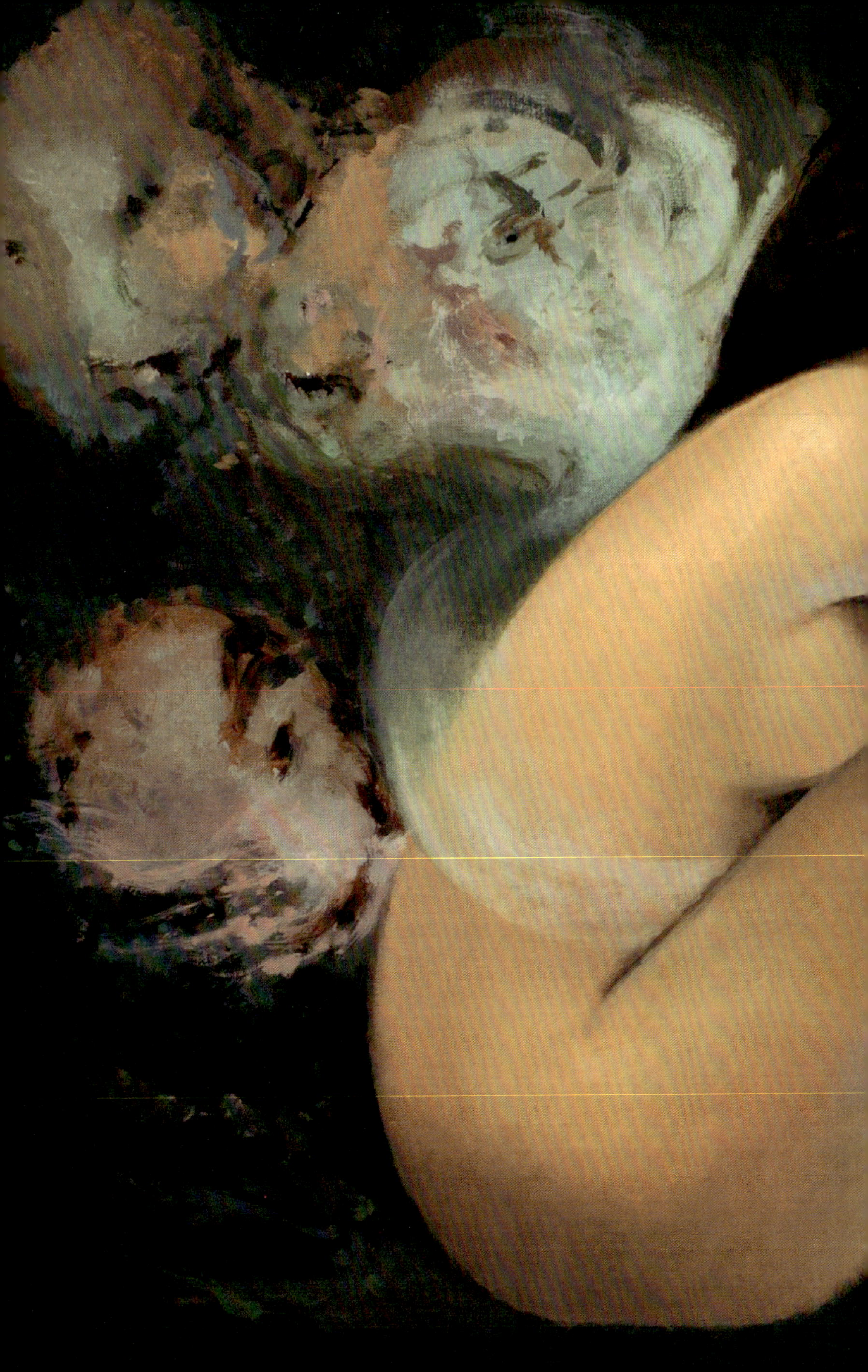

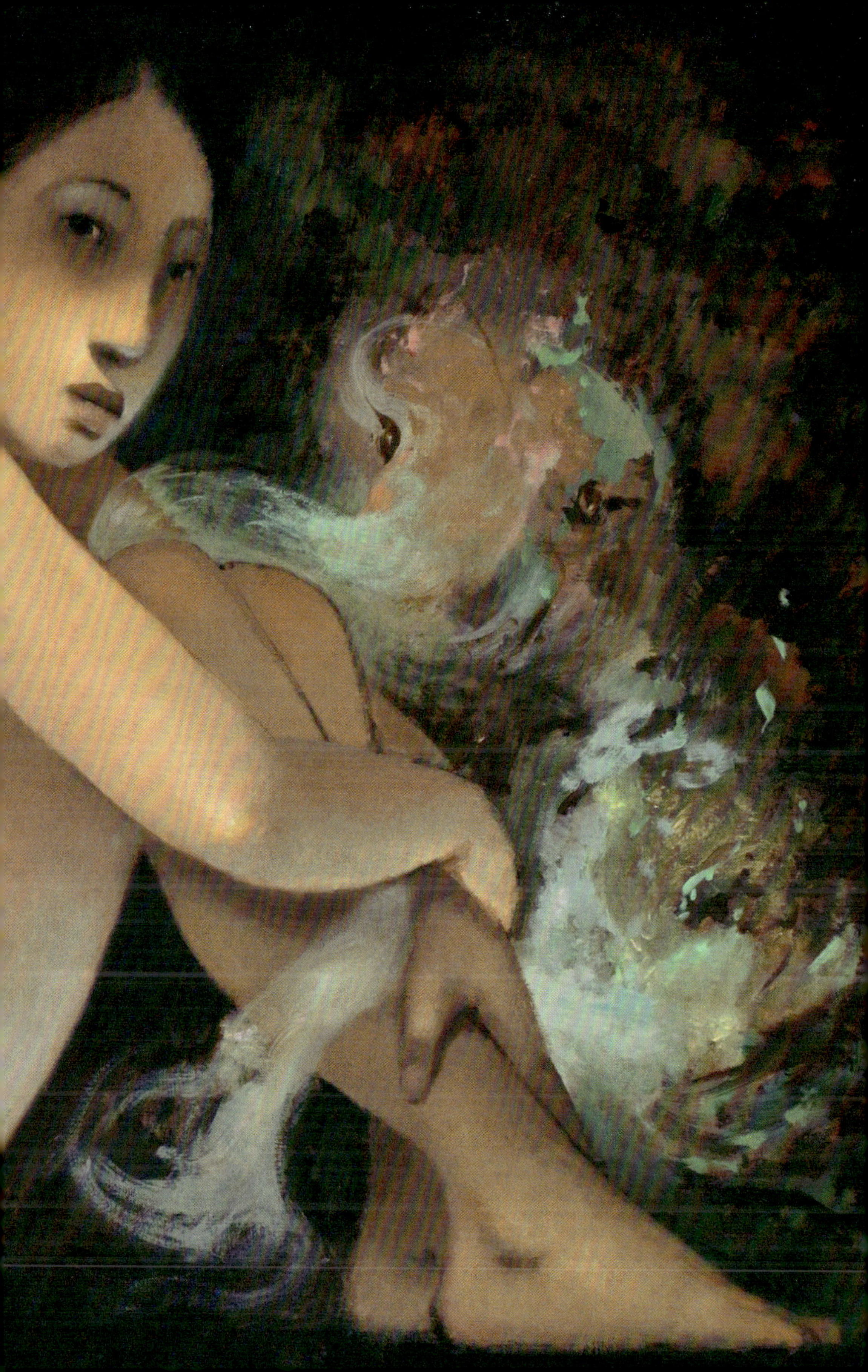

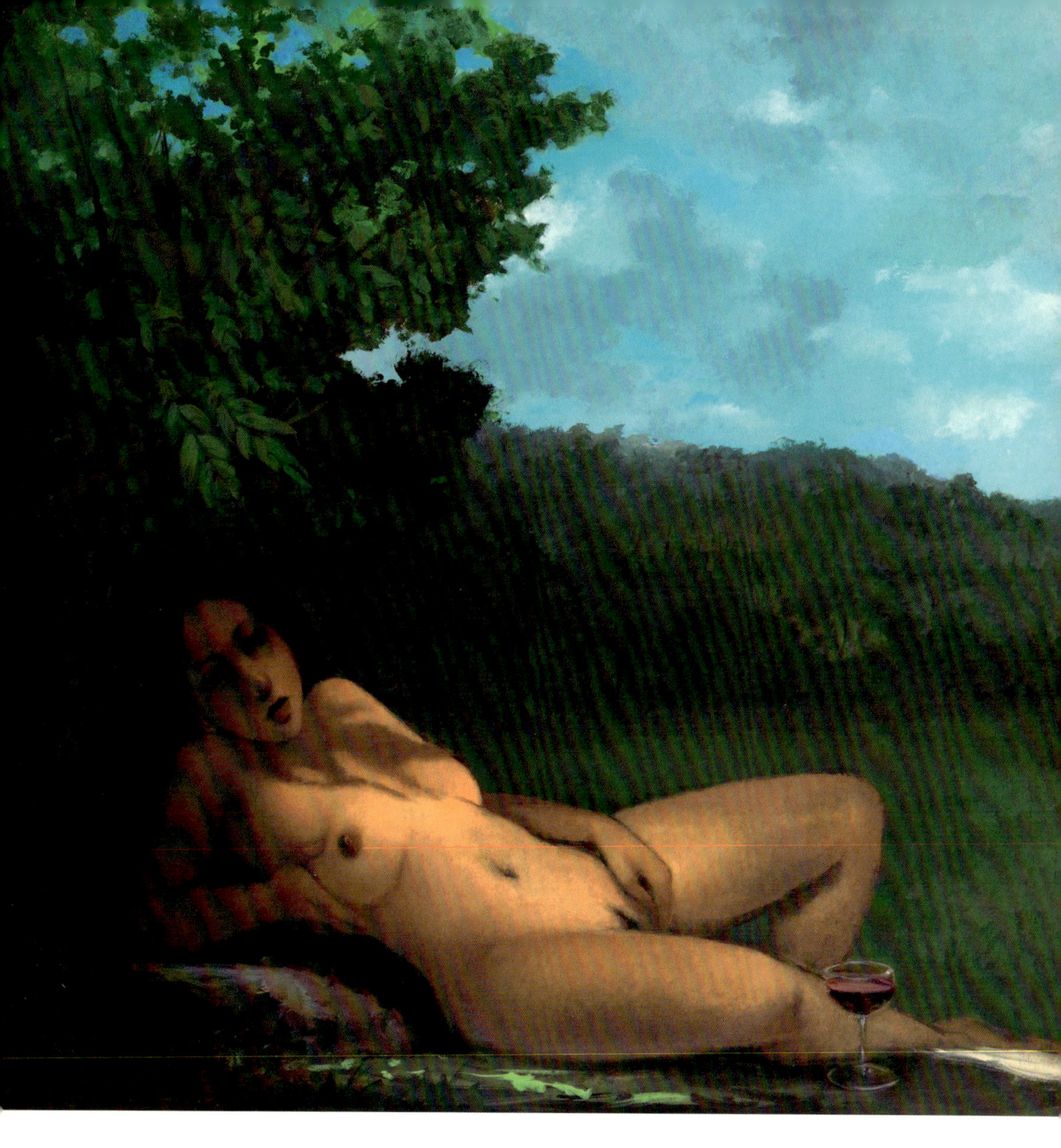

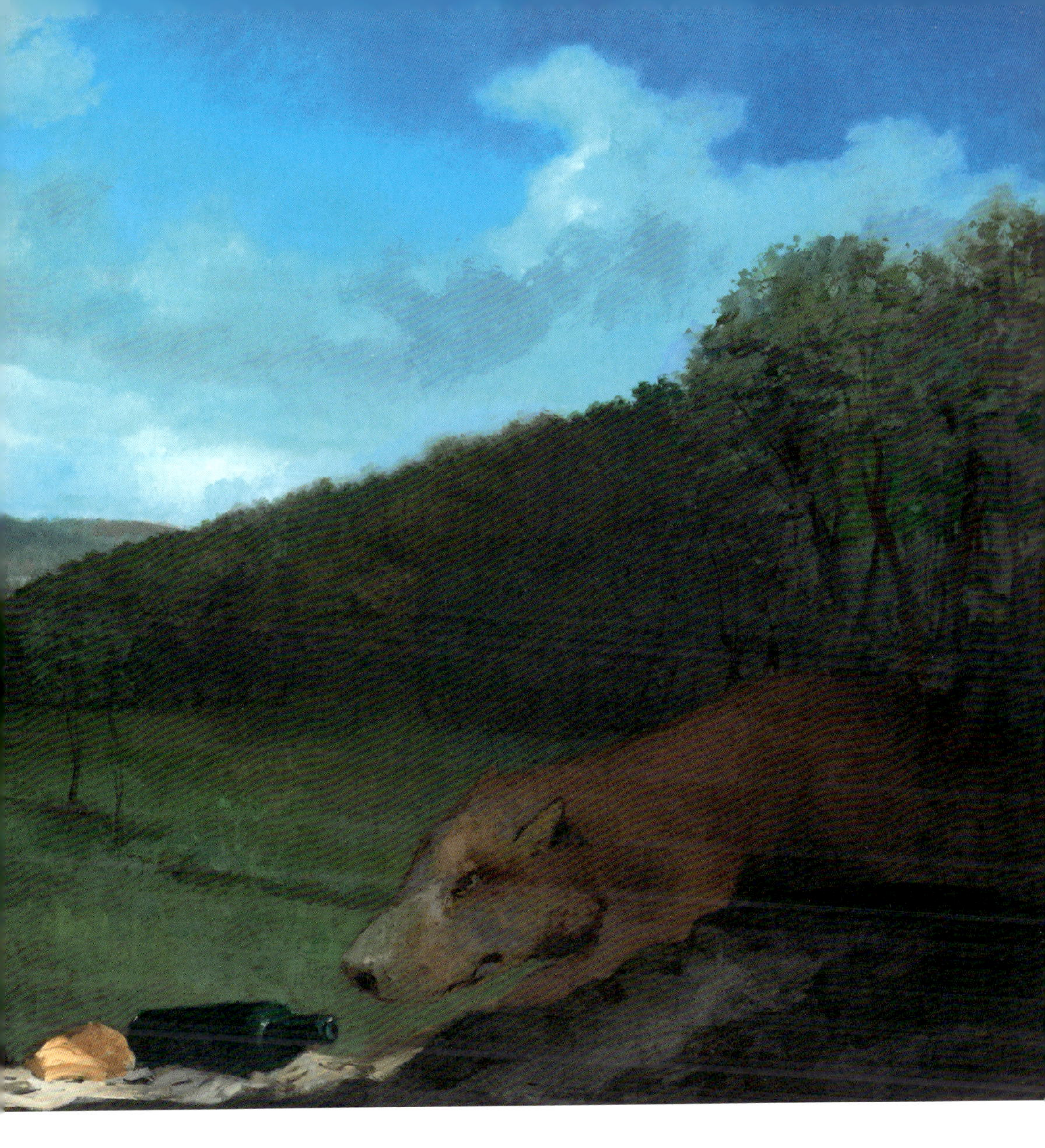

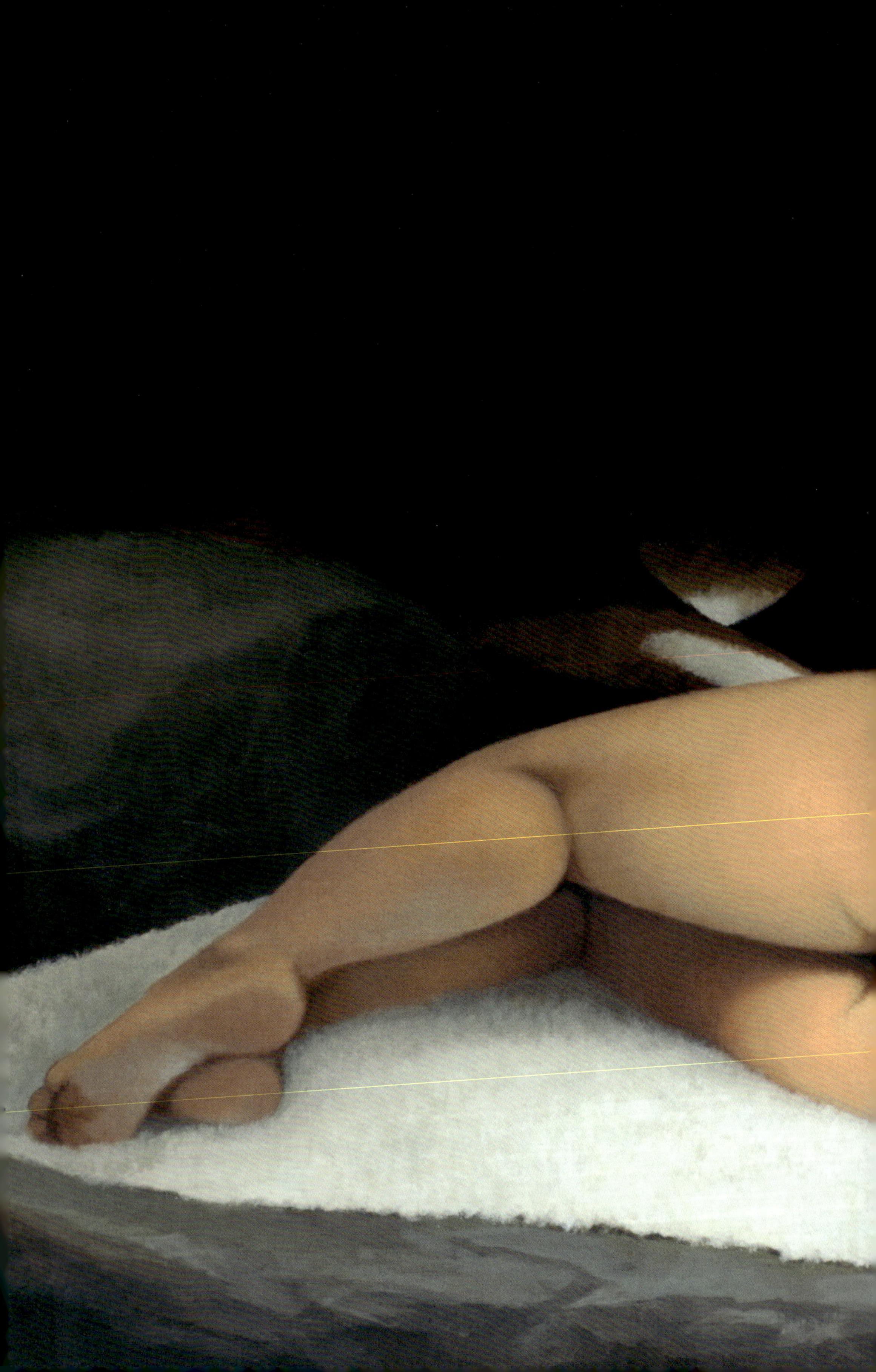

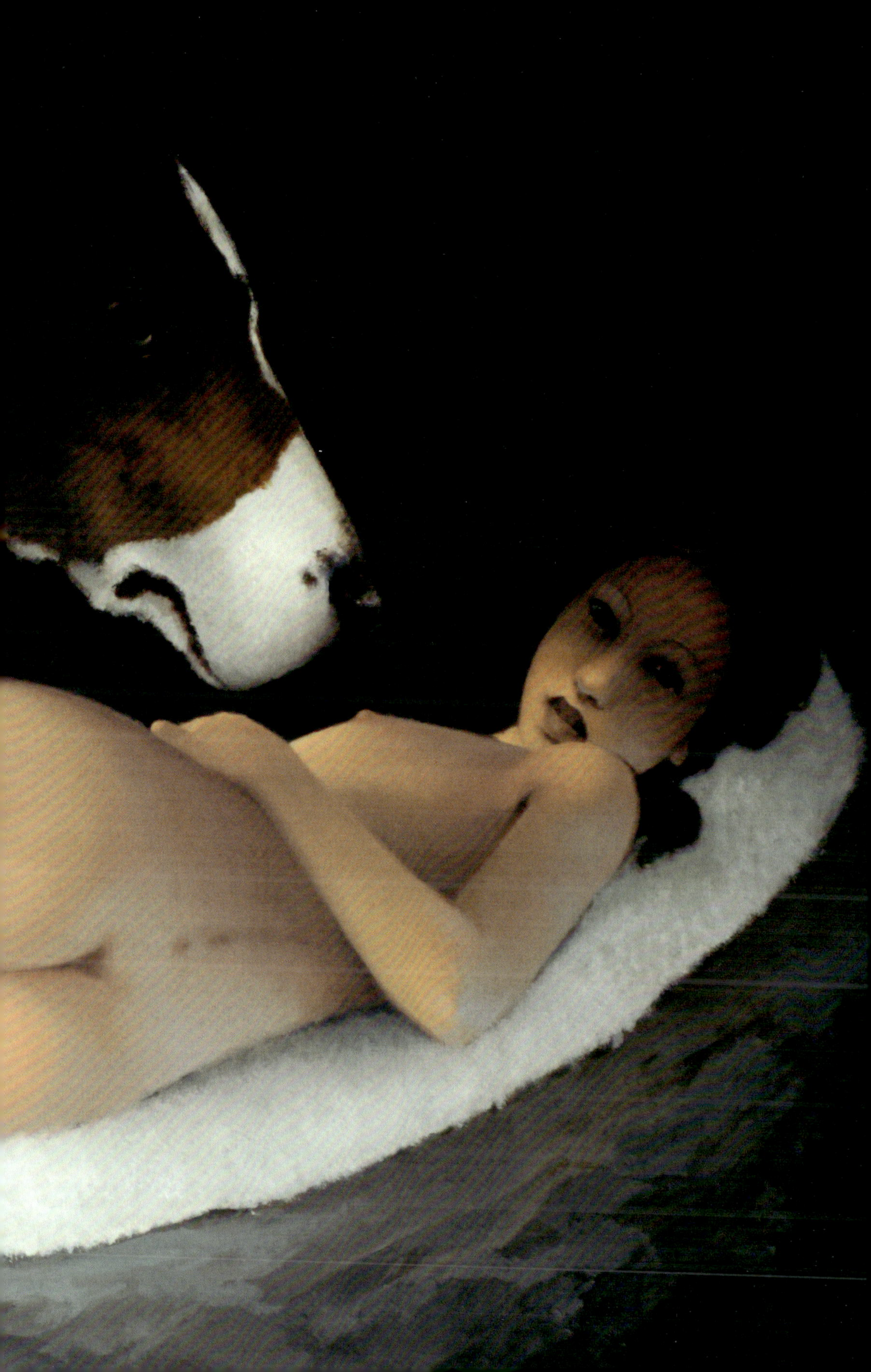

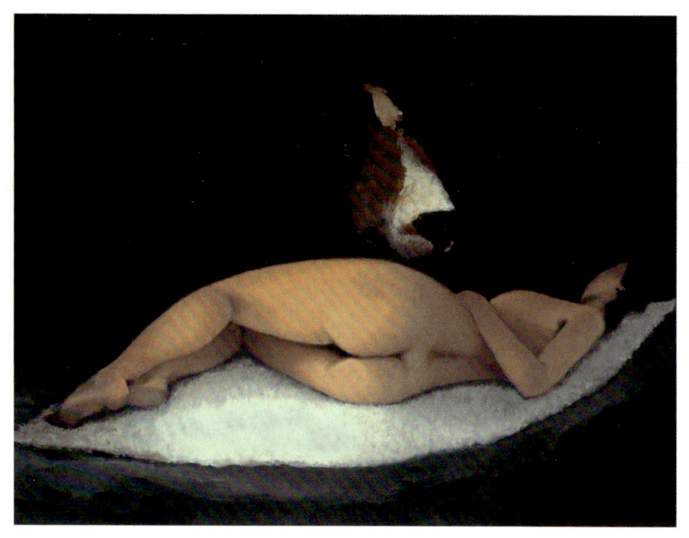

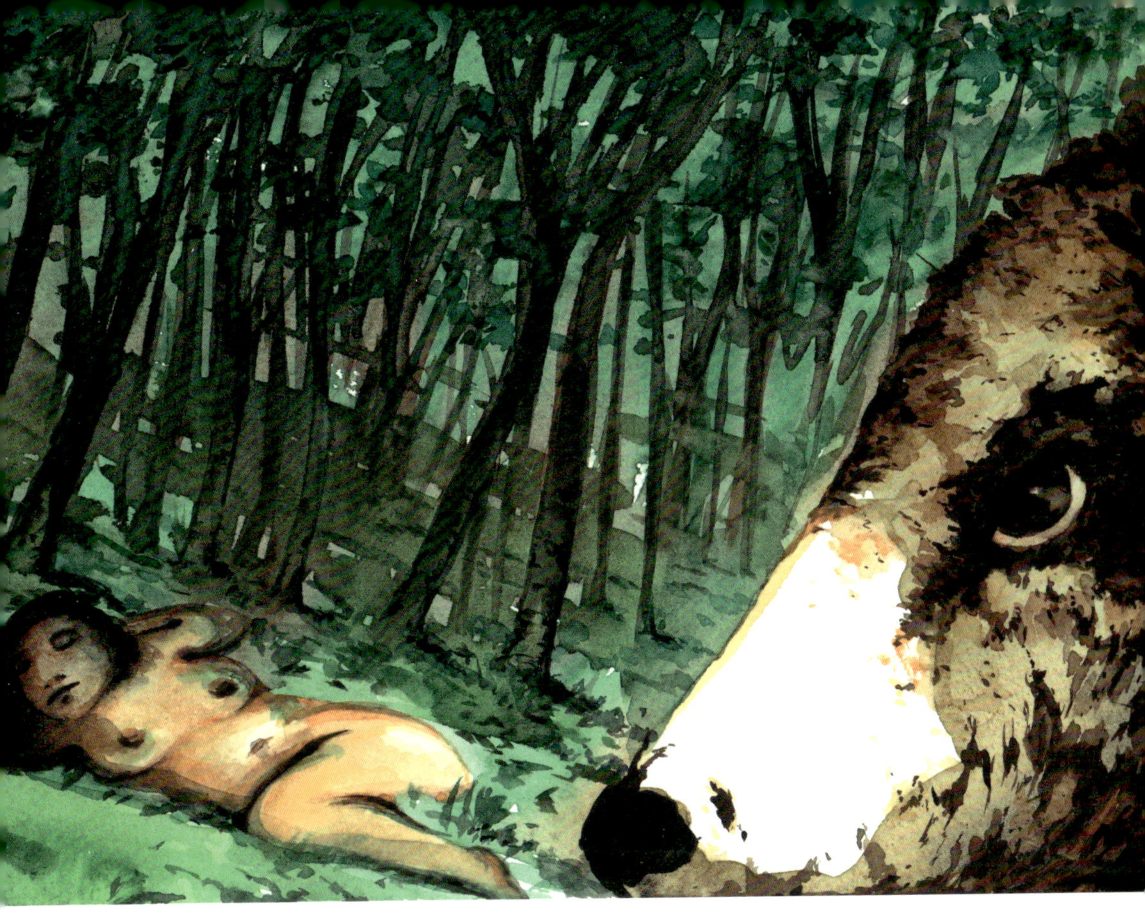

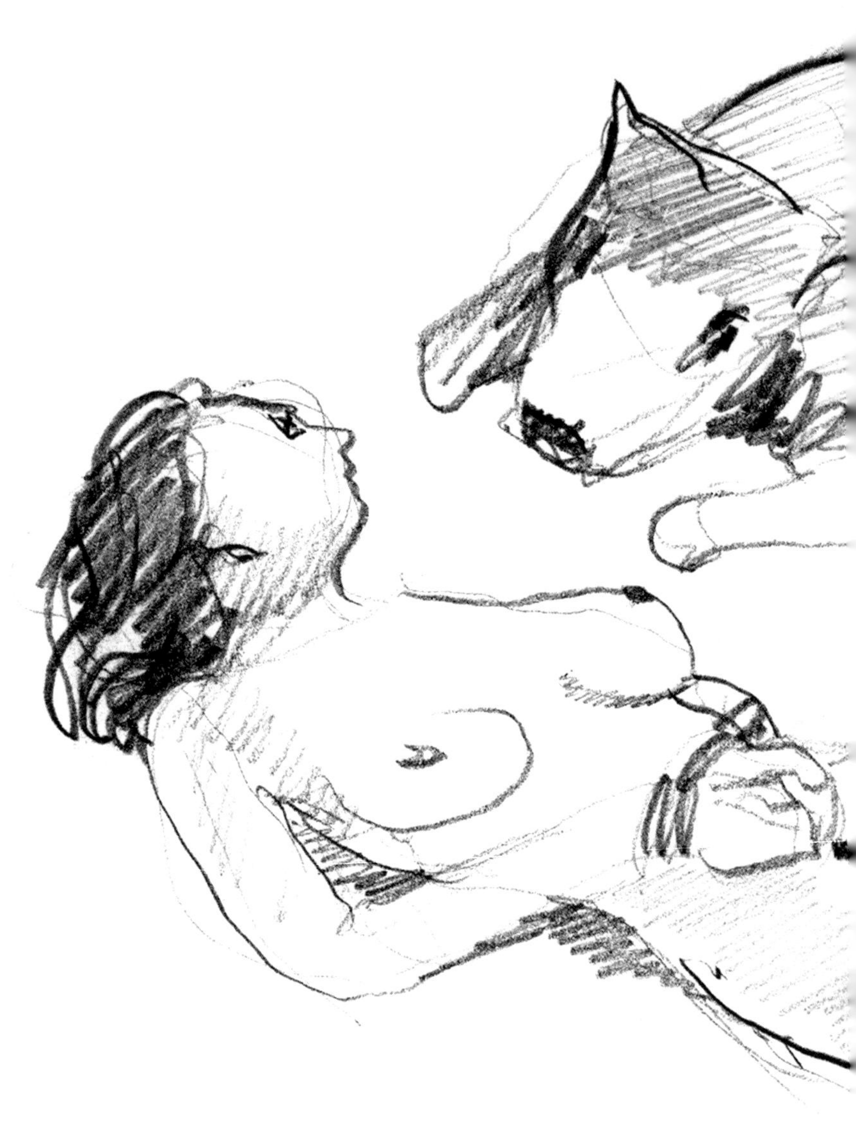

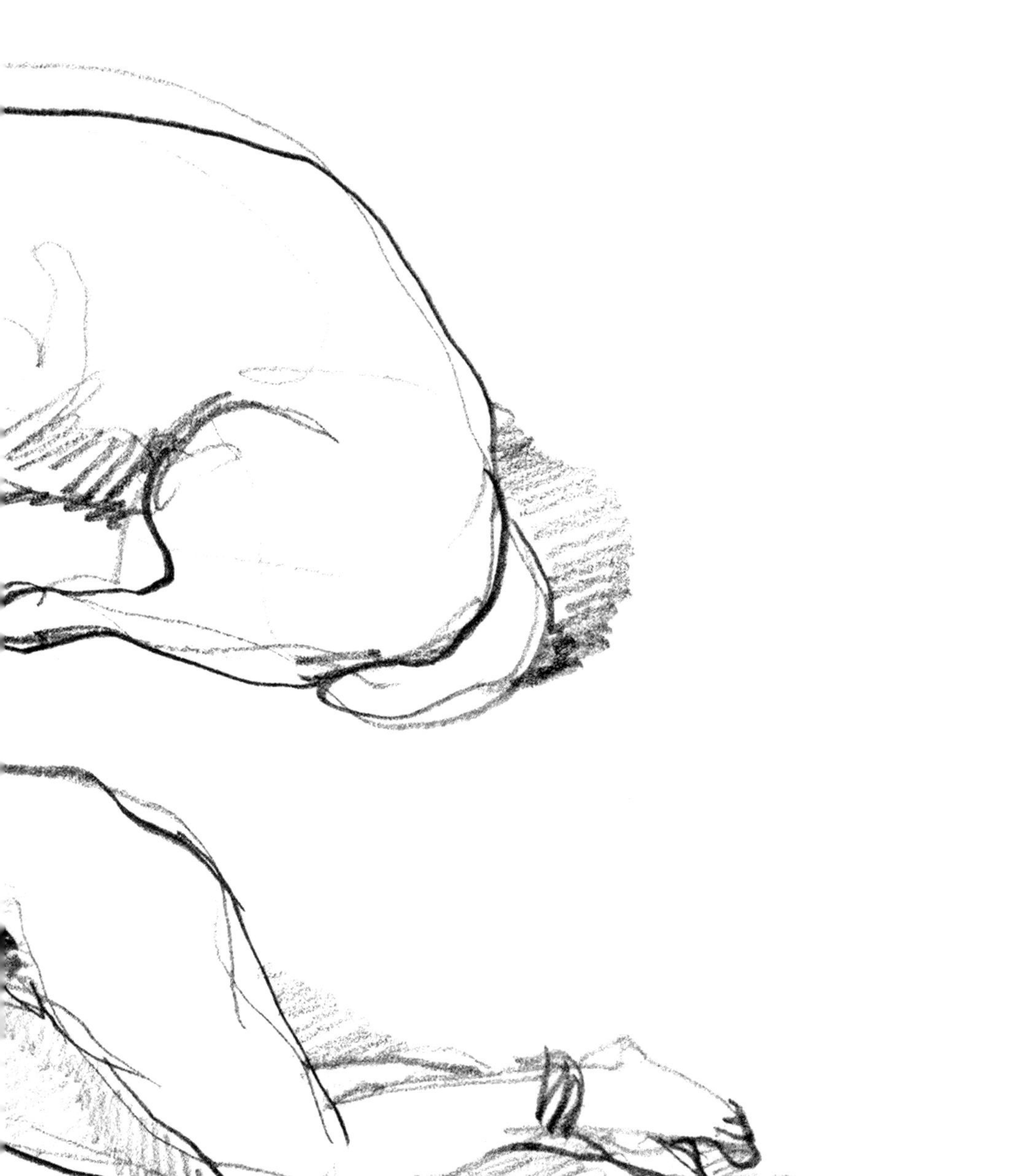

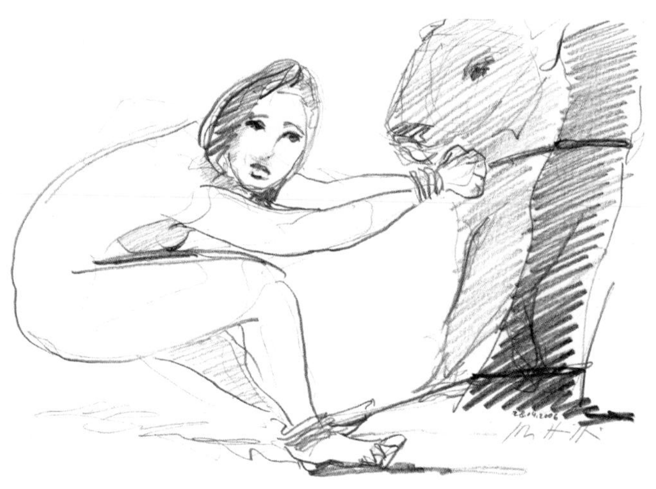

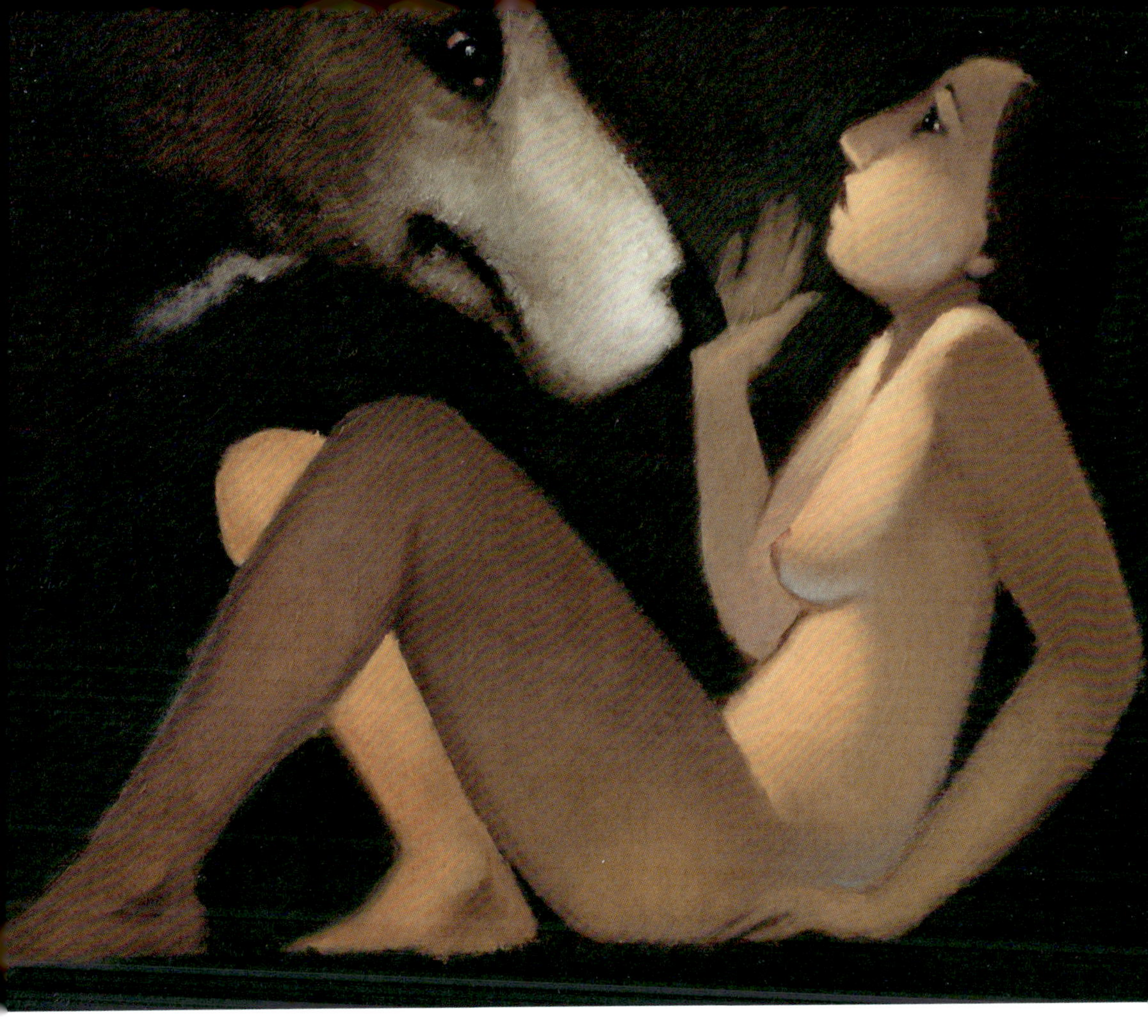

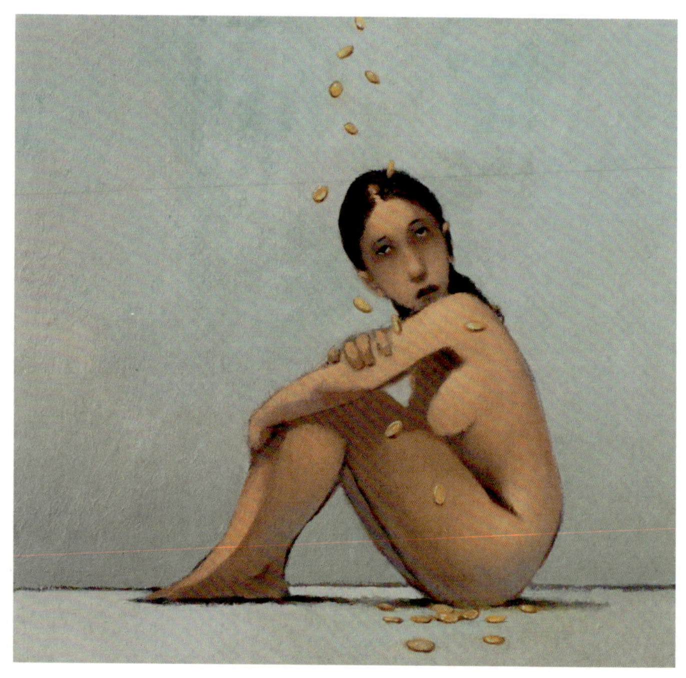

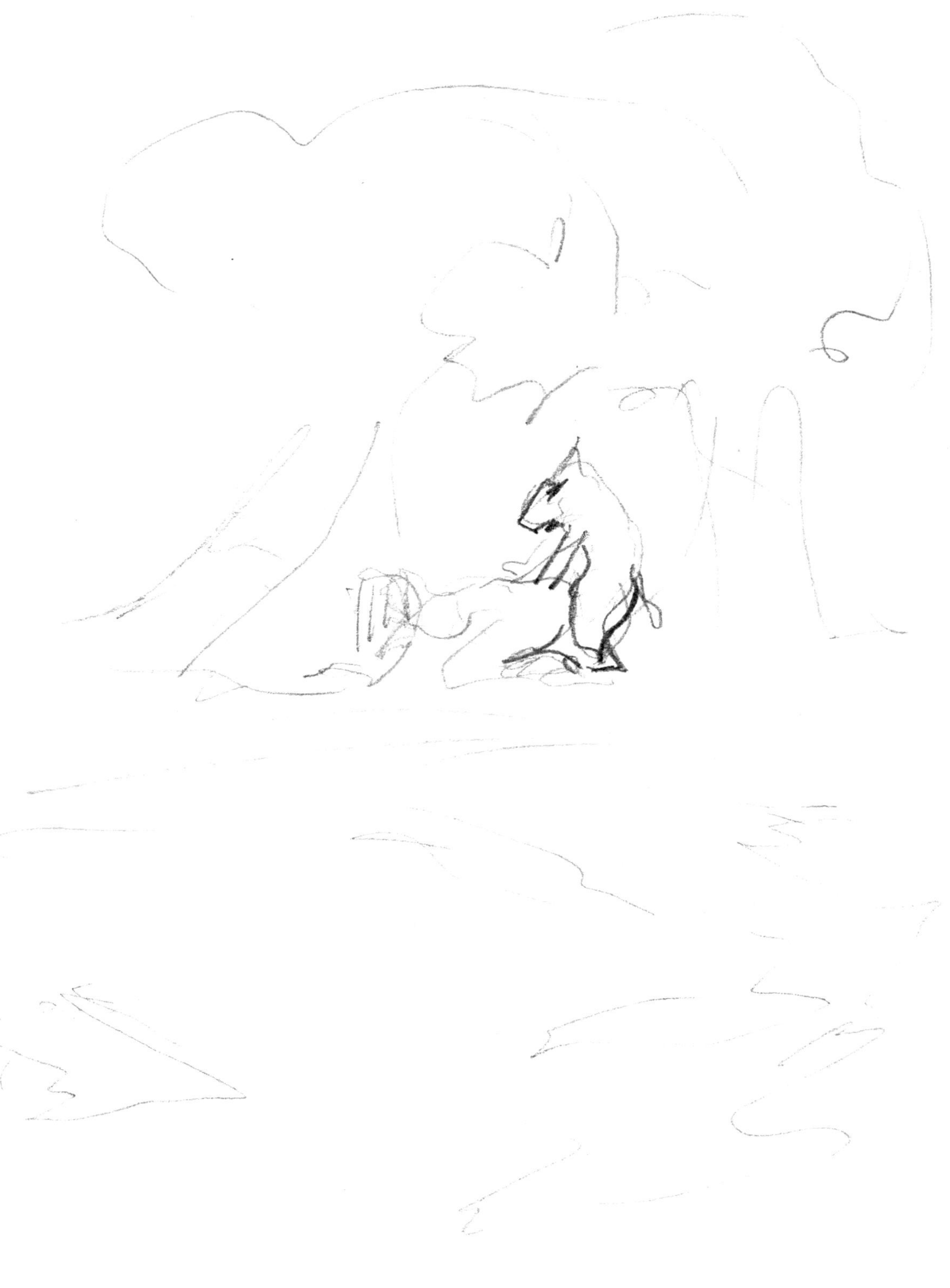

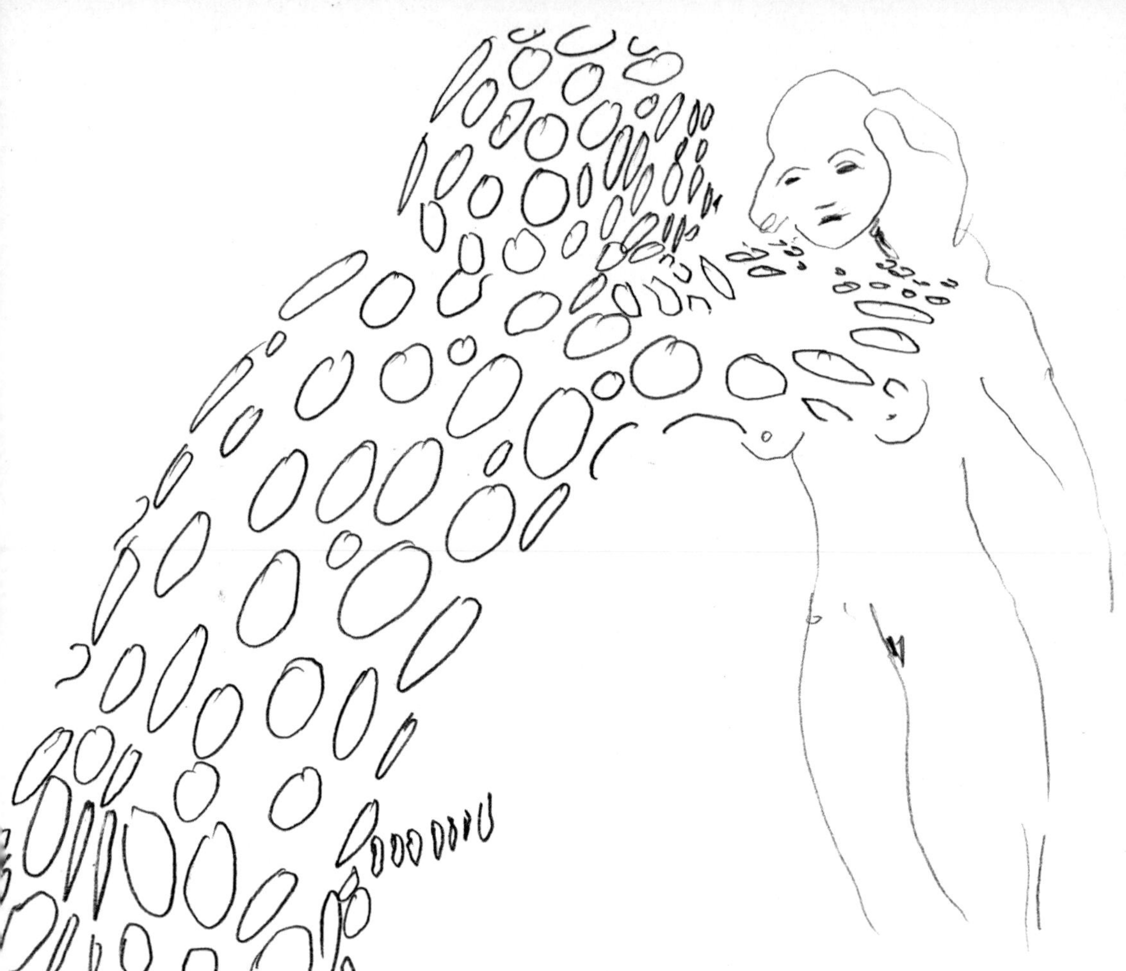

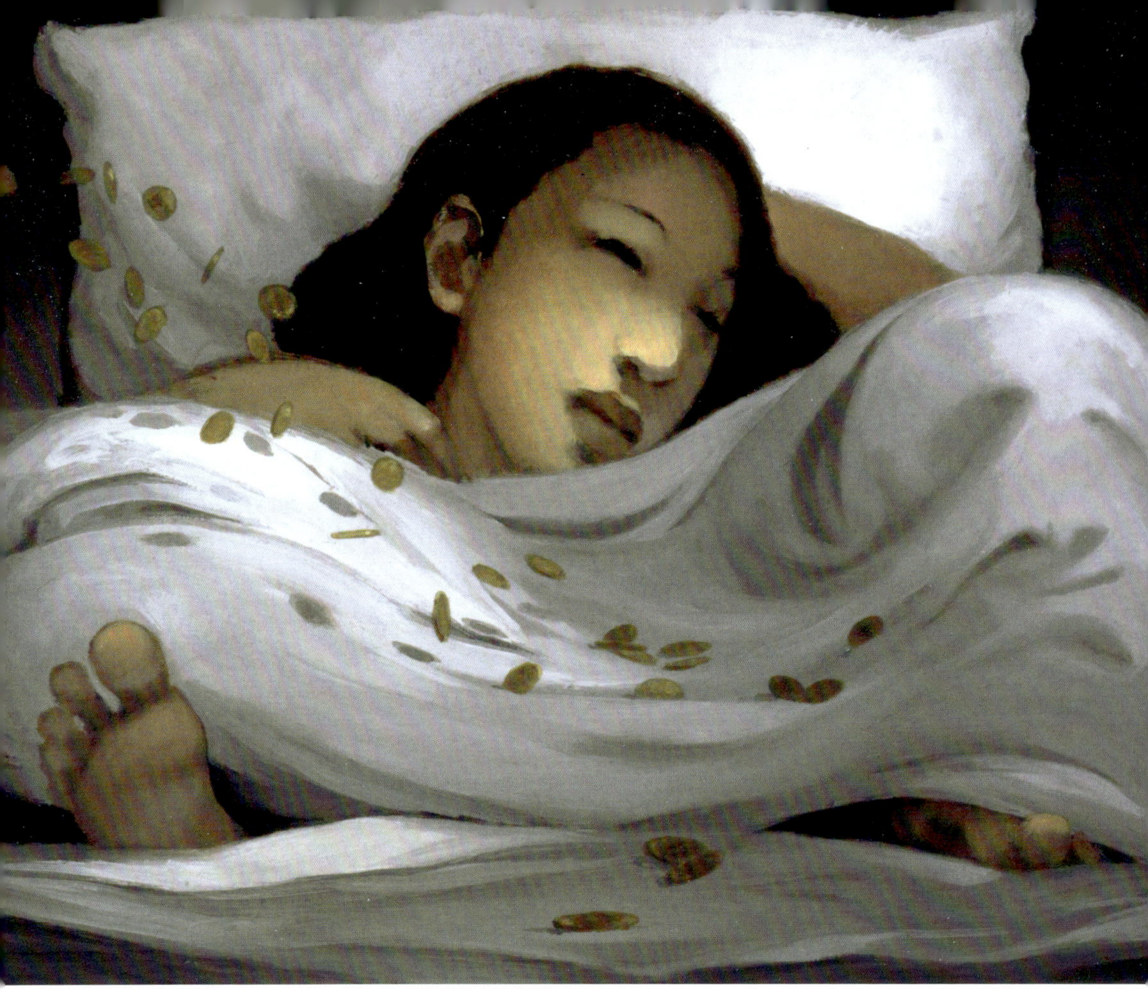

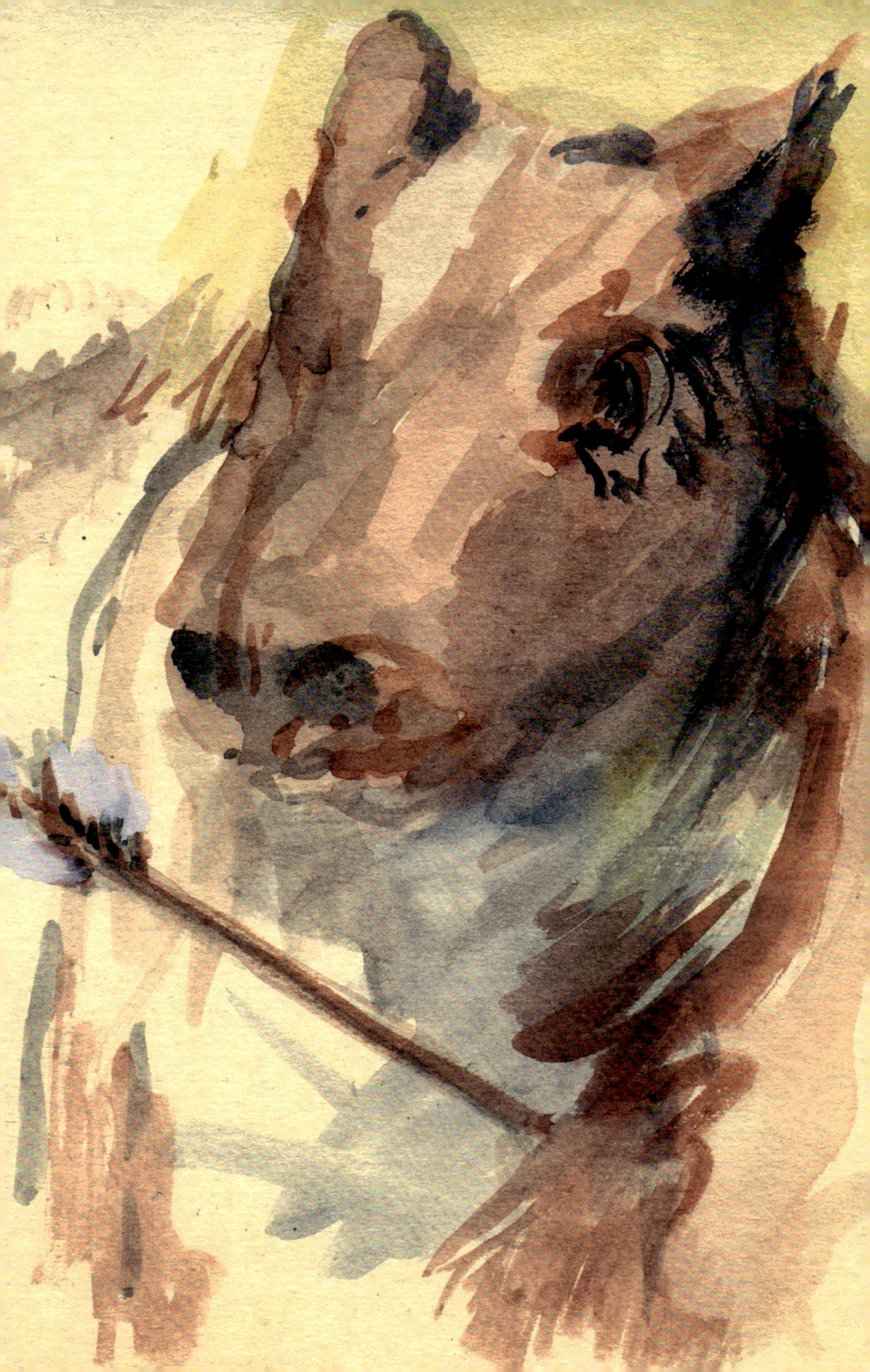

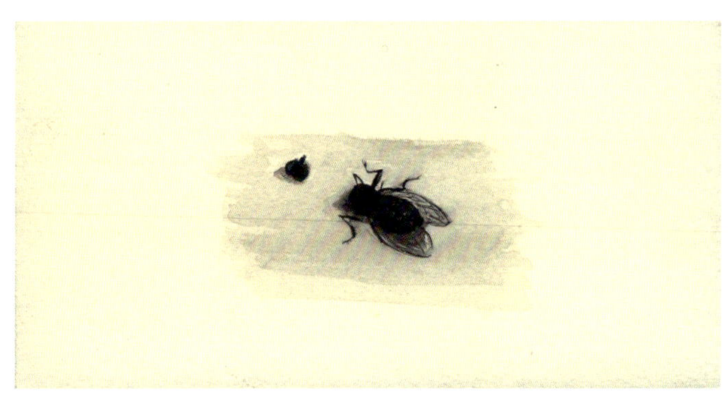

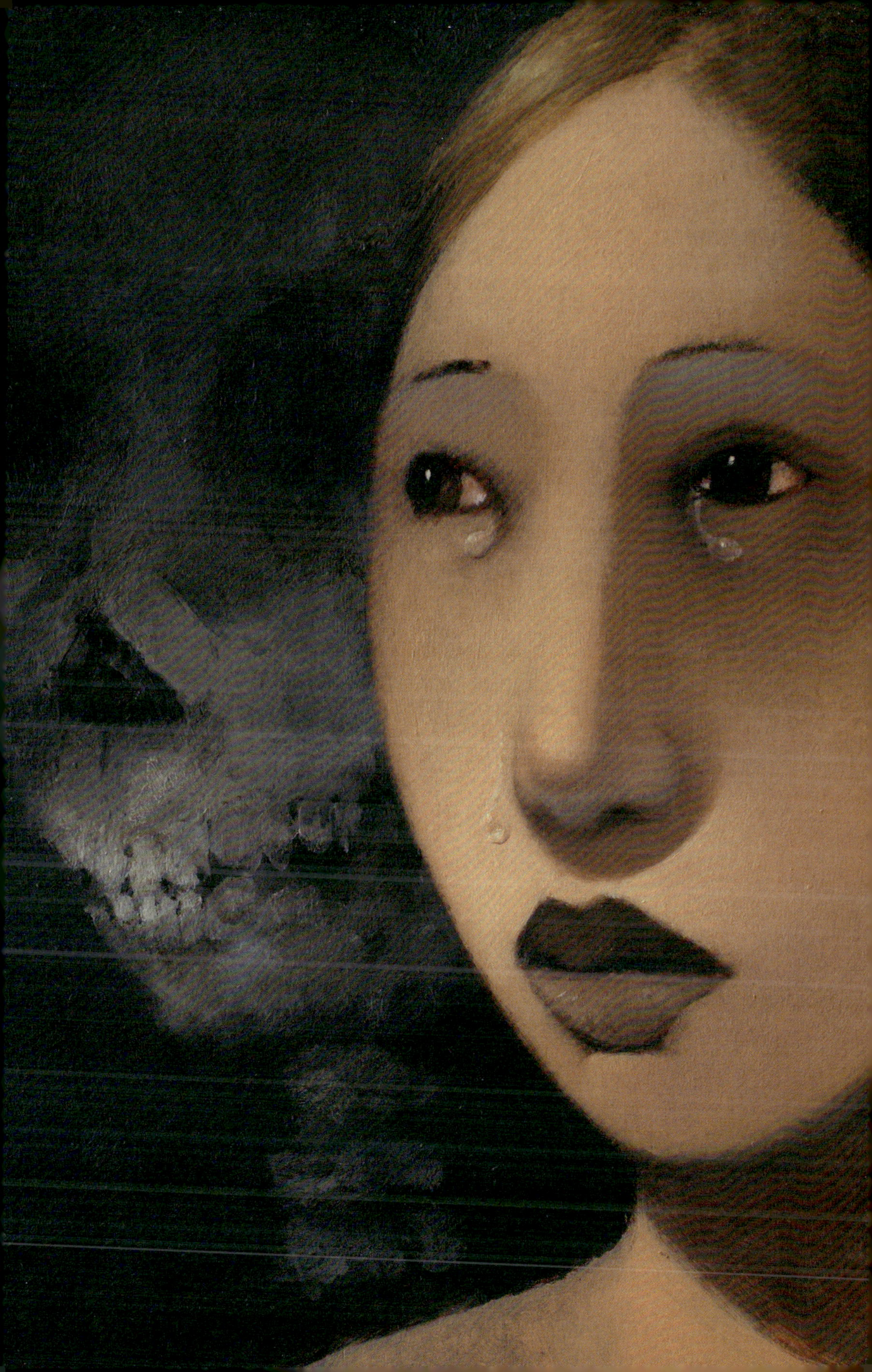

ABBLIDUNGSVERZEICHNIS
LIST OF WORKS

JOHANNES HÜPPI

1965	geboren / born in Baden-Baden
1984 – 1990	Studium an der Kunstakademie in Düsseldorf bei Fritz Schwegler und Dieter Krieg, Meisterschüler / Studied at the Kunstakademie Düsseldorf with Fritz Schwegler and Dieter Krieg, master student
1990 – 2001	Aufenthalt in den USA über eine Dauer von sieben Jahren, unter anderem / Resided in the United States for seven years, among other cities, in New York, Oregon, San Francisco, Los Angeles, Miami
2004 – 2006	Ateliers / Studios in Mexico, Puebla, Oaxaca, Cholula
2004 – 2007	Professur an der / Professor at the Hochschule für Bildende Künste, Braunschweig
2006	Professur an der / Professor at the UDLA, Puebla, Mexico
Preise / Awards	Kiefer-Hablitzel-Preis 1992/3/4, Roy-Lichtenstein-Preis 1997, Preis des Kuratoriums des Mannheimer Kunstvereins (1998)

Lebt und arbeitet in Basel / Lives and works in Basel

EINZELAUSSTELLUNGEN
SOLO EXHIBITIONS

1992	Galerie Klaus Littmann
	Galerie manus presse
1996	Galerie Haus Schneider, Ettlingen/Karlsruhe
	Galerie Delta, Rotterdam
1997	Galerie Hübner, Frankfurt
	Ludwig Forum, Aachen (mit / with Tamara Grcic)
1998	Galerie manus presse, Stuttgart (K)
1999	Galerie Thomas Rehbein, Köln
	paarweise, Ulmer Museum (K)
	Mannheimer Kunstverein (K)
2000	*Kellnerinnen*, Galerie manus presse, Stuttgart
2001	Galerie Michael Cosar, Düsseldorf
	Littmann Kulturprojekte, Basel *Ausstellungsraum*, Münster (K)
2002	*Kellnerinnen*, Museum für Neue Kunst, Freiburg (K)
	Galerie Löhrl, Mönchengladbach (mit / with Thaddäus Hüppi)
	Galerie manus presse, Stuttgart (mit / with Thaddäus Hüppi)
2003	wbd, Berlin
	manus presse, Stuttgart 2004
	paarweise, Institut für Moderne Kunst, Nürnberg
2005	*Stadtkünstler Baden-Baden 2005*, Gesellschaft der Freunde
	junger Kunst Baden-Baden
	Cohabitation, Littmann Kulturprojekte, Basel (mit / with Franz Burkardt)
2006	Museum Gottorf, Aus der Sammlung Carl und Eva Grosshaus (K)
	Galerie Löhrl, Mönchengladbach
	Museum für Moderne Kunst Passau, Aus der Sammlung Grosshaus (K)
2007	Kravets/Wehby Gallery, New York (mit / with Andrea Lehmann)
2008	Galerie Anna Klinkhammer, Düsseldorf
	Kunsthalle Lingen
	Gallery Godo, Seoul, South Korea
2010	Galerie Levy, Berlin
	Gallery Godo, Seoul
2011	Galerie Levy, Hamburg

(K) = catalogue

GRUPPENAUSSTELLUNGEN
GROUP EXHIBITIONS

1993	*Malerei 2000*, Hamburg
	Deckenbild, Rathaus Ludwigsburg (Kunst am Bau)
1996	*Landvermesser*, Mannheimer Kunstverein (K)
	4 Hüppi, Museum für Neue Kunst, Freiburg (K)
1997	*4 Hüppi*, Kunstmuseum Solothurn, CH (K)
1998	*Szenenwechsel XIV*, MMK, Museum für Moderne Kunst, Frankfurt/Main
1999	Galerie Henze und Ketterer, Bern, CH
2000	*portraitartig*, Galerie Thomas Rehbein
2001	*desire*, Ursula Blickle Stiftung, Kraichtal (K)
2003	*Herbarium der Blicke*, Bundeskunsthalle, Bonn (K)
	Das Unheimliche in der Malerei, Städtische Galerie, Delmenhorst (K)
2004	*Punktleuchten*, Littmann Kulturprojekte (K)
2006	*Neue Malerei*, Museum Frieder Burda, Baden-Baden (K)
2007	Museum Kunstpalast Düsseldorf, *Die Kunst zu sammeln* (K)
	Kunsthalle Emden *Garten Eden*
2008	Museum Kunstpalast, *Der verbotene Blick*
2010	Museum Burda *Die Bilder tun was mit mir...*, Baden-Baden (K)

(K) = catalogue

ARBEITEN IN ÖFFENTLICHEN SAMMLUNGEN
WORKS IN PUBLIC COLLECTIONS

Museum für Moderne Kunst, Frankfurt
Museum Frieder Burda, Baden-Baden
Museum Ludwig Forum, Aachen
Ulmer Museum
Sammlung des Bundes, Bonn
Kunsthalle Recklinghausen Städtische Galerie Delmenhorst
Museum für Neue Kunst, Freiburg
Kunst am Bau Deckenbild, Rathaus Ludwigsburg
Deckenbild, *Drei Könige*, Basel

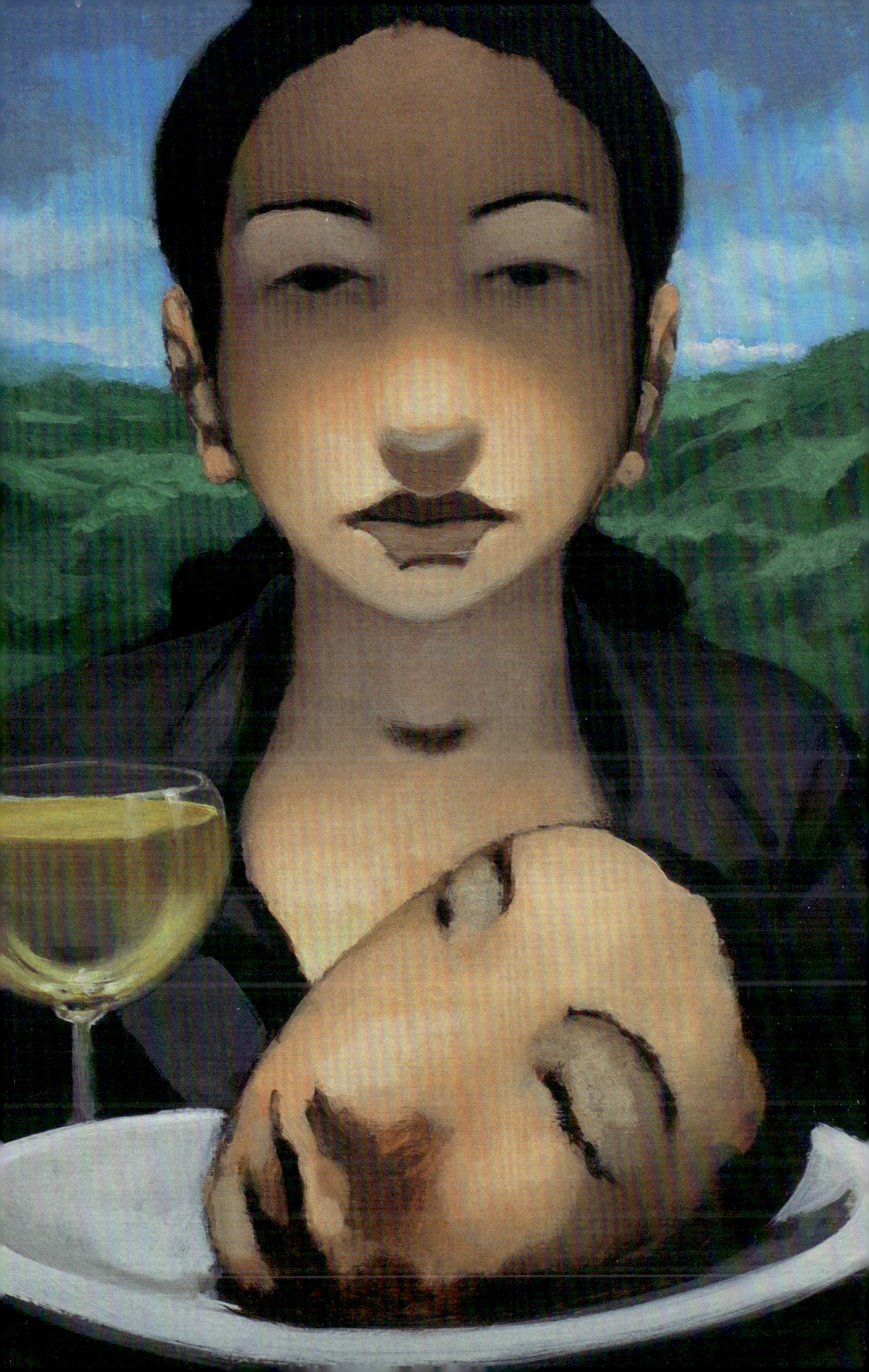

Diese Publikation erscheint anlässlich der Ausstellung / This publication is published in conjunction with the exhibition:

Johannes Hüppi / Fenster zum Hof, 21. 03. – 04. 05. 2011

LEVY Hamburg, Osterfeldstraße 6, D-22529 Hamburg / www.levy-galerie.de

Johannes Hüppi

Herausgegeben von / Edited by Jean-Christophe Ammann; Text / Essay: Jean-Christophe Ammann, Belinda Grace Gardner; Übersetzungen (Dt.-Engl.) / Translations (Ger.-Engl.): Belinda Grace Gardner; Photonachweise / Photo credits: Johannes Hüppi, Studio Gehrig, Dennys Hill, Achim Kukulies, Dirk Masbaum, Reto Pedrini; Grafische Gestaltung / Graphic design: Claas Möller / www.claasbooks.de

Die Deutsche Nationalbibliothek verzeichnet diese Publikation in der Deutschen Nationalbibliografie; detaillierte bibliografische Daten sind im Internet über http://dnb.d-nb.de abrufbar. / The Deutsche Nationalbibliothek holds a record of this publication in the Deutsche Nationalbibliografie; detailed bibliographical data can be found under: http://dnb.d-nb.de

Gesamtherstellung / Printed and published by
Kerber Verlag, Bielefeld
Windelsbleicher Str. 166–170
33659 Bielefeld
Germany
Tel. +49 (0) 5 21/9 50 08-10
Fax +49 (0) 5 21/9 50 08-88
info@kerberverlag.com
www.kerberverlag.com

Kerber, US Distribution
d. a. p., Distributed Art Publishers, Inc.
155 Sixth Avenue, 2nd Floor
New York, NY 10013
Tel. +1 212 6 27 19 99
Fax +1 212 6 27 94 84

ISBN 978-3-86678-540-3

Printed in Germany

Parallel erscheint eine Collector´s Edition mit einer vom Künstler signierten und nummerierten Radierung (16 × 23 cm). Diese limitierte Auflage von 30 Exemplaren ist direkt über den Verlag oder die LEVY Galerie erhältlich. / Parallel, a collector´s edition including an etching (16 × 23 cm), signed and numbered by the artist, and limited to 30 copies is available directly through the publishing house or the LEVY Gallery, Hamburg.

www.kerber-collectors-edition.com

Mit freundlicher Unterstützung von / With friendly support by

swiss arts council
pr⊙helvetia